CHEATING DEATH

Salmon Fishing the Copper River and
Prince William Sound, Alaska

KATHY HALGREN

ISBN 979-8-9911290-0-8 (paperback)
ISBN 979-8-9911290-2-2 (hardcover)
ISBN 979-8-9911290-1-5 (ebook)

First Edition published by Alaska Adventure Books October 2024

Cover photo by Bob Martinson

Before retiring, Bob was a lifelong
Copper River fisherman and
Award-winning photojournalist
whose work has been published worldwide.

His website is
www.bobmartinson.photoshelter.com

Dedicated to the
United States Coast Guard
Helicopter Rescue Teams

In Memory of
United States Coastguardsmen

Lieutenant Ernest P. Rivas
Lieutenant Joseph G. Spoja
Aviation Machinist Mate First Class Scott R. Finfrock
Aviation Machinist Mate Third Class John H. Snyder Jr.

Lost flying a rescue mission
August 7, 1981, on
The Copper River Flats, Alaska.

CONTENTS

INTRODUCTION

THIS STORY IS about my love affair with salmon fishing and a community in Alaska. My adventure began with a vacation in Cordova, Alaska. Surrounded by the Chugach Mountains, Eyak Lake, and Prince William Sound, the town is where I fell in love with the people and their spirit.

The harbor had attracted the Alaska Syndicate, which established Cordova as a railroad town to export copper in the early 1900s. The community grew dependent on the seafood industry when the Kennecott copper mine closed. The town has suffered earthquakes, fires, and salmon-run failures, but perseveres with a can-do attitude and a commitment to long-term sustainability.

My tale begins in the 1970s when the draft for the Vietnam War ended, Nixon resigned, women were burning their bras, and the sexual revolution was in full swing. I participated in the revolution and burned my bra figuratively, but the men I have included in this story shared a relationship of love without the complication of sex.

When I began gillnetting I was one of half a dozen women who fished alone and the only one without a husband or father in the fishing fleet. Not everyone supported the idea of a hippy girl joining the fleet. Those fishermen ignored me, sure I wouldn't last. Most fishermen gave me respect, a couple kept an eye on me, and all of them helped if they saw me in trouble, including those who had shaken their heads and questioned what the heck I was doing with a fishing boat.

I was unfamiliar with boats and fishing. I had recently learned how to tie a boat to a dock. I had no knowledge of how a boat engine worked or how to keep it running. I didn't know how to set an anchor. I didn't know there were five species of Alaskan salmon. Fishing turned into a crash course for me about much more than catching fish. I became a "~~Jack~~ Jill of all trades," and my education continued for years.

I was young, indestructible, adventurous, and too ignorant to have fear. By the time I understood the dangers of fishing, I had fishing in my blood and thought if I was careful, I could avoid the threat of death in the wild. I was careful. I learned from a variety of people and even more from my own numerous mistakes. Struggles to survive, passion, determination, friendship, community, and the beauty of Prince William Sound are a big part of my story.

The problems women report when they break into a male-dominated industry were unfamiliar to me. I didn't share their experience. I was my own boss. None of the 550 fishermen ever sexually harassed me.

On the water equality finds a balance. We all know the other boat might be the one to save our life.

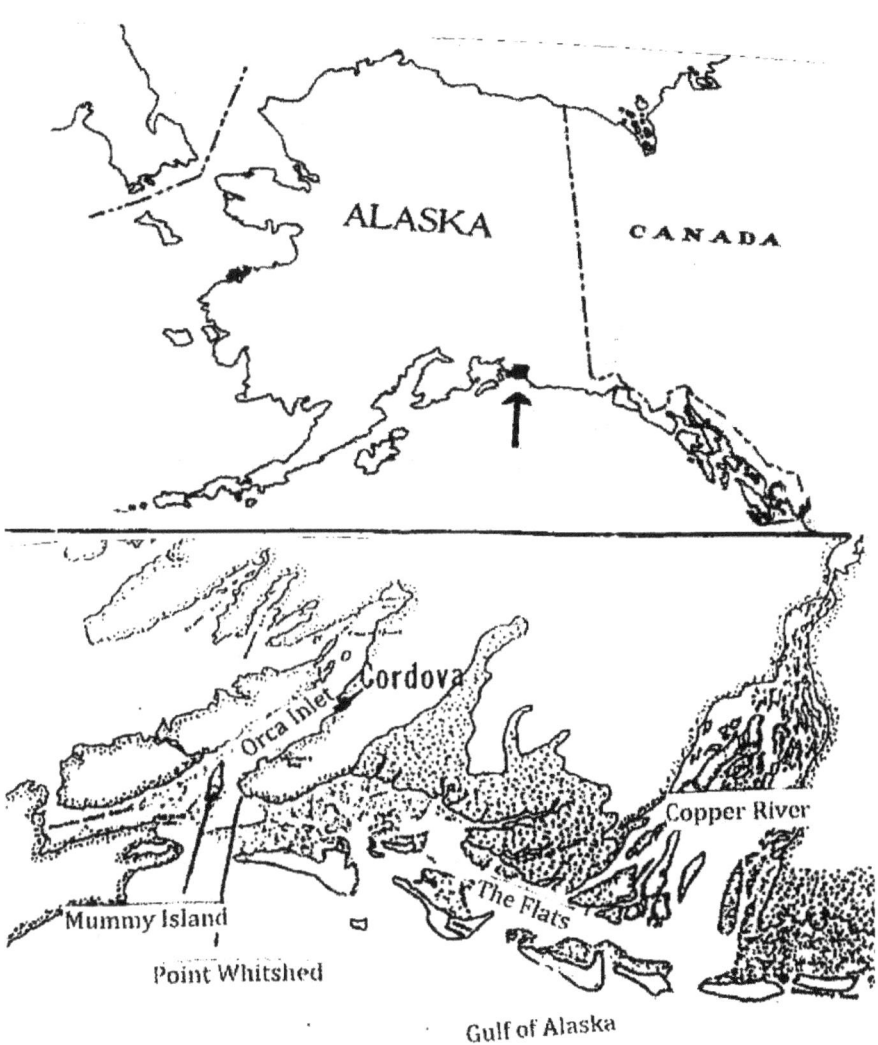

CHAPTER ONE

"KATHY, I'M GOING fishing with Willie. Do you want us to give you a ride to the cabin on our way?" Peggy asked.

"No, I'm afraid to live on the island alone."

"Why don't you come with me and experience the Copper River Flats?" Tom asked. "We'll be cramped, but the weather's good and boats feel larger when it isn't raining."

Before traveling to Alaska, I'd been on a boat twice. I was on an impromptu vacation in Alaska. Why not do what Alaskans do and go fishing? Unknown to me, those waters were the most dangerous for gillnetting in Alaska. Later I learned the Copper River steals at least one life from the fishing fleet every year.

A month earlier, Willie White, brother of a college roommate, came to visit while I lived in Bellingham, Washington. After my roommates and I consumed numerous tacos, we sipped tequila while we enjoyed Willie's stories about life in Alaska.

Willie thought the lifestyle and wildness would be right up my alley. "Kathy, you've had commitments in previous years, but this summer you have no excuse. When I fly back I need to build a new fishing net. If you fly up with me, I'll pay you to hang one of the lines."

I'd heard about Cordova for years, knew half a dozen men who lived in Bellingham and spent summers in Alaska. Recently I had received a rejection letter that made my plans uncertain. Willie was correct. What better time would I have for a two-week vacation? I could do him a favor, tying knots to hold the web to a line, and the reward would cover half the cost of my airfare.

Another shot of tequila, and I asked, "When do we leave?"

The next morning I informed my boss, and two days later, Willie and I left Bellingham. After a two-hour car ride, we arrived at the airport in Seattle when the sun rose. Our flight departed in clear skies, and we enjoyed breakfast while we flew over countless islands dotting the Pacific Coast. Reaching Cordova isn't easy. The flight seemed to stop at every airport large enough to land a jet to deliver the daily mail and fresh milk. All the stops were at towns accessible only by boat or plane. Without airport security, we disembarked, looked around, and reboarded while the airline exchanged passengers and freight. After we traveled about the distance from Los Angeles to Seattle, the plane turned near the top of Alaska's panhandle and followed the coastline west. The scale of the landscape struck me with awe.

"Are we there yet?" I asked with a laugh the fourth time we landed.

"I promise, from here it's a puddle jump to Cordova," Willie said.

Locals called the long flight "the *milk run*." They dread the flight and thought the number of stops was an inconvenience, a wasted day. For me the flight gave me an opportunity to see glimpses of Southeast Alaska. After a brief stay in Yakutat the plane took to the air again. I stared out the window and marveled at the St. Elias range with Mount St. Elias, twenty miles from the coast and more than eighteen thousand feet, which makes it the tallest coastal mountain range in the world, massive, craggy, and inhospitable. I then understood the true meaning of *breathtaking*.

The flight attendants served us sandwiches and cookies while the plane continued along the coast with a backdrop of snow-covered mountains, huge glaciers, endless forests, and hundreds of rivers that emptied into the Gulf of Alaska. The most impressive, the Copper, divided steep blue-and-white mountains with a plume of murky glacial water. It flowed like arteries across the sand, around the barrier islands, and into the gulf with such volume and force the dark gulf water turned a milky gray and carried a distinct river of silty water twenty miles seaward. I pointed at the change in the water's color to Willie.

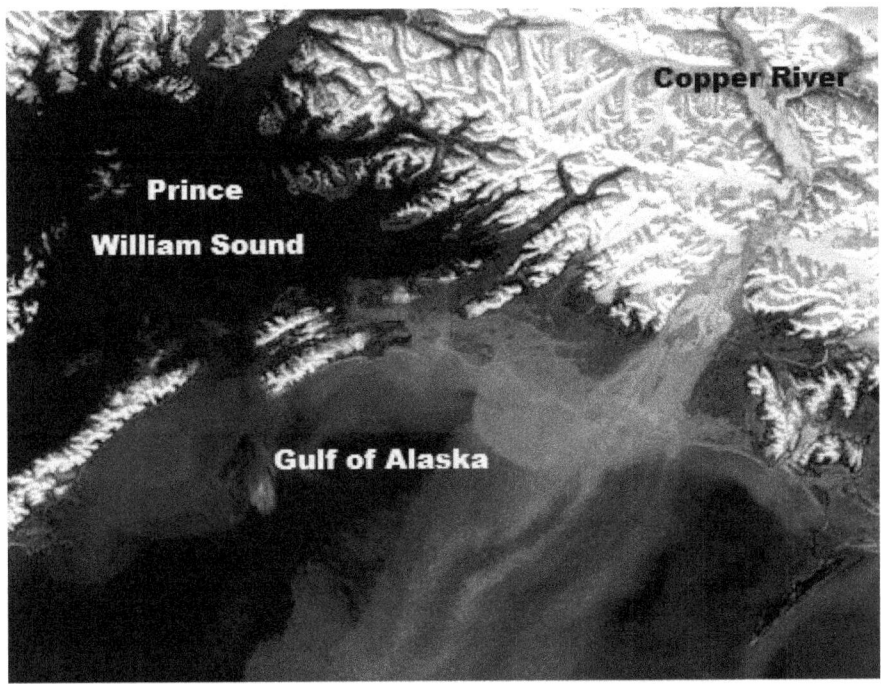

The Copper River Delta as seen from space. NASA

He explained, "Each year the Copper River deposits millions of tons of glacial silt onto the delta, which constantly changes the depth and the lay of the bottom where we fish our nets."

The plane began to reduce its altitude at our first sight of the river delta. We landed at its western edge at an airport that seemed primitive. A set of stairs unfolded from the rear of the 727. I stepped down and felt transported back in time. I don't remember seeing such an undeveloped expanse with no visible signs of civilization beyond the airport terminal, runway, and tower. I felt intrigued. We walked around the wing and across the tarmac to the terminal, a friendly-looking 1950s log cabin a hundred feet away.

We claimed our baggage and loaded it into the Airporter, a stubby 1940s bus. It rolled out of the airport onto a two-lane road that locals called a highway. The road stretched west, straight and flat for six miles across the path of retreating glaciers with a gorgeous view of what remains of them to the north. I remembered Willie's descriptions, but he couldn't have expressed in words the feelings the landscape awakened in me.

The pavement narrowed when it crossed the bridge over Eyak River and wound along the shore of Eyak Lake, where houses and other signs of civilization began to appear. The bus slowed and made a slight turn and the road changed from the Copper River Highway into Cordova's First Street, a main street without any stoplights.

We stepped off in the middle of the two-block town center with structures from the early 1900s, most of them wood, except one side of the street where an entire block had burned in the great fire of 1963. Willie stacked our bags against a storefront and began to walk across the street. I followed him, but hesitated and glanced back at everything I owned sitting unguarded.

"The bags won't move," he reassured me.

He warned me when we walked into the grocery store, "We need to buy enough food to last us a week. Don't look at the prices; you'll lose your appetite, and we'll starve. Mummy Island is a ten-mile boat ride south of town. The cabin is primitive, without electricity. We can buy fresh food to eat for the first few days, and then we have to survive on a canned diet, because without a refrigerator, the ice we haul will last only two or three days."

Canned tuna, vegetables, and fruits were common to me, but cans of bread, butter, and meat were unexpected. An abundance of unfamiliar canned foods lined the shelves of the short aisles, wide enough for one cart to roll on the worn wood floor. I love milk and was delighted when I found canned milk, not evaporated, but the quart of whole milk had the misleading brand name of Real Fresh.

I held a can and asked Willie, "How does this taste?"

"It's not bad if you aerate it by pouring it into a pitcher," he said as he grabbed a case. "You'll like it. And chocolate. We need to buy Peggy some brownie mixes."

We filled two carts and pushed them to the checkout stand. Willie asked the clerk to charge the groceries to a purchase order from his cannery and deliver them to his skiff. The clerk pulled out an invoice and wrote Willie's name, the name and location of his boat, and Morpac across the top. We left after the clerk tallied the items we wanted to pack for a snack.

"Everything in the carts will be on my skiff by the time we arrive," Willie said.

He was confident she'd pack all the groceries, have the boxes delivered, and not overcharge him. He talked nonstop about his girlfriend Peggy. He was in a hurry to reach the island, but not in a hurry to leave town. He looked at his tide book. "Before we can leave, we need to wait for more water."

I guess he saw my puzzled look, because he continued, "Mummy is surrounded by acres of sand at low water. When water covers the sandbars, my skiff can reach the island. Until then, we can go on a hike."

We walked parallel to Orca Inlet, up First Street. A few blocks from the center of town sat two canneries, Alaska Packers and Morpac, the cannery that bought Willie's fish. There the pavement ended, and a dirt road continued up a small hill. We reached the crest and saw a large, empty dock.

"That's where the ferry arrives, the freighters unload, and at the far end is where I fuel my boat," Willie said.

I surveyed the dirt road that continued along the bay, around a steep rock cliff, and went out of sight. I asked, "Why are there no cars on the road?"

"The road ends at Orca, where the New England Fish Company operates, but without a pink salmon season, the cannery is closed, and nothing else is out there."

I'd heard about the poor return of pink salmon to Prince William Sound. The lack of pinks was why Willie visited down south. In other years he would have been fishing from May until September.

We walked down the far side of the hill to a flat area near a stream surrounded by wild grass and ponds. Willie plunked down on a log. "Here's a good spot for a break."

The land rose and became a tree-covered hill with trails. After we sampled a variety of cheeses on hardtack, we hiked the hill and discovered campsites in the woods. Workers had built temporary shelters with pallet boards, scrap wood, and plastic sheeting.

"That's where some of the transient cannery workers live, but without a pink salmon season, they don't have work, so the camp is deserted."

The unusual quiet around me was noticeable. I grew up in Seattle and attended college in three smaller cities, so my ears heard constant noise. I strained to hear, but the background din wasn't audible. The sounds I heard were of the wild: eagle wings flapping; the waterfall behind the trees on the rise of the hill; the water from Orca Inlet slapping against the shore after a boat passed; and a sky full of crows, ravens, and seagulls conversing endlessly. Instead of the smell of the city dominated by exhaust, the air held the aroma of wildflowers that grew on the hill and the fresh saltwater breeze blowing off the inlet.

I looked from the shore when we walked back, and the only signs of humans were occasional boats and some red and black navigational buoys. Hawkins Island dominated the view across Orca Inlet. The island stood about two thousand feet covered with evergreen trees to the shoreline. We retrieved our belongings, which sat exactly where we had left them piled on the sidewalk, and hiked down two hills. The first offered a nice boardwalk, but thereafter, was a dirt road with no sidewalk.

Willie had parked his boat at the far end of the harbor but said, "Let's take the first dock ramp and escape the dust."

We loaded our bags onto a cart and rolled it out the wooden dock to his skiff, parked at the transient float with the other boats that didn't have an assigned slip, a parking place, in the harbor. Boxes of groceries sat stacked on the deck of the skiff, just like he'd promised. Willie climbed on board and started the engine. While it warmed, he transferred the perishables and ice to his coolers. I passed our bags to him, and he packed them into the cabin, while I replaced the cart. When I returned, I untied the lines, climbed on board, and he shifted the engine into gear. The skiff pulled away from the dock, rounded the breakwater, and turned south.

"There's our home for the next couple of weeks," Willie said with his arm extended, pointing down the inlet at Mummy Island. "It's called Mummy because of the natural mummifying caves in those high cliffs."

The skiff traveled at a good clip until about five miles out of the harbor, where the skiff stopped abruptly and the engine died. Willie looked at the shores in the distance and stuck his oar overboard. It hit bottom. The skiff was in less than two feet of water. I was stunned. My experience told me the farther from shore, the deeper the water, the first of many of my beliefs proven wrong.

"We're out of the channel," he casually commented as he searched with his oar over both sides of the skiff for deeper water. "I think I'm too far this way."

I was wide-eyed and suffering culture shock. I didn't understand how he could be stuck in the middle of the inlet in a boat with a dead engine and not be concerned. He pushed a button that tilted the lower unit, which hung off the back of the boat into the water and turned the propeller. With the lower unit tilted up, the boat could travel in less water. He started the engine, shifted it into forward gear, but didn't lift the throttle. At idle speed the skiff inched forward. He continued to push his oar into the water to measure the depth. When he felt no resistance, he exhaled, put down the oar, pushed the switch to lower the unit, lifted the throttle, and proceeded as though nothing had happened. For him touching bottom was nothing. "Digging sand" with his propeller was an accepted navigational technique on those sand flats.

The skiff passed cautiously along the shore into a bay with a little cabin half covered by trees. The island was so quiet the noise of Willie's engine announced our arrival long before we came into sight. Peggy ran down from the cabin to greet us. I'd met her the previous spring when she stayed with us in Bellingham on her way to Cordova. To see her living like a pioneer conflicted with how elegant she naturally appeared. She'd lived on that island in isolation with no way to communicate and no way off the island, even in an emergency. Peggy was excited to see anyone, to hear anything, and especially to welcome Willie home. Her blond hair covered the shoulders of her red-and-black-checked flannel shirt. She wore rubber boots folded at the knees, but when she reached the water, she pulled the boots up to her hips.

She turned her back to me and said, "Hop on. I'll give you a ride to shore."

I hesitated until I thought of the alternative. The transformation of Peggy Parker from a sophisticated urban woman into "Wilderness Woman" had me stunned and impressed. She was completely self-reliant for survival.

Willie backed the skiff deeper and threw the anchor; he had his own pair of hip boots. The beach was a gentle slope of mud and fine sand that became gravel above the tide line. Anchored, the flat-bottom skiff would safely go dry in a couple of hours. When the sand reclaimed the perimeter of the island, we could walk to the skiff and unload the backpacks, groceries, and stove oil we'd brought with us.

A tin roof covered the two-room cabin. I walked in and saw a makeshift kitchen, an old wooden table and chairs, and a bed in the corner. The other room housed a cannery with big sinks, an industrial-sized pressure cooker, and a hand-cranked can sealer. Along the inside wall, short two-by-fours created a ladder that led to the attic.

"You can store your belongings and sleep upstairs," Willie said.

I climbed halfway up the ladder, and he passed me my sleeping bag and pack. At the top I found space without headroom or beds; instead, a tidy pile of foam pads for visitors to sleep on the floor. Comfortable quiet quarters if rain didn't pound on the tin roof.

Mummy Island and Point Whitshed, across the inlet on the mainland, once supplied more than half the razor clams for the country and established Cordova as the Razor Clam Capital of the World. The Great Alaskan Earthquake on Good Friday, 1964, altered the area drastically. The quake centered in Prince William Sound lifted the earth an average of six to eight feet around Cordova and more than thirty feet in other parts of the Sound. When the tide went out and never returned, boats and barges anchored in shallow water sat dry and stranded. Many turned into permanent monuments in the landscape. The minutes-long tremor destroyed an entire industry when the land rose and the razor clam beds dried up. Some of the clam canneries burned. People abandoned others, but because of diligent maintenance through the years, a few, like the one cabin that still stood on the island, were in good condition and perfect for a home-pack operation. We walked on the beach and located Scott's, a former clam cannery reduced to a pile of weathered timbers.

Other than a few huge boulders, the land near the cabin was flat and sloped gently to the water with a view of Hawkins Island. The vegetation above the pre-1964 tideline grew jungle thick, but the beach to the relatively recent tideline was completely barren. A short walk on a path from the cabin led to the other side of Mummy.

Willie pointed to a beach of small rocks with a sunny southern exposure and a view of the ocean. "That's where we'll hang my net."

Willie set up a hanging board, a ten-foot two-by-four mounted at a comfortable height for me to stand and tie knots. A gillnet has a cork line that floats and a lead line that sinks, with nylon web in between. My job was to tie thousands of knots that attached the web to a line that was nine hundred feet long, while he tied knots on the other line. He measured the board and marked the exact spacing.

He stressed to me, "You must tie each knot at the mark and make sure to pull the twine tight. If it slips, it distorts the geometry of the net."

The week went fast and the pile of finished net grew taller. On Saturday's high tide, we rode in Willie's skiff to Cordova for mail, laundry, groceries, and a night on the town. The harbor held a variety of boats. Salmon, herring, and crab were the main seafood harvested by Cordova's fishing fleet, but halibut, black cod, scallops, shrimp, and kelp were also important to the local economy. The boats ranged from less than twenty to almost one-hundred-feet long. As the boats increased in length, the amount of equipment sitting on deck also increased. The rigging, masts, and booms added complexities to the silhouettes. Most of the boats were black, white, or gray, but the bright red buoys, blue and green tarps, and hanging flags created a colorful harbor.

After showers, errands, and chores, we accepted an invitation to a community potluck dinner. People filled their plates and sat at long tables to enjoy the food and conversations. Everyone regardless of age appreciated each other's company. Teenage boys listened intently to an old-timer. I wondered if generation gaps didn't exist because without television, the community had extremely limited news and entertainment sources: the newspaper and one AM radio station, *KLAM*, so they all heard one perspective.

The residents shared fry bread, a local favorite, and a variety of seafood, but few vegetables or fruits. The quality of the produce in town was so poor people from outside joked that Cordova stores sold, at twice the price, what stores in the lower forty-eight threw out. The seafood was the opposite. Delicious crab, shrimp, halibut, and smoked salmon were all plentiful.

The migration to the bars began when the potluck dinner ended. The two-block stretch of First Street hosted three bars. Down the hill stood a fourth. One block farther, a fifth, and a sixth a mile down the highway. Elks and Moose clubs in town with bars served members and guests, all to entertain a town of two thousand that swelled to about five thousand during the summer fishing season. The same people returned each year, so everyone had known each other for years, yet they welcomed me, a stranger.

We stopped at a bar built in 1908, one of Cordova's originals. The Alaskan Hotel and Bar was a long, narrow place with a couple of pool tables, a shuffleboard, and an intricately carved rosewood bar that began at the door and ran more than half the length of the building. I admired the antique bar complete with a brass foot rail, cupboards with leaded glass doors, and a mirrored backsplash that reached fifteen feet up the wall.

"It was shipped around Cape Horn to one of the seventeen saloons in Katalla after the first oil in Alaska was discovered there in the late 1800s," Willie said. "The Katalla Company moved to Odiak, a native village, which became Cordova and the railroad terminal. When the company abandoned Katalla the rosewood bar came to Cordova."

The bartender was a handsome young man, Jimmy, the owner's son. To stoke the party, he rang the bell that hung at the end of the bar, which signaled the purchase of a round of drinks for the house. Sandy, an older woman whose confident, friendly manner reminded me of Mae West, walked behind the bar and helped Jimmy pour the numerous drinks.

"That's Sandy," Willie said. "She was once a military woman. She came to town after she married John, a fisherman from Texas. He was famous for the phrase, 'You don't run; you don't ride.' He was quoted as saying that when he threw his outboard engine overboard because it quit working." Willie sipped his beer and sucked the foam from his mustache with his lower lip. "When John and Sandy divorced, the court awarded her half of what he considered his house, so he took a chainsaw, cut the house in half, and said, 'There's your half. Now get it off my land.' I think the story may have been embellished over the years."

At the end of the bar was a room with a dance floor, a piano, a jukebox, and a small stage. With no seats at the bar, we picked up our drinks, walked to the back room, and sat at a booth off the dance floor. As the evening went on, more drinks went down and people began to play the jukebox. Peggy and I were new women in town and sparked some interest, but most of the men played shuffleboard, shot pool, or talked fish.

An older man, George Andersen, made sure the few women had a chance to grace the dance floor. He remained seated for the fast songs, but when the slow music began, he was the first person on the dance floor with a different woman each time. He stood about five-foot-seven and was heavy, not fat, but solid, with a round face, a glowing smile, a boxer's nose, and cauliflower ears. George alone had been the police force in Cordova in territorial days. He'd been a champion boxer, which explained his features and his ability to glide across the dance floor.

The gathering at the bar felt like a private party, because everyone knew each other. The locals were tolerant with a laissez-faire attitude. To explain or dismiss any unconventional behavior, people said, "Oh, that's just so-and-so." I guess with familiarity comes predictability and acceptance. I didn't know at the time that within a few years, they'd say, "Oh, that's just Kathy." I felt myself falling in love with the community and its friendly people. The warm emotions I felt quenched a thirst that surprised me, because I hadn't been aware of the yearning.

The sun was rising when the bars closed at four. We walked to the harbor, where I slept in a bunk on the *Sugar*, a boat that belonged to friends from Bellingham. When the tide was right on Sunday morning, I crawled onto Willie's skiff, and we motored back to Mummy Island with enough of town to last us all week.

I appreciated the quiet isolation on Mummy Island. The news we heard was local from *KLAM*. Sunshine on a private beach, Willie's thought-provoking conversations, and Peggy, who brought us coffee and treats, made the days fly.

Hanging a net is tedious work, so we also reserved time for hikes. I was told that for generations the caves on Mummy Island served as the final resting place for indigenous royalty. Regional tribal members wrapped the bodies of their respected leaders in sea-otter skins and laid them in the natural mummifying caves high in the cliffs above the cabin. We found what had been an entrance to a cave on one of our hikes. In previous years descendants sealed the cave entrance with large boulders to preserve the sacred spot. Some visitors to the island felt uncomfortable so close to the ancient spirits. To me, Mummy Island felt peaceful and became one of my favorite locations on earth.

My two weeks were over. Willie was absolutely correct. I loved life in Alaska and never wanted to leave. While we were in town on the weekend for laundry and food, I called my parents and sent a check to my roommates for rent.

The canneries and the fishermen couldn't agree on a price per pound for the fish. Willie's net was finished and wound on his reel. The gillnetters, although fired up and ready to catch salmon, stayed *on the beach*, meaning they didn't go fishing, they were on strike for an acceptable price.

A group of friends joined us on Mummy Island. I knew some of them from Bellingham, where they spent their winters building their boats. The days dragged while the gillnetters waited to resolve the price. We needed a project to keep the fishermen occupied and chase away the restlessness of the strike.

Peggy suggested, "We should build a banya (an Alaskan sauna). We can use wood from Scott's Cannery."

The grandfather of John Scott, nicknamed Bean, once owned Scott's Cannery. Bean had heard stories of his grandfather's life decades earlier when razor clams were plentiful and numerous canneries operated on Mummy Island and at Point Whitshed. Those stories were part of what had drawn Bean to Cordova. He returned each spring to fish for salmon until fall. He worked winters as a carpenter, so we named him supervisor for construction of the banya.

"The timbers from Scott's Cannery are straight and solid," Bean said. "We can use heavy twine to lash the beams off the ground between those four trees. The entrance from below will minimize any loss of heat when people go in and out."

Photo by Tom Copeland

A gillnetter brought a surplus diesel stove, a fuel tank, and some stovepipe from his locker. The banya builders mounted the stove on the platform that rested on the beams. Soon the walls stood and the roof went on. The banya was almost ready to light when news came across on the radio that the gillnetters were going fishing. The skippers heard the news, dropped everything and scrambled to their boats. Peggy and I found ourselves alone on Mummy Island, thankful we had a supply of food.

A boat can reach the island in the last couple of hours of high tide, but we didn't possess a boat. We remained captive on the island. Our one means of communication was *KLAM* on a transistor radio. That evening Peggy and I walked to the far side of the island and watched the boats power across the shallow water that temporarily covered the sandbars and then disappear, melting into the horizon. The boats fished for five days while we hiked, read, finished the banya, and relaxed in the solitude of the island. At the end of the week Willie stopped at the island. He arrived on the high tide early in the morning, anchored his skiff, and fell asleep.

When we woke, Peggy pointed to Willie's skiff. "We're going to town on the next tide. Let's load the boat."

With the skiff dry, Peggy and I loaded the garbage bags, empty fuel jugs, and our overflowing pile of laundry into his skiff. In the afternoon, the skiff floated. When Willie woke, he ran the boat with Peggy and me to Cordova.

Saturday night the town celebrated the completion of its indoor heated swimming pool. In a community dependent on harvesting seafood, swimming is an important skill that few Cordovans possessed. For years the residents wished for a pool so their children could learn to swim. The community celebrated the grand opening with a shower of fireworks. The abundant catch of salmon the gillnetters harvested that week heightened the excitement.

After the pool party, Peggy, Willie, and I walked a few blocks north of town with Bean and Tom, another banya builder. We hiked the hill behind Morpac to a military surplus tent. Complete with walls and an oil stove, the tent sat on a plywood platform. Bean and Tom kept their town basecamp there for the summer. Hidden by the trees, the tent offered a warm, dry place to seek shelter from the rain, which began late that night.

CHAPTER TWO

IN THE MORNING when everyone prepared to head out fishing, I knew I didn't want to live on the island alone. I accepted an offer to go with Bean's fishing partner, Tom, an entertaining storyteller with a good sense of humor. His twenty-one-foot skiff was a flat-bottomed wooden rowboat. He powered the skiff with a "kicker," an outboard engine that hung off one side of the stern. The other side held the rollers, three wooden cylinders that formed a U shape, open at the top, which guided the net in and out of the boat. A piece of plywood bent to fit across the bow formed a cave-type shelter for the cabin. Fishing equipment and fish storage crowded the remaining limited space.

Tom's skiff plied down Orca Inlet past Mummy Island, where he turned the skiff east and entered the mudflats of the Copper River Delta. The shoreline changed from trees to sand, the water clear to muddy. The dominant color was gray.

"Welcome to the Flats," Tom said.

I knew nothing about fishing, but the area appeared welcoming, with the calm wind, flat water, and sunshine. Tom ran the skiff east within the shallow channels between sandbars of various sizes and heights. After about a half an hour, he slowed the skiff and ran it as shallow as possible to a beach. He turned the boat 180 degrees and threw the buoy, attached to the end of his net, off the stern. In a well-practiced routine, he grabbed and dropped a pile of net and lines overboard and powered the skiff away from the shore. The net unwound from the reel, flowed through the rollers over the stern, dropped into the water, and followed the trail of the skiff. Tom shifted the kicker out of gear. The momentum of the skiff slowed. He eased the last of the net into the water. He attached the end of the cork line to his tow post, and when the line came tight, the skiff jerked and swung abruptly in the direction of the current. Tom shut off the engine.

"Now we drift and wait for the salmon to hit. Watch the cork line."

The cork line dotted with red and white corks floated on the surface of the water between the skiff and the shore. Willie's net was long when we hung, stacked, and loaded it. Tom's net, the same length, looked short floating in the water. My erroneous perception of distance on water became obvious. A red cork separated the white corks every ten fathoms, or sixty feet, but the distance on the water appeared to be ten feet. The cork line suspended the web, which created an underwater fence of diamond shapes that caught the salmon by the gills when the fish swam into the web.

"See the corks bobbing?" Tom asked. "That's salmon."

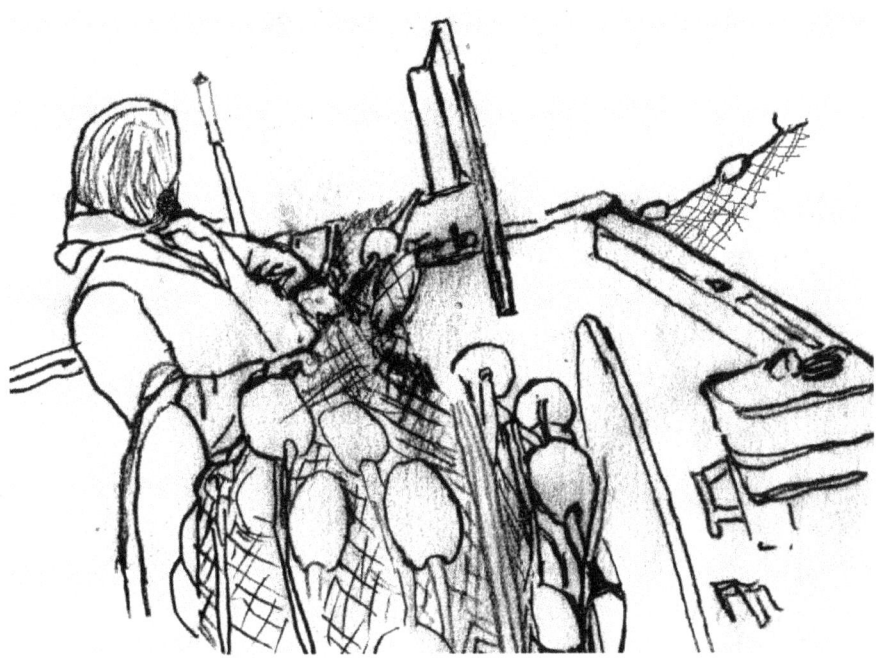

Once we drifted a certain distance, Tom placed a plastic garbage can on the kicker to hide the propeller and keep it from tangling in the web. He pulled in the net, picked a dozen coho out of the web, removed the garbage can, ran the skiff back to the shore, set the net, and then loaded the fish into his hold.

The time that the net drifted in the channel, called a *set*, varied from ten minutes to two hours, depending on the speed of the current. When the flood tide ran hard, the skiff and net raced up the channel toward the Fish and Game boundary line with fishing closed markers. The ebb tide washed the net down the channel toward the ocean bar and the breaking waves.

"I want to avoid my net drifting above the markers or out the bar through the surf."

Between the marker and the ocean bar, he needed to avoid snags. Trees and branches drifted down the river and tangled in the nets or became saturated and sank. Sometimes a piece of wood "sanded over" and didn't budge. The snags grabbed the lead line, and the net became anchored until the strain broke the line, the current switched direction, or the line pulled the chunk of wood free. Tom worked his net continuously until once every six hours at the change of tide set. The current slowed and the net ultimately stopped for a few minutes before the direction of the current reversed. On those sets, we paused for a coffee break and a quick meal. By then our stomachs growled.

Disappointed with his catch, Tom said, "I want to run farther east, but the tide is low. The inside passage is too shallow. We'll have to run out the ocean bar, through the breakers, and head east in the gulf."

Six major barrier islands separate and shelter the river delta from the Gulf of Alaska. The ocean meets the coast on the outside shore of those islands and expresses her mood with either gentle surf or monstrous waves. Deeper water interrupts the line of surf between the "sand islands," where the water calms. Those channels are deep enough for shallow draft boats to navigate between the gulf and the delta in nice weather.

Tom ran the skiff out a channel that led us beyond the breakers into the gulf. He ducked in and out through the breakers at each ocean bar and continued to run the skiff east in his relentless search for more coho. When he ran in one of the channels, I glanced at the stern. My eyes opened wide, my mouth dropped open, and my heart raced. A wave crested above Tom's head. My expression must have shown my fright, because he glanced over his shoulder and sped up to outrun the wave. The wave broke with a thundering crash inches behind his stern, while the skiff slid to safety inside the ocean bar.

We both exhaled in relief. "Whoa!"

We traveled about forty miles to the east end of the delta by midweek. The fishing improved, but more boats crowded the area than in the other channels. Every night Tom delivered his catch to a tender, a boat hired by one of the canneries. Tenders bought and hauled salmon to town and supplied fishing boats with water, fuel, food, and weather reports.

"A storm is brewing in the eastern gulf headed in our direction—a severe storm," the tenderman warned us Thursday night.

Early Friday the thirteenth, the CB radio hummed with chatter about the storm. Fishing remained open until Saturday, but with the intense atmospheric low approaching, the skippers planned to quit fishing and race to town. By daylight the water had become too wild and dangerous for the skiffs to travel in the gulf. The gillnetters needed to wait until the tide rose enough to allow their skiffs to travel the inside channel, the channel inside the barrier islands.

The sky to the east continued to darken. Tom laid his net for a morning low-water set. At the minute the tide book predicted the change of tide, the wind began to blow. The gusts blew hard against the stern, and the cork line yanked tight. More than one gust splashed water over the stern. Salt water dripped from his black beard. He delivered his salmon to a tender and filled the fuel tank before he threw his anchor to wait for more tide.

The storm was rapidly approaching. Tom's outboard-powered skiff was too puny to carry me and stay ahead of the storm. Joel, another banya builder and the gillnetter who owned the cabin on Mummy Island, offered to ferry me in his skiff, the *Clam Burger*. It was longer, wider, and more powerful, with an inboard/outboard engine.

All the boats needed more water to travel across the river delta. That water also covered the sandbars that afforded the skiffs some protection. When the tide came in and enough water flooded under the shallowest draft skiffs, skippers, including Tom, began to leave the anchorage. He dropped me off on the *Clam Burger* and began his run. Joel's skiff sat deeper in the water, so he waited another twenty minutes before he pulled his anchor.

The wind increased with the tide. That morning the so-called protected route to town didn't seem protected. The water inside the sandbars was rougher than the open ocean earlier in the week, complete with swells and foam. The water threatened the *Clam Burger* when it crossed the channels that ran in from the ocean. There the swells intensified. The skiff swayed and bounced like an airplane in turbulence. Enormous powerful breakers rolled across the entire bar entrance. Tall, white, loud, and frothy, the breaking waves made the bars impassable.

The *Clam Burger* bow plowed into the swells. Its speed slowed while the engine struggled to power the skiff through the wall of water until the bow broke through and the skiff fell into the sea on the far side of the swell. At times waves crashed over the bow and splashed icy salt water in our faces.

In one spot the route followed a shallow channel between two sandbars. The tide covered a portion of the outside sandbar with loud, pounding surf. Although Joel's skiff was larger than Tom's, it felt tiny. Eventually Joel made his way behind the Egg Island sandbar, where traveling was easier, but by no means pleasant.

At the western end of the delta, Mummy Island marks the spot where the route to town turns north. There boats travel behind Point Whitshed into the sheltered waters of Orca Inlet. With the wind screaming at their sterns and Mummy Island in sight, the boats raced toward the Hump, the shallowest spot on the inside passage. The waters were unmarked. Skippers made their best guess of where the water was deep enough to cross. When the lead boats bumped the sand and stuck, the pack of boats following dispersed and tried their next best guess. The wind howled. The tide was in high flood. The boats aground soon blew across the shallow stretch and reached the safe side of Point Whitshed.

The *Clam Burger* rounded a point on the leeside of Mummy Island. Joel's cabin and a few anchored skiffs came into view. Joel ran his skiff close to the shore. I jumped off the bow. He backed his skiff away from the shore and threw his anchor. More boats joined us, ready to fire up the banya.

Rain battered the island. The wind persisted and picked up speed. We filled the banya oil tank, lit the stove, and the party began. When we splashed water on the hot granite rocks that surrounded the stove, billows of steam filled the banya and forced our tight muscles to loosen. All of us felt exhausted from a strenuous week of fishing. We listened to the rain pound and wind roar while the heat soothed our aching bodies. We had escaped the Flats. We could relax. We knew we were safe from the fury of Mother Nature.

When I left the banya and faced the wind, I struggled to breathe. The rain pelted my body like slivers of glass, and hearing above the wind's wail became hard. While Willie stayed inside and baked, we cooled in the rain, sought shelter in the cabin, and exchanged stories from the week of fishing. We noticed Willie stroll past the cabin with steam rising from his silhouette. He passed again on his return to the banya with the six-pack of beer he retrieved from his skiff.

Within minutes we heard him yell, "Fire! The banya's on fire!"

We ran out of the cabin toward the banya and saw a glowing hot spot on the roof by the stove stack. The wind blew hard on the roof fire and created intense heat but little flame. Before anyone could react, the sun-scorched two-by-twelve timbers lit up like giant wooden matchsticks. In minutes flames consumed the banya. We had no way to fight the blaze. We backed away. When we remembered the oil tank hanging on the wall, we retreated farther.

For the first time, I appreciated the dime-size raindrops and prayed they continued to fall from the sky. The fire burned with intense heat. I worried the whole island was going to erupt in flames.

The stove oil ignited in one quick burst of fire, not with the explosion I feared. The vegetation around the banya was green and saturated with rainwater. The plants barely dried and never caught fire. When the flames burned to coals, the rain doused the banya and reduced it to ash.

Photo by Tom Copeland

The exhaustion from the week of fishing, the anxiety of the day, and horror of the night left everyone drained and ready for sleep. The skippers walked to their skiffs that sat dry while the tide was low and slept until the tide flooded over the sandbars, floating their boats for the ride to town.

I said to Peggy, "I wonder if the ancient spirits didn't mind us seeking solitude but objected to the island becoming party central because of the inviting banya."

WHEN WE HEARD on *KLAM* that the Department of Fish and Game closed the salmon season for the year, we cleaned the cabin for the winter. Willie ran his skiff with Peggy and me to Cordova. In town, the gillnetters unloaded their nets, pulled their boats out of the water, and moved everything into storage. A few of the larger boats stayed in the water so the skippers could go deer hunting on the remote islands. The crews of the largest boats switched equipment and were prepared to fish the winter.

Willie pulled his skiff at Morpac. The cannery had numerous buildings: the fish processing buildings, several storage warehouses, a bunkhouse, and a cookhouse. Peggy and I hauled multiple loads upstairs in a warehouse to Willie's locker. I knew another Morpac gillnetter, Dick Becker from Bellingham. Over time we'd become good friends. Every fall when the gang returned from Alaska, Dick threw a party at his house on the lake in Bellingham, and Willie barbequed a king salmon. Dick was the person I called when I wanted to do something, but not alone. He was always ready for an adventure.

Since childhood I've had girlfriends, but also appreciated my friendships with boys. I never wanted to be a boy, but activities planned with boys were often more fun, exciting, and likely to cause mischief. I developed enjoyable friendships with boys before we were interested in "the other sex." When music classes began in grade school, I inherited the trumpet my three older brothers had played. I was the only girl to leave for music class with the brass section. I still cherish some of the friendships that I had with boys. In high school when Dave and Donnie knew I was going to be stood up for a dance, they dressed in their finest, and I had two dates. Two girlfriends dressing up and taking me wouldn't have had the same effect on my broken heart. I enjoy the special men in my life, and Dick had become one of them.

He planned to drive south on the Alcan, the Alaskan Canadian Highway, a familiar drive twice a year for Dick and his passenger Larry, another gillnetter. That year Dick intended to haul equipment and leftover materials from the previous spring when he had lengthened his fiberglass boat, the *Pagan Queen*.

"Are you interested in coming?" Dick asked. "Larry doesn't drive. If you want to share the driving, you're welcome to come with us."

Dick explained, "Vice President Agnew's last vote broke a tie in the Senate, which approved the Trans Alaska Oil Pipeline lease. Fishermen fought the terminal being located inside of Prince William Sound. We sued but settled when the oil companies promised ultramodern tankers and rapid response to any spill. We heard jobs were available and plan to stop in Valdez and Fairbanks to sign up for employment at the labor halls before we drive south. I don't know what's involved or how long the trip will take. We might not reach Washington for two weeks."

At that time people didn't need identification to board planes. I sold my open return ticket to another woman and, with the cash, was off to see more of Alaska. Dick packed the back of his truck full, with fiberglass resin and cloth, a space heater, tools, and tarps. We found enough cracks to cram in a sleeping bag and one backpack each. We departed on the ferry late at night, grabbed our sleeping bags, rolled them out on the top deck with the other travelers, and fell asleep. In the morning the ferry docked in Valdez, where we enjoyed a hot breakfast at a cafe.

"I'll leave my truck in the grocery store parking lot and meet you there after Larry and I go to the Labor Hall," Dick said.

I explored the town, a town without any historic buildings. At the original Valdez, the sand and gravel suffered liquefaction during the four-minute Good Friday earthquake. The harbor and a portion of the town slumped into the fjord. The slide displaced a large volume of water and triggered a local tsunami. Thirty- to forty-foot tsunamis from the earthquake followed. The longshoremen and everyone on the dock perished. Residents relocated Valdez on higher, firmer ground four miles west of the original site.

I met Dick and Larry at the truck in the afternoon. We bought food for instant meals, and drove to Valdez Glacier for a picnic.

"That plaque memorializes the men, women, and pack animals lost when they attempted to cross that glacier during the gold rush," Dick said.

I stared up at the frozen wall of ice and said, "I hope I never experience their desperation."

After we finished our dinner the three of us crammed into the front seat of the El Camino. Dick began the drive to Fairbanks.

He stopped in the middle of nowhere at a turnout. "This spot looks good for a nap."

We unpacked our sleeping bags for a night under the stars, which were much more visible than in a sky close to the lights of civilization. The beauty of the bright stars made closing my eyes hard, especially when I thought about bears. After we woke we continued toward Fairbanks. Dick pointed at Denali, Mount McKinley, in the distance with its summit hidden by the clouds. "Get a look at that! We can enjoy this view because the south slope rises seventeen thousand feet in twelve miles. The mountain is high enough to create its own weather, the most severe in the world, which makes the summit an unusual sight."

We stopped at the six-million-acre park that surrounds the mountain, where wildness is the chief attraction. On the inner roads, Denali park limited visitors to park busses. The ride was like visiting a zoo where the wild animals roamed free and the cages held the people.

We traveled into the interior, where the landscape showed hints of the gold mining era, with abandoned equipment on the hillsides. When we reached Fairbanks, we chipped in for a motel room with two beds. Larry and Dick slept in their sleeping bags on top of one, while I enjoyed the luxury of a long, hot shower, crisp sheets, and a real bed for the first time since leaving Bellingham.

Dick and Larry signed up for future jobs at the labor hall in the morning while I slept. They returned, and we began the drive to Washington. Before we lost sight of the highest mountain in North

America, we looked above the clouds and captured a rare sight of Denali's summit.

We rode for hours and watched the scenery change while we crossed the continent. The landscape in low areas said the season was summer, but the leaves turned orange, red, and yellow in the passes. In the next valley the leaves looked late-summer green. We drove for a couple of days on gravel roads that kicked up clouds of dust. Dick and I traded driving every few hours and stopped for nights under the stars.

Dick surprised Larry and me one afternoon when he parked the truck, switched off the ignition, and announced, "We're due for a soak."

A path through the trees ended at Liard Hot Springs. We soaked in the steam pools lined with rocks. The smell of sulfur floated in the air, but the heat relaxed our stiff muscles, a fair trade for the stink. When we heard the next group of visitors on the trail, we slipped into our clothes, hiked down to the truck, and continued the long drive. Either Dick thought of fewer things to show us, or the roads were better, because from the hot springs south, the miles flew. We reached the Canada–United States border at the Peace Arch and counted the minutes until we'd enjoy our first home-cooked meal in a week.

We hadn't showered or changed clothes since Fairbanks. Dick's tight blond curls, without a barber's touch since early the previous spring, had grown out as wild as Einstein's in his older years. Larry's straight black hair hung to his shoulders, and they both wore beards. U.S. Customs agents glanced at us, decided we looked like hippies, and instructed Dick to pull his truck into a special lane. An agent marched us inside, and after an officer searched our pockets, he allowed us to return to the truck.

We found Dick's load sprawled across the entire parking lot. He expressed both doubt and hope that he could fit the entire load back into his truck. He climbed in, crawled to the front of the canopy, and called out articles by name. Larry and I surveyed the piles and passed the requested items into the truck. Dick smiled with relief when he hopped off the tailgate with his load stowed once again.

We continued to Bellingham without any further delay. Dick drove me to the house I left in August. Kris was at work, but Jym welcomed me to the contents of the refrigerator and a fresh cup of coffee, eager to hear about my visit to Alaska. My two-week vacation had lasted almost two months. The isolation, the wilderness, and the people with their can-do attitude and spirit of helping one another awakened in me a different reality. I lost interest in reapplying to graduate school and changed my priority to returning to Alaska as soon as possible.

My boss hired me back, and I was grateful for the income. My vacation cost far more money than I expected. After working to pay the money I owed to my parents and with some startup money saved, I wrote to Peggy and asked about the availability of jobs in Cordova.

CHAPTER THREE

WHEN WE CLOSED the cabin for the winter the previous fall, Peggy moved to an apartment in Cordova and found a job with the local newspaper. In response to my letter, she wrote that three of the canneries in town were processing crab, and jobs were available. She encouraged me to come and invited me to sleep on her couch until I found a place of my own.

I spent most of a day in March flying to Cordova. Unlike my first flight with Willie, a thick cloud cover obstructed my view. Spring had arrived with daffodils blooming in Bellingham. I landed in Cordova and found a fresh layer of snow covered the streets with an accumulation of old crusty snow everywhere else. The temperatures stayed cold enough to keep the snow from melting.

I dropped my bags at Peggy's and went to Morpac cannery. It hired me on the spot to work on a tanner crab processing line. The job involved standing at a conveyor belt and stuffing cooked crab halves, complete with legs and a claw, into a plastic bag. Working on a conveyor belt was the hardest I'd ever experienced. Physically the job required minimal effort, but mentally, the task was mind numbing. After I stared for hours at that never-ending supply of crab on the belt, my eyes played tricks on me. The half crab turned into a bird. The crab claw, through my conveyor-belted eyes, changed into a bird beak. The vision of birds gasping for air when I stuffed them into plastic bags made me stop, shake my head, and readjust my focus. My coworkers broke the trance when they cracked a leg and ate the crab. I concluded the only reason workers stayed on that line was for the endless amount of crab they consumed during their shifts.

My first night at Peggy's apartment, we woke and found sheets of ice on the inside of the windows. The oil-burning heater had quit working. Peggy called the property manager to no avail; he was out of town until the next day. We tinkered with the carburetor on the furnace but failed at creating any heat. When the manager returned, he ordered parts, but days passed before the parts arrived.

Life became a search for warmth. The restaurants were warm, but after the first day we knew seats that required a purchase were too expensive. Peggy and I found refuge in the library when it was open. When it closed, we sought the warmth of the laundromat. People sitting in the library or waiting in the laundromat are common so we could sit there unnoticed. When both closed, we went home and crawled into our sleeping bags.

Peggy's second-floor apartment stood a half block down the hill from the main street. Two south-facing picture windows gave us an unobstructed view of Orca Inlet, where we watched the sun move along the horizon from Mummy Island to Hawkins Island, setting farther north each night. The daily change in the sunrise and sunset became dramatic after the spring equinox. Daylight increased by several minutes each day. I saw the promise of spring everywhere.

The canneries that operated year-round switched from crab to herring and then to salmon. My life on the processing line was shorter than crab season. I was waitressing at the Reluctant Fisherman by the time Dick arrived in town. When he returned from seining herring in Prince William Sound, he hired me to work on the *Pagan Queen* for salmon season. My first task was to help Dick hang his new sockeye net. We climbed the stairs in one of the many Morpac warehouses and found the gear loft, an area with a smooth floor and large enough to stretch a net. Although not as scenic as the beach on Mummy Island, the cannery provided coffee breaks for workers and fishermen seven days a week at ten in the morning and three in the afternoon, with pastries and cookies baked fresh each morning in the cookhouse kitchen.

Willie, Tom, and Bean arrived with the flood of gillnetters, and the cannery bustled with activity while the fishermen prepared for the season opener. They painted their wooden hulls, hung or mended nets, replaced or repaired engines or reels, and a few, including Bean, rushed to finish work on a new boat. The gillnetters possessed different priorities and deadlines, but everything had to be ready for May 15 the season opener by regulation. From then until September, our lives revolved around *openers* when we fished and *closures* when we did maintenance, made repairs, and replenished our bodies and supplies. The two openers were Monday at six in the morning and Thursday night at six. That year, fishing legally began Thursday evening, but when the gillnetters actually went fishing depended on how the price negotiations progressed between the fishermen and the canneries.

Cordova Aquatic Marketing Association, CAMA, established in the razor-clam days, negotiated the price contracts between the fishermen and the canneries for crab and salmon. Nearly every night CAMA called a meeting where Bob Blake, a gillnetter, seiner, crabber, and CAMA president, presented any new price offer. At my first meeting, Dick and I walked into the school gym with the bleachers pulled out from one wall and filled with almost the entire fishing fleet. Members in the audience expressed their feelings about the price and the market in passionate speeches to the crowd. Some spoke softly and deliberately, while others screamed about cannery collusion. Spirited debates went on for hours, before Bob called for a vote, which decided the will of the majority. When the offer failed to meet the majority's approval, fishermen kept their boats tied to the dock, declaring a strike. The gillnetters accepted that they wouldn't set their nets Thursday night because of the low price offers. They were hopeful about fishing on Monday morning.

After a long winter, the fishermen were out of cash. They lived on purchase orders, which were credit from the canneries. To apply pressure when the strike began, the canneries stopped issuing purchase orders. The threat of a strike gave gillnetters an incentive to be prepared. Dick's boat was ready and well stocked with food. Without money or credit, gillnetters caught in the middle of an unexpected engine replacement or a new but unfinished boat suffered immensely.

The previous winter, Bean had shared a farmhouse near Bellingham with Tom, his wife, Merrie, and their son, Jesse. Bean built a new boat in the barn, a fiberglass bow-picker, the *Equinox,* and he needed money to finish it. Morpac cannery financed the boat, but when the strike began, although the boat wasn't finished, Bean's cannery credit was.

The local processors refused to offer an acceptable price for the salmon. Days went by without a meeting. Tensions around town grew stronger over the weekend when skippers realized they wouldn't set their nets, taste their first bite of spring salmon, or make any money on Monday morning.

Bob Blake, a highly regarded negotiator, tried to bring new buyers into town to purchase salmon. A week into the season, he called a CAMA meeting. He found a packer from Pelican, a tiny town on the other side of the Gulf of Alaska, with an offer Bob thought the fishermen should consider. He explained the offer, and CAMA members debated their options.

Pelican Seafoods operated two tenders that held fewer salmon than the anticipated catch. The eager membership agreed to limit their catch, or at least their sales. If the fishermen accepted the offer, they agreed to divide the tenders' capacity equally among the CAMA members. They figured each member could deliver six hundred pounds of salmon, about a hundred fish. The rest of each gillnetter's catch would be a free home-pack for the freezer or the smokehouse. A limit of one hundred sockeye isn't much, but the fishermen would have some much-needed cash and a taste of salmon.

The discussion didn't drag on for hours, because the gillnetters knew a limited amount of time remained to catch the tide for the opener that evening. After they debated the details, the membership voted. When Bob Blake announced the majority accepted the offer, the room exploded with a stampede to the harbor. A flurry of activity erupted everywhere in town. The main street became crowded when people spent their bottom dollar and loaded trucks with last-minute supplies and groceries. The harbor emptied in no time as the boats hurried past the breakwater and rushed toward Mummy Island on the flood tide.

After I untied the lines, I leapt onto the *Pagan Queen* as she pulled away from the Morpac dock. Dick steered down Orca Inlet past Mummy Island. Instead of turning east and running across the Hump, he continued south to the ocean, running out Strawberry Channel with small breakers on each side.

"I never run Strawberry Bar on the ebb. It's too unpredictable," Dick said.

The water looked predictable enough to me. Gentle waves washed to the shore in slow motion. I watched Dick study the area as though seeing the channel for the first time.

"Take a good look; Strawberry Bar is never this calm," he said.

I asked, "How did an ocean bar ever get the name Strawberry?"

Dick pointed west. "On that beach a profusion of strawberries grow wild. People also named Egg and Grass Islands because of their unique characteristics. Egg Island has thousands of Glaucous gull eggs, and beach grass covers the sand dunes on Grass Island."

"What are the names of the other islands?"

"Pete Dahl bears the name of a Swede who fished there and operated a store at the head of the slough that also bears his name." A slough pronounced slou, is a secondary channel of a river delta that is flushed by the tide.

The two sand islands at the east end, Coquenhena, or Kokenhenik as we know it, and Softuk are Alaskan Native names, but I don't know their meanings. I think Coquenhena may have been a chief's name."

People began fishing commercially in the lakes and rivers after Seward purchased the territory from Russia in 1867. The area fished hasn't changed since the 1920s, when the feds kicked fishermen out of the rivers and lakes. The inside boundary line stretched across the delta five-hundred-yards off each mouth of the river. Tom fished the "inside" waters, between the barrier islands and the grass banks. The waters of the district extended offshore of the barrier islands into the Gulf of Alaska, and skippers referred to that area as the "outside."

Almost all of the gillnetters fished small skiffs on the inside, in the shallow channels and small waterways surrounded by sand. In his fiberglass boat, larger than most and with two engines, Dick fished outside the barrier islands. I tried to imagine how the gillnetters knew their location when surrounded by only water and sky in every direction. Few boats had a compass, and even fewer had a depth sounder. Dick's boat had both, but Tom's skiff didn't have either.

Dick set his net outside of Egg Island at six. The anticipation of catching his limit in the opening set turned to disappointment when we watched the quiet cork line. After we drifted for a couple of hours, he pulled the net in. Dick's enthusiasm dropped, but he kept an optimistic attitude. "Maybe when the tide changes."

Fishing outside the sandbars in the gulf was more relaxed than drifting the inside channels. Dick didn't worry about catching snags, drifting into the breakers, or illegally flooding above the fishing closed markers. The net drifted east, then west. The sets lasted longer with less stress, except when the net drifted too close to the outside beach, the breakers, or a navigational buoy.

Early Friday morning Dick ran the *Pagan Queen* inside the ocean bar with about sixty salmon on board. He set the net in the middle of the Egg Island Channel for low water. The cork line would hardly move for at least an hour, the perfect time to crank up the stove and fry some bacon, potatoes, and eggs for breakfast.

After Dick caught his limit in the morning low-water set, we tied to a raft of boats behind the tender and waited to deliver our sockeye. The weather that day was unusually calm for the Flats. We stood on deck and soaked up the sunshine while we visited with the other waiting skippers. We shuffled boats for three hours before we delivered our six hundred pounds. Other gillnetters caught more than their limit. The skippers kept a few for a home-pack, saved some to share in town, and gave their extras to gillnetters who came up short. Dick kept his extras. "The chore of cleaning these fish will pay off next winter when I open my freezer and select salmon for dinner," he said.

Dick ran the *Pagan Queen* to town loaded with his extra catch. After the Morpac office closed for the day, we unloaded the salmon and spent the entire night on the dock cleaning Dick's extra catch of sockeye and all of the king salmon. We packed the salmon and in the morning, sent the boxes by airfreight to Dick's sister, with one seventy-pound box to my parents.

Throughout the weekend closure, the town feasted on fresh salmon. The two tenders bought as much salmon as the boats could pack. The gillnetters brought their extras in to share with the community, a tradition influenced by the Alaskan Native culture. The entire town celebrated spring and the return of the salmon.

The limited tenders and restricted catch continued, but the gillnetters were eager. For the first opener, the *Equinox* wasn't ready. Bean fished his skiff. With money from the first fishing opener, he wasn't able to finish every project he'd planned for his boat, but he completed the necessities. Saturday he launched the *Equinox* with a new net on board and ready to fish. That night I went with Peggy and a group of friends and celebrated with Bean and Tom in their tent above the cannery.

Bean's new boat was revolutionary, and the group discussed the many recent changes in the fishery. The most significant in Alaska's history was limiting the number of salmon-fishing permits. Another change was boat construction, swapping wood for fiberglass. The most innovative switch was from skiffs that picked nets from the stern to bow-pickers, boats like the *Equinox,* with nets worked off the bow.

"Nothing is forever. Change is our only guarantee. I need some change to buy enough gas to catch some salmon," Bean said.

We laughed and emptied our pockets to fill the *Equinox* fuel tanks. No one cared about their money. No one kept count, except Bean. We felt privileged to play a small, but instrumental part in sending Bean's new boat fishing.

Bean welcomed Peggy to join him for the Equinox maiden voyage and offered her a home-pack from their catch. We all knew Peggy loved her job writing for the newspaper, but she missed the fishing life. The scheduled fishing periods were on weekdays, workdays for Peggy. Memorial Day, a holiday and a scheduled opener, was her one chance the entire season to go fishing.

"We can catch my limit and your home-pack and return in time for you to be at work on Tuesday," Bean said.

Sunday morning the town was dry and dusty, but the weather changed before noon. Low clouds wrapped the mountains to the south that protect Cordova from the Gulf of Alaska. The clouds slithered around the mountain range and into town, growing thicker and darker. A storm strengthened on the gulf. The wind began with occasional gusts and then blew in earnest. The forecast predicted the weather to worsen. The old-timers' boats at the Morpac cannery float stayed tied to the dock. I learned to watch and listen to the old-timers. They knew plenty from having fished the Flats for years and survived to experience growing old.

Nervous about losing my job, I went to talk to my skipper about not going because of the weather. Before I reached the boat, I saw Dick walking up the dock. His hands were covered in grease.

"One of the engines isn't running," he blurted, "Johnny Dollar doesn't have the part. I called south, the weasels aren't open on Sunday. Monday is Memorial Day. The shop won't open until Tuesday. We're screwed."

Johnny Dollar was the fishing fleet's nickname for John French, owner of the outboard shop in town. He earned the nickname Dollar because without competition, he felt free to charge whatever he thought a part was worth. Dick was desperate and would have happily paid double top dollar for the part he needed.

I felt relieved. I hadn't lost my job, and I didn't have to go out into the storm that continued to build. When I told Peggy I wasn't going, she told me Bean was confident in his new bow-picker. It was longer, wider, and more suited for fishing in tough weather. Peggy wanted a home-pack and Bean was desperate to catch some salmon and finish his projects on the *Equinox*. They pulled away from the dock with most of the boats on the Sunday evening tide.

Many of the boats stopped short of Mummy Island at Point Whitshed, the last protected anchorage before the shallow river delta sprawls across the northern shore of the Gulf of Alaska. Past Point Whitshed, few places offer a spot to hide. The tide changes the depth of the water up to eighteen feet every six hours, which complicates navigation. A five-foot change makes the difference between sitting on a dry sandbar or navigating a channel with plenty of water. The tides pressure skippers to travel when they have the water, regardless of the weather. The boats need to be on the correct side of the sandbar where the salmon are when the storm lets up. That night many of the gillnet boats anchored on the leeside of Point Whitshed, on the wrong side of the Hump, and waited for the wind to diminish. We heard Bean and Peggy crossed the Hump while the tide was high enough to reach Egg Island. They anchored behind the sandbar, where they would check the weather in the morning.

The wind blew unobstructed across the gulf onto the delta. Mountains block the town and afford far more protection, but the wind screamed. The gusts pulled tight on the lines that held the *Pagan Queen* to the dock. The wind jerked the lines, which kept the boat in motion and awakened me throughout the night.

In the morning Dick and I woke to the sound of loud panicked voices on the dock. We rushed out on deck to hear what happened. Tom Madsen, a local pilot, needed someone with experience to spot from a floatplane for him.

"Bean and Peggy are in trouble. I'm grounded, but the minute visibility improves, we need to go rescue them."

Floyd, another gillnetter, went with Madsen to the city airport at Eyak Lake, where they waited for flying conditions to improve. The rest of us stood by, waited for news, and prayed Peggy and Bean would survive the experience. Tom ran his skiff to town and tied up at the Morpac dock. He heard on the radio that Bean had gone overboard. He told us the skipper of a fifty-eight-foot boat tried to run out the Egg Island bar to give assistance but turned back after a breaker broke out his windows.

We heard a chartered helicopter was in town with a crew doing geological exploration on the coast east of the delta. The crew members were eager to finish their work, but high winds and lack of visibility kept them at the airport on the lake. Tom Madsen called the city airport and reported spotting Peggy. When the helicopter pilot, Lucky, heard the call on the office radio, he volunteered to fly out and attempt a rescue.

News came that Peggy was at the hospital. Dick drove Tom and me there to comfort her. When we walked to the front of the hospital, I surveyed Peggy through the window. She sat quiet and motionless, like a statue. The doctor talked to her, but her body looked lifeless, her face expressionless. When we walked in and hugged her, she came to life. She was desperate to leave the hospital. Tom escorted her out.

The doctor told me, "Physically she is okay, other than the multitude of bruises. I worried about shock, but because of her reaction to you and Tom, I think she'll be okay."

I caught up with Tom and Peggy. We walked to the Reluctant Fisherman Restaurant for a cup of coffee. We sat at a corner table.

Peggy began her story, "Bean ran the *Equinox* out the Egg Island bar and down the beach to a hole in the breakers." She tried to explain to Tom where they had gone, but she was unfamiliar with the outside beach and had limited visibility. People later confirmed Peggy and Bean had been at the Mousetrap.

Peggy was unemotional and spoke in a monotone as though she reported from her field notes. "On the opener Bean threw the buoy off the bow and began to lay his net. Before it was completely out, he stopped. He told me even with his new, improved boat the wind and water were too wild for fishing."

She said Bean considered cutting the net but hesitated because the lines were new. The wind and the surf pushed the *Equinox* farther into the beach and the breakers. Bean made the decision to cut the net, but before he did, the wind calmed, giving him the opportunity to bring in the net and escape the breakers. Bean began to haul in the net, prepared with his knife to cut the lines if necessary. A rogue wave, a sneaker, hit the port stern quarter of the *Equinox* with enough force to roll it more than 180 degrees before it righted itself.

"I sat inside the cabin on a stool. The roll of the boat threw me from my perch. I picked myself off the floor and searched for Bean through the window. I didn't see him on deck."

She thought Bean was against the fish hold. She told how she scrambled out of the rear entrance, held her body tight to the side of the cabin, and crept to the front deck. It was empty. Her eyes scanned the water where she caught sight of Bean struggling in the distance.

"The wave washed Bean forty feet from the boat. He raised his arm and called to me from the water, 'Hurry.' I threw the life ring. It went nowhere near him. The strong current and powerful wind pushed us farther apart. I searched for a knife to cut the net. Bean's hung on his belt around his waist. All I could find was a butter knife. I knew he was helpless and losing strength, but I had no way to reach him because the net acted like an anchor. In desperation I called out on the radio. Skippers responded, but I wasn't sure of our location."

I was in shock and resisted listening. I didn't want to hear her story. I didn't want her story to be real. My mind filled with images of Bean when I last saw him, his excitement, and the pride he showed in his new boat.

The server came by and filled our cups, which brought me back to the present. The next thing I heard, the *Equinox* was free of the net. Peggy threw the boat into forward and raced toward Bean. Another powerful wave struck the boat. The *Equinox* bucked up out of the water and slammed down. Peggy held on for her life. A crushing wave of water pounded her. The engine died. She couldn't restart the engine. When the froth cleared, Bean was no longer visible.

"I rushed back to the radio," Peggy said. "I didn't know what was wrong with the engine. A voice on the radio told me to throw the anchor before the boat washed onto the beach."

She described how she made her way to the bow, tied off the anchor, and threw it overboard. The boat spun around tight on the anchor and slammed down with a deafening shudder. She gripped the side of the boat, crept to the stern, and crawled into the cabin. She described how the waves threw her around the cabin. The radio was dead. She was alone on a dead boat. The captain she trusted was dead.

"I looked out the window at a gray world, absent of life. I felt certain I too would be dead soon. The time seemed an eternity before the wind calmed slightly and the sky lightened. Out of nowhere a sea otter popped up beside the boat. The otter's black eyes focused directly on mine. The otter was a sign that life existed in that gray world and gave me hope I might survive."

She heard a plane. She poked her head out of the cabin, unsure the sound was real. She couldn't shift her eyes off the plane. "I asked myself if it was actually there."

She explained how the plane flew around and buzzed the *Equinox* until she saw the face of the pilot, Tom Madsen. Peggy said she was relieved when she saw the face of a friend. She knew then she was going to live. Madsen knew where she was, and she trusted him to make sure someone rescued her. A plane can't land in twenty-foot seas. When the plane flew toward town she understood help was on the way.

After what seemed forever, she saw a helicopter. She noticed it wasn't the Coast Guard. She didn't question when a line dropped. After several attempts, she managed to grab the line that dangled from the helicopter and whipped in the wind.

"I seized the rope, cinched it around my waist, closed my eyes, and held on for my life. I told myself, 'The next thing I'm going to feel will be hard sand under my feet.' While I dangled below, the helicopter flew above Egg Island and lowered me onto the sand. The pilot landed, and I ran to the helicopter. When the helicopter reached town, a local drove me to the hospital."

She reported her story without emotion. We sat stunned. We were in shock. I wanted to deny her story. Tom had lost his best friend and fishing partner. I couldn't imagine what Peggy experienced. Bean was dead. Peggy witnessed his death. She escaped with her life and haunting memories that awakened her for many nights.

People were looking for Bean, but Peggy knew he was dead. He called to her, but she'd been unable to save him. She felt an unfamiliar helplessness, which changed her forever. Those who have witnessed a tragic death in war or fatal accidents are familiar with the helplessness and unforgettable memories.

That afternoon two gillnetters from the Village of Tatitlek fished outside Strawberry Bar and shouldered the dreadful task of catching Bean's body in their net. They wrapped him in a sleeping bag, pulled in the rest of their net, and ran their boat to town. The experience left them shaken.

Tom and I were at Peggy's apartment when Mike, the state trooper, called and requested someone come to identify Bean's body. Tom offered to go to the funeral home. He'd treasured a close friendship with Bean since college. He and Bean were partners in the tent on the hill, a locker at Morpac, and the *Sugar*, a seine boat in the harbor. Tom needed to see Bean to believe the loss of his fishing partner and best friend.

Tom felt responsible because he'd encouraged Bean to come to Cordova to fish. Bean was drawn to the land he remembered from his grandfather's stories about Mummy Island and razor clams. All of us felt the loss of John "Bean" Scott. We remembered the night he launched the *Equinox* and the pride he showed in his new boat. We recalled how we helped Bean fuel the *Equinox* for her maiden voyage. We felt privileged at the time.

We remembered his words, "Nothing is forever. Change is our only guarantee."

A few of us slept that night in Peggy's living room. In her nightmares she heard Bean's voice call to her, but she was helpless. At times she couldn't close her eyes, because of the vivid pictures.

Peggy woke from her nightmares and said, "I keep seeing Bean in the water with his arm up. He keeps calling out my name."

CHAPTER FOUR

THE EQUINOX DRAGGED anchor and washed onto the outer beach of Egg Island. When the storm broke and the seas were down, Wally Raber and Ric Schultz, known as Schultzy, flew out to retrieve the *Equinox* and run her to town. Schultzy suspected that when the hull flew out of the water and exposed the propeller, the engine over revved, which broke the rotor. The fact that a one-dollar part sealed Bean's fate was hard to accept.

Schultzy repaired the engine with the new rotor he'd packed. Wally reconnected a loose wire, which fixed the radio. Schultzy pulled the anchor and Wally blasted the *Equinox* off the beach. A wave caught the boat and launched her into the air. Wally cut the throttle. The *Equinox* landed. Another wave hurled her back up in time to meet Schultzy falling from the first wave. He landed face first on the front deck. His arm in front of his face received most of the impact, but the terrific force, even cushioned by his forearm, split Schultzy's face open and knocked out his front teeth. He ignored the blood and pain while Wally powered the boat away from the beach. When the boat reached deeper water, Wally radioed a float plane to meet the *Equinox* at Whitshed and fly Schultzy to the hospital. Wally ran the *Equinox* to Morpac cannery while the doctor stitched Schultzy's face.

I SPENT MOST of my time at Peggy's apartment. We talked when she felt comfortable. I don't think she found any comfort when she learned that even an ace mechanic couldn't have fixed the engine without the necessary part.

"At the time I felt like I should have been able to do something to save Bean. If I'd known how to fix the engine, maybe I could have saved him. How much do you know about the *Pagan Queen?* Do you know where the fire extinguisher is?" Peggy asked. "You need to know how to run the boat and work the radio. I didn't know which lever was the shift and which one was the throttle," she confessed. "An emergency isn't the time to learn. If people are going on a boat as a passenger or crew member, they have the responsibility to know more than I ever thought to question."

Peggy was correct. I had steered the boat and followed a compass heading, but Dick shifted the boat and accelerated to cruising speed before he gave me the wheel. After my talk with Peggy, I learned how to work things on the boat instead of depending on Dick.

THE CANNERIES SIGNED the CAMA price contract in early June. The additional buyers and tenders energized the fishermen. Without a limit, gillnetters could fish the whole opener and sell all the salmon they caught.

Dick started the engines on the *Pagan Queen,* I untied the lines, and we headed out. The sun rose along with the tide, but the sun failed to shine through the thick, dark clouds. Floyd also pulled away and fell in with us for the run down Orca Inlet, past Point Whitshed and Mummy Island.

"Strawberry looks turbulent. We are too early on the tide to cross the Hump, but I don't want to run Strawberry," Dick said.

He turned the *Pagan Queen* east and skimmed across the shallow water until the slight V-shaped hull bumped and slipped along the sandy bottom. The propeller stirred up the muddy water and dug until the boat stuck. A stiff wind blew, so Dick dropped his anchor. Floyd, in his flat-bottomed skiff, waved and grinned when his skiff passed us. Not far ahead of us, his prop bumped. His skiff stopped. He tilted his lower unit, and with his propeller, dug sand across the shallows until the skiff dropped into deeper water on the far side of the Hump. He lowered his propeller and streaked off.

We waited half an hour until our boat floated. Dick ran the *Pagan Queen* behind Egg Island and turned south at the channel. The boat bounced and swerved when we traveled across the bar. The surf crashed with a deafening thunder. Waves broke on both sides a long distance into the gulf. Dick turned east beyond the breakers, and outside of Pete Dahl, he set his net.

The rough water made seeing fish hit and jiggle the cork line impossible. I retreated to the cabin and began to prepare breakfast. The next thing I knew, my body lay flat on the deck with my head over the side, feeding the fish. I experienced terrible chills that were relieved only when I puked. The vomiting caused my temperature to rise, which triggered a sweat that generated the chills. The cruel cycle persisted. I thought I was going to die. At times before we reached shore, I wished I could die. I'd never felt so sick. I'd never fished in a rough ocean. When we reached the dock, I scrambled off the boat. When I stood on shore, I felt sick again. The land moved beneath my feet. Half the day went by while I tried to remedy my dehydration and regain my balance.

The old-timers encouraged me. "You just need to find your sea legs."

"Stick with it, and you'll get used to the motion."

"With some experience, you'll feel better."

I enjoyed the independence, the long hours, and the physical work in the fresh salt air. The fishing experience was new and stimulating, and the sunsets, when visible, were the best. To be honest, most of my time fishing on the ocean I remained on the deck with my head overboard. Dick, a patient skipper, believed I would adjust.

Bean's family wanted to lease his Limited Entry Permit to cover some of his fishing debt. Bean's brother asked Tom if he could find someone to fish the permit. That season was the first that the state required a Limited Entry Permit, and most gillnetters qualified for one. Those without a permit thought a month into the season was too late to make any money. A short summer fishery in the Sound and the fall coho harvest was all that remained of the gillnet season. The most profitable part of the year was past, and interest in leasing Bean's permit was nonexistent. Tom pursued every option but found no interest by any experienced gillnetters. He tried to persuade Merrie. She agreed to come to Cordova with their son, Jesse, to live and fish on the *Sugar* in the Sound with him, but she refused to lease the permit. Tom continued to search, but every prospect came up dry. Convinced no other possibilities existed, he came to me with an offer. He heard I'd quit the *Pagan Queen* because I never found my sea legs.

"I also suffer seasickness on the ocean," he confessed. "That's why I fish inside on the Flats."

"Nice to know I'm not alone."

"Your problem is that gillnetters who fish on the inside don't need a deckhand. If you want to fish inside, you need to fish on your own."

The idea sounded interesting but impossible, until Tom said, "To begin you can lease Bean's permit from his family. You can give fishing a try on the Sound where you won't feel seasick."

When I didn't turn him down flat the way everyone else had, he continued, "The Copper River Flats are unforgiving, but Prince William Sound is the opposite. A fishery opens for three weeks at Coghill, in the northwest corner of the Sound. It has deep protected waters, slow currents, no breakers, and it's forgiving."

Bean's death brought home the fact that one mistake on the Flats can be fatal. Coghill sounded like the perfect place to learn. I wouldn't suffer seasickness in protected waters, or at least that is what Tom convinced me.

He sweetened the deal. "I'm going seining with the *Sugar*. You can use my skiff and a net of Bean's that's almost new. We can outfit you in a float coat, hip boots, and raingear from the extras stored in the locker."

Tom is an optimistic person. He has a knack at making an impossible task sound feasible, even routine. He knew he had me hooked on the idea, and he reeled me in.

"If you catch two salmon, one of them is yours. It'll be like a paid vacation."

He'd keep half of the money from the salmon I sold and pay all of my fishing expenses. I would pay Bean's family for the permit from my half of the catch.

Tom made the offer sound like a voyage filled with pure pleasure. He said, "It'll be a vacation without a care in the world. You can set your net and then drift and dream."

"I don't know anything about how to keep an engine running, and I don't have a clue about an outboard."

"The problem with kickers is the fuel. It's always the fuel," Tom assured me. "Check the fuel line connections first. Make sure the lines are tight. If the problem isn't the fuel, check for spark, but it's always the fuel. If you have fuel and spark, you can always make a kicker run."

"Other things go wrong with outboards. How about the gears in the lower unit?"

The fishery would open soon. Tom was desperate for someone to pay Bean's family to use the permit. He added a spare outboard to the deal. "If the engine needs repair, you can send it on a tender to Johnny Dollar's. The spare kicker can be stored on a tender, an instant engine replacement with two clamps."

Sixty miles across Prince William Sound to Coghill was out of range for the skiff with the small fuel tank and inefficient outboard engine. The skiff required a tow from a larger boat. Tom, confident I would accept his offer, had already arranged a tow with Joel, the owner of the cabin on Mummy Island.

The previous fall Joel sold the *Clam Burger.* He moved to Bellingham, where he built the thirty-two-foot *Mummy Mist,* a gillnet boat large enough to seine.

"The *Mummy Mist* won't notice the strain of pulling the skiff across the Sound," Tom said.

The overwhelming opinion of people at Morpac coffee breaks was that the opportunity wasn't a money-making proposition. To me, a newcomer, the offer was an expense-paid vacation drifting in the beauty of Prince William Sound. With little knowledge of mechanics, fishing, or boats, and even less about navigation, I considered the offer. I could survive anything for three weeks except seasickness. I went with a handful of quarters to find a pay phone and money to lease Bean's permit.

My parents were visiting my father's family in Sweden, so I called my brother Jon. I told him about the opportunity and begged him for a loan. He thought the adventure sounded exciting, and he had the money to loan me.

"I'll send a check right away."

I found Tom and accepted the deal. We walked to the Fish and Game office, where the woman in charge reviewed the numerous documents that Tom had brought. She filled out an emergency transfer form and handed me a carbon copy. With a book of fishing regulations in hand, we went to his skiff, the twenty-one-foot *Any Day Now,* my home for three weeks on the other side of Prince William Sound. The cabin at the bow was tiny, without headroom to stand. The one spot to sit was on the bunk. From there I could access everything I needed to live. Clothes fit under the mattress, food under the bunk, a water jug sat outside the door, and at my feet sat a diesel-burning stove. Aft of the cabin the fish hold consumed the full seven-foot width of the skiff. Aft of the fish hold off to one side sat a reel.

Gillnetters called the reel a Lankard, after a local man, Glen Lankard, who assembled the automated reel about ten years earlier with a three-horse-power Briggs and Stratton engine connected to a 1951 Studebaker car transmission with a belt tensioner that engaged the gearbox that turned the spool. Gillnetters operated the transmission in first gear to pull in a heavy load of salmon, second gear for normal operation, and third gear for frantic times, when the net drifted too close to a fishing area boundary or the breakers. Lankard's reel is an example of the ingenuity of the fishermen. They invented things to fit their particular needs and improve their lives. The gillnetters had pulled their nets by hand for a hundred years, but when they saw the reel work, they knew they needed one. It revolutionized gillnetting on the Flats, and before long all the skippers equipped their skiffs with one of Glen Lankard's reels.

Glen's invention gave women, who often were without enough strength and stamina to pull a net in by hand, the ability to join the fishery. There is no way I, that hippy girl, would have considered gillnetting if I'd had to pull 150 fathoms of net out of the water by hand. The unintended consequence of the reel was the "Girl Netter."

Tom used the skiff to fish one more period on the Flats. When he returned to town on Wednesday, I met him to take charge of the skiff. We discovered a problem; I couldn't tilt his fifty-horse outboard. I tried and tried, hung onto the engine with all my weight, but the kicker didn't budge. Tom realized the fifty-horse was way too heavy. Luckily he had more outboards in his locker and replaced the engine with a forty-horse that was plenty heavy, but I was able to tilt.

Responsibility for the *Any Day Now* was mine, which involved bailing water, including the frequent rain. The skiff didn't have a bilge pump, so I used a bailer, a wooden scoop that fit between the ribs. I began a life where the hour of the day became irrelevant; the tide book ruled my life. My first challenge was to position the skiff on the grid, a rack of twelve-by-twelve timbers laid parallel and fixed perpendicular to a dock. After tying the skiff to the pilings at high tide, I waited hours for the tide to recede and the skiff to sit dry on the timbers. When the water went out from under the timbers, I squeezed under the skiff, scrubbed the bottom, removed the moss, scraped off the barnacles, and then applied a coat of bottom paint to retard their return. I hurried to cover the last spot with paint while the rising water lapped at my boots.

While I waited for the tide to float the skiff, I walked to the post office and found my fishing license in the mail. I wanted to share my excitement with Peggy. I stopped at the newspaper office to show her my entry permit, a plastic card with my name embossed on it. The newspaper office printed the weekly paper on Thursday. When I walked in, Peggy beamed and pulled a *Cordova Times* hot off the press. With the same intense thrill, she showed me the newspaper. Her name appeared in bold letters on the front page above a story she wrote reporting about the four tenders damaged in severe weather on the Flats. The article represented her first byline. Our documented victories etched that moment in our minds forever.

When the *Any Day Now* floated off the grid, I moved the skiff to a boat slip in the harbor. I stretched Bean's net on the dock in front of my boat. After I battled to start the Briggs and Stratton engine, I wound the net onto the reel and loaded the skiff with groceries and everything I needed to live for three weeks.

The following day, Joel would tow the skiff to Coghill with the *Mummy Mist*. According to the dock talk, I'd send in a grocery list each Friday with a tender. The grocery stores filled boxes with the gillnetters' orders and delivered them to the tenders. The tenders returned on Sunday, anchored in a bay, and distributed the boxes on Monday when the crew pulled alongside each boat to purchase its salmon. If a boat broke down, the tender delivered the part so the gillnetter could complete repairs before the fishing opener. If skippers ran out of groceries or were desperate for mail, they visited on Sunday after the tender anchored. I listened to the dockside advice and thought I knew what to expect. I was unaware of the fishermen placing wagers on how long I would last.

SUNDAY MORNING I fired up the skiff, ran it out of the harbor, and as scheduled met Joel and the *Mummy Mist* outside the breakwater. I passed him my towline, turned off and tilted the kicker, and then climbed on board the *Mummy Mist*. Joel secured the skiff towline and shifted his boat into gear from the controls on the back deck. We stood and watched his boat's wake slap against the skiff. He adjusted the rigging until the bow of the skiff rode high on the crest of one of the stern waves the *Mummy Mist* created. When he was satisfied with how the skiff towed, we moved inside his cabin for the daylong ride across Prince William Sound.

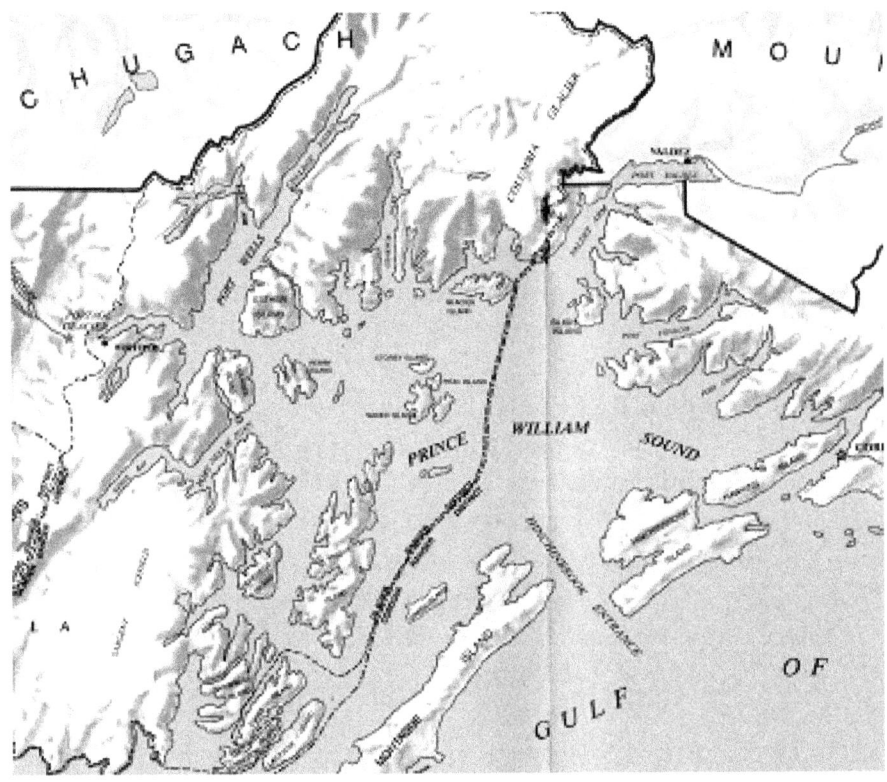

The *Mummy Mist* traveled north. The steep snow-covered mountains on both shorelines of Orca Inlet limited our view. When we rounded Salmo Point on Hawkins Island, the shoreline fanned out in front of us, which made the view expansive. The sandbars disappeared, and the depth of the water plummeted from feet to fathoms. To the west the waters of the Sound extended beyond the visible horizon. The highest points of land came into view when we traveled farther. We saw an island, at first a speck hardly visible in the distance. After an hour the island stood taller and wider as the curvature of the earth allowed us to see more. Every navigational buoy hosted a well-fed sea lion, or a family of them, basking in the sun. The sea lions glanced at the boat when it passed. I imagined the lazy look they gave us meant I hope I don't have to move, and usually, they didn't. We saw whales breach, other whales blow, and porpoise play around Joel's boat. The porpoise swam alongside close to the surface and took turns zipping across in front of Joel's boat.

"Don't you worry you might smack one? They're quite close when they cross your bow."

"The porpoise surf underwater on the pressure wave coming off the front of my hull. It's a carnival ride for them," Joel reassured me.

One porpoise after another surfed across the bow, alternating sides. They swam around to the stern and found a spot in line for another ride. They traveled in groups, swam with the boat, and then disappeared. Miles in front of Columbia Glacier, we cruised past icebergs of various shades of blue, some larger than the *Mummy Mist*.

Joel said. "We call the smaller chunks of ice growlers."

The ice drifted toward the sea and crackled while it melted in the frigid water. Halfway across the Sound a snow-topped mountainous island, Montague, dominated our view to the south. The island is one of three that separate the Sound waters from the Gulf of Alaska. Montague is rugged and wild, and the few stories Joel knew involved bears and fatalities. Farther west, glacier-covered blue mountains became visible in the distance and set the backdrop for a dozen more islands. After about eight hours of marine entertainment, the *Mummy Mist* reached the Coghill district. Joel towed my skiff to a bay at the south end of Esther Island, where Tom suggested I begin my "vacation." I climbed on board my skiff while Joel untied the towline and tossed it to me.

Joel was continuing north for ten miles to anchor with a boat skippered by his girlfriend, Sylvia. Her mother, father, and three of her four brothers fished their own boats. She financed her winters at a college in New Mexico by gillnetting in the spring and seining on her dad's boat over the summer.

I drove the skiff to the middle of a few anchored boats, turned off and tilted the kicker. After I dropped my anchor, I sat in the bow, leaned against the cabin, and watched the *Mummy Mist* travel out of the bay around the point and out of sight. Listening to Joel's boat engine fade to silent, my reality struck me. I was alone, floating next to a cliff, in not much more than a plywood box. I was responsible for my survival, but that fact felt insignificant compared to how much I appreciated the silence, the fresh salt air, and the gentle motion of the skiff.

The depth of the water was unknown to me. The skiff didn't have a depth finder. I lacked knowledge about proper anchor scope, which a tight anchor line tells by its angle. A problem wasn't obvious to me when the anchor line went straight down. All I knew about anchoring was to tie off the line before I dropped the anchor overboard. Ignorance is bliss. I relaxed and slept like a baby. After a few hours a banging noise startled me. I slid into my boots and burst out of the cabin dressed in the red long johns I slept in. The skipper of the boat my skiff banged into came out of his cabin. He pushed his hair away from his face, wiped his eyes, and appeared confused.

I apologized. "I must have anchored wrong, but if you want to give me a few pointers, I'll try again."

"Give me a line from your bow," he muttered. "I'll tie it to my stern, and we can both catch some sleep."

IN THE MORNING the skipper I woke at midnight stared at me with a puzzled look. He must have thought the bump in the night had been a dream. He tossed me my line.

He said, "Good luck" as he drove away.

From his expression I imagined him mumbling under his breath, "You're going to need it." And I did. With minutes until the opener, I didn't know where to set my net. Even if I knew where, I didn't have the confidence to throw my buoy overboard and run the skiff for nine hundred feet in a straight line without stopping. Dick steered his boat with a wheel like a car. I steered with a handle that poked out of the side of the engine mounted on the stern. I moved the stick side to side and the skiff zigzagged out of the anchorage.

Boats crowded the area outside the bay. Some drifted close to the shore while others drifted out deep. A blast of boat engines broke the morning silence. The skippers threw their buoys overboard and powered their boats. The nets flew off the sterns and claimed the water for the opening set.

I slowed my skiff and tried to stay out of everyone's way. Within five minutes a maze of nets filled the area. Boats set their nets out from the beach. Off the buoy that marked the far end of the first net floated another buoy, which marked another net. That net stretched out, and beyond it another. All around me were strings of gillnets. Relief ran through me when I saw a familiar boat, the *Shirley H*. The skipper, Ron, gillnetted but would equip the boat to seine later in the season. I pulled the skiff alongside.

Ron stood on deck and looked surprised to see me. "What are you doing here?"

"I'm not sure. That's why I haven't set my net. I'm not even sure where I am."

Ron laughed and reached out his hand. "Toss me your bow line. Stay for a cup of coffee."

I knew Ron, Larry's younger brother, from the Morpac cannery. Like Dick, Ron grew up fishing with his brother and father. Nowadays they fished their own boats. We tied my skiff alongside his boat, and I climbed on board the *Shirley H*. I told him about my anchor mishap, and he taught me about anchor line angles.

"Farther into the bay on the opposite side, you'll find a shallower anchorage we call Mosquito Bay. This early, bugs aren't a problem, but later in the season you'll understand why the bay has that name."

Ron pointed to the main landmarks, bays, and boundary lines, "See the Fishing Closed signs on the beach? You need to keep your net on the outside of those markers, out of the bay."

He handed me his binoculars. The line was easy to imagine between the two markers on opposite shores. The boats on the outside edge marked the offshore line. The marker line ran one mile off Esther Island, but the line was arbitrary, because none of the boats had any electronics to tell them their distance from shore. The gillnetters believed one mile offshore was when the trees on the island weren't clearly distinguishable. More importantly, protection officers agreed.

Ron downed the last of his coffee, looked at his net, and said, "My net's flagged out. It's time to pick up."

"Your net's what?"

"The wind blew on our boats, which pulled my net straight out behind us, parallel to the shore. The salmon swim parallel to the shore. I need to reset my net perpendicular to the beach."

"I'll cut loose and try to stay out of your way."

"It won't take me long, if you want to stay tied alongside."

Ron picked his net and showed me the three species of salmon he caught, keta and pink salmon I wasn't familiar with yet, and sockeye, the most plentiful in his catch that early in the season. To my untrained eye the salmon all appeared the same, shiny silver-colored fish. On the Flats the difference in weight made kings and reds easy to separate. People made identification more confusing because they used two or three different names for each of the salmon. The chinook salmon is also a king. The sockeye is a red. A humpy is a pink. A coho is a silver, and a keta can be a chum, a dog, or an alligator. The difference was in the price the canneries paid us for them.

Ron picked a pink and slid it across the deck toward me, "Here's a pink."

He picked a keta. "See how much smaller that salmon is? Notice the size of the scales? If you ever catch a big fat one, you can tell by the spots on the tail."

Ron was correct; the pinks at half the size with small scales and spots on their tails were unmistakable; however, some time passed before I learned to look at the gills to differentiate a keta salmon from a sockeye.

Ron prepared the lines to reset his net. I felt more confident and cut loose of the *Shirley H.* I ran the skiff past the end of numerous nets until I found an empty spot, pointed the skiff toward a distant boat, and dropped my buoy overboard. The buoy trailed through the water on the end of the line. I tugged on the net, pulled it off the reel, and tossed the lines and web over the stern until enough net fell in the water to drag more. The net spun off the reel, and I concentrated on the skiff tracking straight.

Backlash! The net snagged on itself. The cork line jerked tight. The reel jolted to a stop. I shifted the kicker into neutral, grabbed the sides of the reel, and tried to slow the momentum of the skiff and ease the strain on the net before any of the web ripped. The lines jerked hard enough that they wedged under the remaining net. I pulled some net in by hand, relieved the tension on the lines, and then yanked until the lines pulled loose from the remaining net. I found the cause of the backlash. The web snagged and twisted around a cork. When I untangled the cork, the reel spun freely. I shifted the kicker into gear. The engine died.

I looked over the stern and saw a thick gob of web and lines that wrapped the propeller so tight it was unable to turn. Winding anything in a propeller can be serious. The skiff sat dead in the water at the mercy of the wind, current, and tide. I shouted a few choice words, but knew I was in no danger. If I cut the web out of the prop, the chore of extricating the prop would be easier, but I needed to use the net for three weeks, and that set was my first. I gathered some tools, hung over the stern, and reached out to the end of the shaft. I was glad Tom made me rehearse removing the propeller on the spare kicker, but the task had sure been easier when the parts held still and were visible, dry, and not upside down.

I dug through the tight web and grasped the end of the cotter key, a metal fastener with two tines that reminded me of an industrial-strength bobby pin. When I pulled out the key, the cone unlocked and lifted off the end of the propeller shaft. Through layers of web I tapped on a blunt-ended punch with a hammer and removed the shear pin. The metal rod locked the propeller to the shaft. Once loose, the propeller rolled out of the web. A boat wake slapped the stern while I tried to fit the prop back on, and I watched the shear pin roll overboard. I brought the propeller back on board and searched the cans full of spare parts under the bunk. I rejoiced when I saw Tom's abundant supply of cotter keys and shear pins. In the time spent clearing the prop, the wind blew the skiff and the short length of net parallel to the beach. The net worked like a sea anchor, not a fishing net.

My jacket sleeves dripped salt water after I removed the propeller, but when I picked up the net, a flush of salt water poured down the inside of my sleeves to my elbows, cold, wet, and not a single salmon. Ready to try again, I idled into position, tossed my buoy overboard, and helped the lines and web over the stern. The boat crept forward, I watched for another backlash and tried to keep the skiff going straight.

I reached the other end of my net, attached the cork line on my tow post, and exhaled a deep breath of relief. I was fishing.

I changed into a dry shirt and hung the wet one with my jacket near the stove, poured another cup of coffee, sat on the fish hold, and looked around at the scenery. Tom's description was accurate. The fishery on the Sound was in calm water, with gentle currents. The scenery was like going from black and white with a view of gray water and sand on the Flats, to Technicolor with the view of green trees and a backdrop of blue and white mountains. The fishery was the extreme opposite of the Flats. Most important, I wasn't seasick. I picked up and set my net again, changed into another dry shirt, and drifted in utopia with the sun shining on a view of water as far as I could see, interrupted by landmasses with vegetation that grew down to the shore. My body felt nourished from the hypnotic motion of the boat and fatigued from the physical work.

The boats fished from Monday morning for five days straight. The skippers practiced a routine that came from years of experience. Nothing about fishing was routine for me. I questioned my every move and proved most of my answers wrong.

The *Tamnik* drove by Monday night and asked, "Are you ready to deliver?"

"Yes, I want to deliver and sleep for a few hours."

Ken and Jerri named the *Tamnik* after their daughters, Tami and Niki. The boat fished crab in the winter, harvested herring in the spring, seined salmon in the summer, and tendered in the spring and fall. Ken gillnetted, while Jerri skippered the *Tamnik,* tendering for the gillnet boats on the Flats and the Sound. She'd tender for a few more weeks until the family went seining. Although their children were young, they were helpful workers on deck. Duane, one of the crab crew members, operated the deck equipment on the *Tamnik* and knew me from crab season in Cordova. A familiar face greeting me was a pleasure.

The crew tied my skiff alongside with our fish holds in line. I gave Duane my permit card and he turned on the hydraulics and moved levers mounted on the back of the *Tamnik* cabin. The brailer rose, swung over, and lowered in between the two boats. The brailer, a three-foot wide aluminum ring, hung from lines strung through the rigging. A heavy black net hung like a basket from the ring into the water.

I appreciated that when Duane looked in my fish hold, he didn't laugh. I doubt he'd ever received such a small delivery. With his help sorting, I picked the sockeye out of my hold and dropped them splashing into the brailer. With the sockeye unloaded, I called out the number of reds in the brailer.

"Coming up." Duane called out.

He pushed a lever that lifted the bag of reds out of the water and into the air. Another lever swung the brailer over until it hung above the open *Tamnik* fish hold. He paused and squinted at the weight on the scale that hung above the brailer. I guess he didn't want me to feel discouraged, because he read the weight aloud as though I should be proud. He turned and called the number and weight of the sockeye to Jerri in the cabin. When she repeated the numbers back to him, he lowered the brailer, reached under the bottom of the black net, and pulled a fine chain. The bottom of the brailer fell open and released the sockeye splashing into the *Tamnik's* fish hold.

Duane shrugged at the few salmon remaining and said, "Pitch those on deck, and I'll give you a five-pound average for the pinks and ten for the chum."

He offered a healthy average. I estimated the weight at four and eight pounds. I laid them on the deck. Niki and Tami picked up the salmon and counted aloud when they dropped them into the chilled water. Duane called those totals to Jerri. When she called the numbers back, the girls hosed off the brailer and the deck. They asked whether I needed fuel, water, or groceries. Tami reached for my empty water jug, and Niki passed me the gas nozzle. I added oil to the fuel tank and pumped in the gas. We traded again, the gas nozzle for the full water container. While I washed my fish hold, I entertained Duane with the story of my anchor mishap the previous night.

He told me, "If you ever anchor there again, try closer to shore."

Jerri came out of the cabin and passed me my entry permit card and a fish ticket. It reported the number and weight of the salmon I'd delivered and the number of gallons of gas I'd pumped. I cut loose of the *Tamnik* and ran to the anchorage Ron told me about earlier. I dropped my anchor, knowing to check the angle of the line. With the anchor set, I didn't anticipate disaster and relaxed for a few minutes. After I set my alarm clock, I collapsed on the bunk.

The next thing I knew the alarm rang. I shut it off and strained to hold my eyes open. If they shut for a second, I'd be fast asleep. I made a thermos of coffee and drank a cup while I ran the skiff out of the bay. The area looked familiar, compared to the previous morning. I set my net and cooked breakfast while I waited for the salmon to hit.

Dick and Tom made catching salmon look effortless, but salmon thinner than the diamond mesh swam through my web. Oversized salmon bumped into the net and swam around it. The state of Alaska didn't allow us to use monofilament web, single-strand web that is clear, like fishing line. We used web with multiple strands of nylon. Gillnetters had their own preference for color that ranged from shades of gray to blue on the Flats and every hue from yellow to dark green on the Sound. With the water clear, many of the correct-size salmon saw the colored web, swam around it, and escaped. Catching salmon wasn't easy.

A fisherman told me, "That's why they call it fishin' instead of catchin'."

Although salmon were a challenge to catch, long streaks of seaweed, sticks, and logs that drifted in the water required no skill or experience to get lodged in the net. I made a set at the edge of a bay where at high water numerous sockeye swam out of the bay, along with huge rafts of pop weed kelp. I set my net at the border of that bay every high water and cringed while I watched the rafts of seaweed drift toward my net. I told myself the salmon I'd catch would pay my wages as a gardener.

My net also caught a variety of the oldest multi-organ creatures, jellyfish. Red, purple, white, or orange, the gelatinous umbrella-shaped creatures that existed before dinosaurs did, pulsated through the water trailing poisonous tentacles. The tentacles fire harpoon-type structures that penetrate the skin when touched. The sting is a jelly's defense and the way it captures prey. The tentacles shoot poison even when separated from the jellyfish. Invisible mashed jelly clung to my gloves and jacket cuffs, causing a painful sting whenever any hint of jelly touched my skin. The white jellyfish are mild; the more color, the more poisonous.

Red jellies are the worst. In addition to the pain, the jellyfish made my eyes water, made me sneeze, and made my nose run.

Fred, Sylvia's father, summed up the fishermen's feeling about jellies when he posed a question to them, "If you are up to your neck in shit and someone throws a jellyfish at you, do you duck?" The fishermen knew without any thought that they would instinctively duck before they allowed a jellyfish to splat in their face.

When my net came on board, it brought in gallons of water, jellies that accumulated in the bilge of the skiff and a few salmon, which I was still learning how to pick. When the water in the skiff became uncomfortable around the knees of my hip boots, I paused and bailed the water full of jellyfish overboard. Without a bilge pump, bailing the water out of the skiff one scoop at a time was a strenuous job. Mornings when the outboard and Briggs were cold, I pulled on the starter rope and practically wore out my arms before the engines started. I pushed and pulled to keep the web and lines evenly wound on the spool every time I picked the net. I developed muscles I never knew existed. Each night, exhausted and hungry, I ran the skiff to the anchorage. I suffered with sore hands, cold feet, and wet clothes, and my face and wrists were on fire from jellyfish burns.

I asked myself, "Why did I choose this torture for a vacation?"

The physical exhaustion, coupled with mental overload because everything was new, caused me to sleep well. I treasured nights rocking in my warm, dry bunk. After a few hours of sleep I felt refreshed and ready to tackle another day.

One evening I found the *Tamnik* in the bay anchored for the night. After I delivered my catch, I accepted Jerri's offer to hang my skiff on a line off the tender's stern, which spared my exhausted muscles the effort of pulling my anchor.

In the morning Duane heard me yank on the kicker. I appreciated when he jumped on board and said, "Save your hands for picking salmon." He pulled on the rope and started the outboard engine.

Another night, I was ready to deliver my catch for the day, but the *Tamnik* was busy a couple of miles away. I went to where the tender normally anchored. I planned to sleep until the *Tamnik* came in, deliver, and then go fishing. Remembering what Duane told me, I ran the skiff near the shore and dropped my anchor. It grabbed before I ran out of line. I changed into dry clothes and collapsed into my bunk.

Duane's shouting woke me. I poked my head out of the cabin. He hollered and pointed toward the bottom of my skiff. I stretched out farther to see what he pointed at with such panic. When I looked over the side I saw green moss instead of water. More than half of my skiff sat on a flat moss-covered boulder. A gentle wake from the *Tamnik* washed over the rock. I moved to the low side, and on the third wave, the skiff slipped off the mossy rock into the water with a splash. We both howled with relief. I pulled my anchor, and he dropped his. While I delivered my fish, we amused ourselves with comments about how perfect that boulder was for my skiff to sit on.

My first week went by without too many disastrous events. I picked weeds, bailed jellyfish, and spent too much of my day hanging over the stern, removing my net from the propeller. My reaction to the constant solitude surprised me. Within hours I began talking to myself. Although I don't talk a lot, I need to converse. I had no one to share a conversation with except the tender crew when I delivered my fish once a day. With too much time to think, I experienced my own pain of Bean's death and thought about him often.

CHAPTER FIVE

WHEN I DELIVERED my salmon Friday night, Duane told me, "The best anchorage for the weekend is at the north end of Esther Passage. It is deep and well protected."

I unrolled my chart and found the entrance to the passage at the southeast corner of Esther Island, a fifty-square-mile rock snugged up to the mainland and separated by a ten-mile waterway. The entrance at the south end stretched more than a mile wide, with two islands at the mouth. I turned the skiff to enter, but two more islands blocked my view of the passage and gave the illusion the entrance was a bay. Behind the distant islands the passage narrowed, and the first turn obstructed any farther view. Mountains sloped down and changed from rock to green lush alpine valleys. The island's steep rock cliffs dropped to the shore and maintained their rapid descent, which made the waterway narrow and deep. Few rocks plagued the bottom, which was good, because I couldn't stop staring in awe at the island's massive rock walls that towered above me. The narrow passage wound for miles before it widened with two slight bays on the mainland shore.

"Stay close to the mainland when you see the anchorage," Duane had warned me. "Off the shore of the island lies a reef not far below the surface. The rocks hang into the passage quite a distance. Cut that turn wide; stay close to the mainland."

The shore of the island at the anchorage stood tall with sheer rock. The mainland shore dropped and changed to low green meadows that sloped to a gravel shoreline. Trees outlined a ridgeline to the north, and beyond more blue and white mountains were visible. A spit, a sliver of land projecting into the water like a tiny peninsula, divided the two bays. I navigated around it and was surprised to see a logging operation tucked in on the shore, which explained the brown patches and ruts on the hills. The patches highlighted areas where the loggers cut trees. Brown ruts ran down the hill across the green meadow and marked the path where the loggers skid trees to the shoreline. No one was logging at the time and the beach was quiet. In the bay a dozen fishing boats sat anchored and silent for the weekend closure.

The skiff needed shallow water to anchor. I idled toward the mouth of a creek until I saw the bottom. I backed off to where I lost sight of the mud and gravel and dropped my anchor. I had survived the week. I felt emboldened because some days I questioned if I could tolerate making one more set. I felt sure the week lasted more than five days. I learned things at an accelerated rate that never entered my mind when Tom described a relaxing vacation in the wild. His description of the beauty, calm water, and that I wouldn't be seasick was accurate, but his description of the experience as "drift and dream" was far from my reality. Sleep that night without the pressure to wake and set my net was long and rewarding.

In the morning I watched three boats idle to the shallows at high water. With their bows near the shore, they dropped their anchors. After I ate breakfast and enjoyed a makeshift shower, a stress-free nap was irresistible.

The tide was out when I woke. The three bow-pickers sat on a sloped gravel beach. One sat dry for repairs. The other two skippers helped each other pull their nets onto the shore. I watched the gillnetters mend their nets in the sunshine, with constant conversation, some laughter, and a few beers. The gillnetters reloaded their nets while the tide lapped at their sterns. When the water floated their bows, they reversed, pulled away from the beach, and dropped their anchors in deep water. I was desperate to talk with someone, anyone, but didn't know any of the other skippers. The noise of the day faded to silence. Eating, sleeping, and preparing for the next five days of fishing was the priority for the weekend. I slept off and on for the entire two-day closure.

On Sunday afternoon, boats began departing. A few headed south, but most went north. I thought about which way I wanted to go in the morning and pulled out my chart. The anchorage at the north end of the pass divided the Coghill fishing district in half. A couple more turns, and the passage intercepted Port Wells, about one-third of the way up the fjord. I fell asleep with anticipation, imagining what was to the north.

I pulled my anchor at four Monday morning, ready to explore. The narrow passage limited my view to the near shores covered with evergreen and alder trees and below, blueberry and salmonberry bushes that grew above the gravel beach. When the skiff rounded the last corner of the passage, the northwestern entrance exploded with breathtaking scenery. Glistening water stretched for miles across Port Wells. I could see beyond the far shore, up Barry Arm, full of glaciers that sparkled in the sun, and miles into the Chugach Mountain Range. The vista to the south reached beyond Port Wells to distant tree-covered islands. The fjord to the north narrowed with endless rugged blue mountains smothered in glaciers.

I turned north and motored another ten miles, past boats drifting where the skippers planned to set their nets. The majority of the boats congregated on the eastern half of the fjord, in front of the lagoon at Coghill Point. The shallow lagoon led to the mouth of the river, which ascended to Coghill Lake where the sockeye that escaped our nets spawned the next generation. Sockeye swam into the area over the weekend and milled around the lagoon. Gillnetters caught the buildup of salmon in the first set or two. A steady stream of boats then headed south to harvest the salmon where the fish entered the district. High in the fjord, the water was calmer compared to the more open waters at the south end. The tranquil water combined with the scenery held me with magnetic force, content to catch the sockeye that made their way past the nets cast twenty miles in front of mine.

The Department of Fish and Game posted boundary markers on Coghill Point and the eastern shore, which closed the waters inside the lagoon. I watched boats set their nets outside of the Fishing Closed marker on the point. The nets caught the salmon that swam in and out of the lagoon past the point. Boats lined up for a turn on that marker set. The skippers gave each other fifteen minutes from the time their buoy touched the water until the next skipper set a net on the marker line in front of the previous net. The second net intercepted the salmon. The fishermen call the act *corking,* laying a net in front of another, cork for cork and intercepting the fish. The behavior is acceptable only on marker sets, although fishermen complain, "some net corked me," no matter where the boats are fishing.

Waiting at the marker is a gamble. While the boats wait in line, the skipper isn't catching salmon. The sets made on the marker line can sink a net or be a *skunk,* an empty net. The crowd of boats in line disappeared when sockeye quit swimming past the point. I refused to wait for a turn at the marker because I would suffer embarrassment when the skippers watched me set my net, which might consume my whole fifteen minutes before the next net made a set and corked me. Instead I drifted south of the point and intercepted the salmon on their way to the lagoon.

One afternoon I heard a loud flock of birds and glanced toward the point. A flurry of birds squawked and darted to the water and then flew up, not high, squawked, circled, and dove to the water again. I pulled in my net and ran closer to see what the bird activity meant. I was ecstatic when I saw Willie, who owned the *Philip L.* He'd set his net at the marker and drifted around the point and up College Fjord.

"Set your net! Sockeye are everywhere," he shouted from his back deck. "Set your net here; you're bound to catch some. They're everywhere."

I set my net, but the cork line remained quiet. I watched the activity around Willie's net. The cork line sank in places; in other spots sockeye splashed. The explanation for the bird celebration became obvious. The seals ate salmon out of the nets, and birds ate the scraps from the seals. I watched, fascinated by the seal and bird activity. Willie's net caught a sockeye at the cork line. One-third of the salmon's body cleared the surface of the water. The birds claimed that salmon, not merely the scraps from the seal feast. The birds dive-bombed a seal that contested their claim. A brave bird tried numerous times to lift the salmon out of the water. A seal seemed to use that sockeye for bird bait.

"The reds are coming in like grapes," Willie hollered when he began to pull in his net.

His net glistened emerging from the water and climbing over the stern. I thought the net looked like a giant's solid silver necklace. I watched him pick. I'd never seen sockeye caught in such mass, birds in a frenzy, or seals enjoying such a picnic. I picked my net with a few stragglers. Willie stopped picking for a moment and motioned me over. He dropped his rain jacket off his shoulders, wiped his brow, and resumed picking.

When my skiff floated off his stern, he yelled, "Go to the point and set your net."

Running the skiff down the fjord, I dodged nets in the same situation as Willie's, loaded with sockeye that hung like clusters of grapes. The seals and birds continued their banquet dinner. The line of boats was gone from the point. I went to the marker and threw my buoy overboard. The gillnetters set their net as close as possible to the beach. My buoy floated a disappointing boat length or more from the shore on my first attempt, but I made the marker set. I was the one active boat and caught some of the salmon that remained. The other skippers continued to haul their nets on board full of salmon. The gamble of waiting in line paid off. Willie caught more sockeye in that one set than I'd caught in the previous week and a half. I paid more attention to the activity around Coghill Point from that day forward.

A fjord with fifteen more glaciers stretched north beyond Coghill Point. Nineteenth-century explorers named most locations in the Sound, so the name College Fjord puzzled me. I solved part of the riddle when I read the names of Seven Sisters colleges for the glaciers to the northwest. At the head and the east side, the glaciers bore names of Ivy League colleges. I learned the Harriman Expedition named the glaciers in 1899. When the expedition traveled up College Fjord, John Muir, one of Harriman's invited guests, wrote, "The scene was wild and rugged in the extreme." After more than a century his description is still accurate.

The mountains glowed from the sun's reflection on the glaciers and the previous winter's melting snow. A distant roar farther up the fjord occasionally shattered the silence. The noise sounded like thunder or a shotgun blast. The noise turned out to be glaciers calving, icebergs that broke off the face of a frozen river and fell into the fjord. The volume of the noise directly related to the size of the chunk of ice. Icebergs in various hues of aquamarine and white shimmered while they drifted down the fjord. Most noticeable was how much noise the ice made when it splashed and crackled while it bobbed and rolled with the current. With ice all around me, the air held a crisp chill in spite of the brilliant summer sunshine.

When fishing was slow, the tendermen found time for entertainment. One skipper sent cards every Christmas that pictured him as Santa perched on an iceberg. I watched in the distance while the tender pulled up to a chunk of ice larger than the boat. The skipper lowered himself dressed in his boots and Santa hat onto a shelf of the iceberg. He climbed to a prominent spot, posed for a few snapshots, and hustled back aboard the tender. The iceberg rolled when the boat pulled away. Maybe the prop wash from the boat caused the iceberg to roll; I don't know. The skipper, an old salt, would have performed any trick to add a bit of excitement for his crew.

I was so tired toward the end of the week that when I sat to rest for a moment, I passed out from exhaustion. When I woke after a couple of hours of deep sleep, my net had gathered an assortment of icebergs that floated snug against the cork line. I pushed the growlers away, but the large icebergs presented a problem. One iceberg snagged the cork line and rolled. The berg lifted the cork line and web twenty feet into the air. After the noise faded from the splash of the iceberg when it rolled, I heard the web rip when the iceberg bounced in the water.

"Go back to sleep and drift until the iceberg melts to a manageable size," is what I imagined Willie might say.

When I pulled a few chunks of ice on board with my landing net, the weight of the smaller pieces surprised me. Even the smallest chunks, tiny bits barely visible, were substantial and a chore to lift on board. After I broke the chunks with a hammer, I packed the pieces in my cooler. I crushed the ice into smaller bits and added shards to a drink. The effervescent ice made a constant crackling noise while it released entrained air captured by snowfalls in centuries past.

A trick I learned for cold, wet mornings was to remove the spark plugs and warm them on the stove before I replaced them, at least on mornings when the stove worked. The days the stove refused to work made my time with the tender even sweeter, because the tender crew offered hot coffee. Most days the tender crew was my only human contact. When gillnetters are on the fishing grounds, tendermen are their lifelines. The tenders stocked common supplies: paper towels; spark plugs; and an assortment of nuts, bolts, and various sizes of cotter keys. The tender skipper talked to town on radios and ordered anything not in stock. The gillnetters relied on the tenders for information, fuel, food, parts, assistance, a tow, and more. A unique relationship developed between the tendermen and the fishermen dependent on them. The fact the tenders were on the grounds to buy and transport our salmon to the canneries seemed secondary to keeping the fishermen fishing, fed, and informed.

Several canneries bought salmon, each with its own fleet of tenders and fishing boats. The relationship between the fishermen and their cannery goes deeper than the choice of a tender. For some the commitment involved lines of credit or boat financing. The canneries also offered winter storage of the boats and fishing gear, a locker, and a bunkhouse room.

That year three of the canneries formed a partnership they called the Combine. Morpac and the New England Fish Company operated their processing facilities, while Alaska Packers Association organized the tender fleet. The Combine worked well for the gillnetters because the tenders didn't compete. Instead, each tender worked a specific area. If a gillnetter was part of the Combine, which more than half of us were, a tender visited daily. Unlike on the Flats, the tender crew tied onto the fishing boats and unloaded the salmon while the nets continued to fish. If fishing was slow, the tenders stopped to visit. Many times the crew fed hungry gillnetters and offered hot coffee on cold mornings and ice-cold soda or beer on hot afternoons. If a fishermen experienced a problem, the tender crew offered assistance. After the tender supplied the gillnetter with water, fuel, and groceries, the crew traveled to the next boat.

Toward the end of the week I watched the *Tamnik* pull up to a gillnet boat not far from mine. Dressed in raingear, the captain sat at the helm asleep with the engine idling. He sprang up, bustled out of the cabin, and walked off the deck of his boat. He woke when he hit the chilly water. The *Tamnik* crew tied on, fished him out, and after he changed into dry clothes, warmed him with a cup of coffee. Gillnetters sneak catnaps while fishing, but by the end of the week many suffer severe sleep deprivation.

I needed my sleep, but when I napped, more often than not I woke with my net wrapped around my skiff or an iceberg. I suffered physical and mental exhaustion and worked best when I anchored at night for a few hours of high-quality sleep. One evening I ran from the river toward the north end of the pass. I planned to make one more set before I anchored. I ached for human interaction and was thrilled to see Willie set his net. I stopped to say hello and hoped he wanted to visit.

He greeted me, "I'm going to cook some dinner. You wanna set your net off mine and share some?"

We combined our food and enjoyed a hardy meal. The *Philip L,* a combination gillnet/seine boat, was smaller than the seine boats that tendered. It felt double the size of my skiff. We could stand in his cabin.

When the time came to pick up our nets, he said, "If you want to, you're welcome to stay tied on for the night instead of anchoring."

I pulled in the net and picked the salmon gills free from the web and laid the fish on deck. While I loaded the salmon one by one into my fish hold, I considered Willie's offer. I would save myself the half-hour run in and out of the anchorage. Even better, I wouldn't have to pull my stubborn anchor in the morning. When Willie reset his net, I pulled alongside, and he passed me his bow line.

"Your skiff tied on is an advantage for me in case I drift over my net during the night. My prop is on a shaft on the bottom of the hull," he explained. "To remove the net, I need to find a tow to a shallow, flat beach, wait for the tide, and cut the net from the propeller with a knife. It's another long wait for the *Philip L* to float before I'm back to fishing."

"If you get your net in the wheel at low water, are you out of commission for eighteen hours?" I asked.

"Yeah. My other option is to strip down, jump in, and cut the net out of my propeller underwater. Tom claims the chore takes him several dives, each no longer than about ten minutes, and then he warms up at the stove and eats a bunch of candy bars before he can try again."

"Can't hypothermia make people so weak they can't climb onto the boat?"

"Yeah, I think Tom talks too casually about going in the water. I'll bet days go by before his body temperature returns to normal. I don't dive. I keep my net away from my propeller."

After a few hours of sleep, I set my net off the end of Willie's. When I saw him begin to pick up his net, I began to pick up mine. He pulled his buoy on board and cruised to the stern of my skiff with a look of disappointment, I guessed because of the few salmon he'd caught.

Off my stern he called to me, "I'm headed to the south end of the island. If you want to come, I'll give you a tow."

He understood the tedious effort of running a skiff with a loud, slow kicker for any distance. I picked the rest of my net while he brewed some fresh coffee and readied a towline. We tied the skiff on the line, and I climbed aboard the *Philip L*. He chose a course southwest around Esther Island, instead of through the passage, unseen territory for me. The *Philip L* wasn't any faster than my skiff, but the ride was more comfortable than standing next to an outboard engine spewing exhaust. We sat on top of the flat cabin at a steering station and drank coffee while he pointed out the landmarks and features of interest. We traveled past Granite Bay full of huge boulder-shaped islands. The chart showed a reported reef south of the bay. Few vessels navigate inside Prince William Sound, so the charts for the area aren't specific or updated. Chart notes of "position approximate" or "reported" are common.

He held a wide track. "It's here, all right. I know of nets shredded by the shallow ridge of rocks that extend from that shore."

The fishing boundary ran one mile offshore, but few boats fished in the waters west of the island. When we rounded the southwest corner at Esther Rock, a city of boats appeared. Willie struggled when he drove through the maze of gillnets. The tenders hadn't begun their rounds that early. We found one anchored in Island Bay and delivered our salmon. Willie had been waiting to hear news about the purse seine fishery. That season would be his first seining the *Philip L,* and he was eager to begin.

"The pink catch is strengthening," the tenderman told him. "We haven't heard an announcement for seining yet, but everyone expects one soon. I've heard reports of pink salmon spotted everywhere in the Sound. Maybe we'll hear this weekend."

With that news we left the tender, and that evening after fishing closed, Willie came by my skiff. "I'm headed to town to exchange my gillnet for a seine net, power block, skiff, and crew." He winked and gave a laugh. "If seining doesn't open in other districts of the Sound, I'll be back to set my seine net in front of all you gillnetters."

THE SEINE BOATS used for tenders were sufficient for the thousands of sockeye salmon the gillnetters caught. For the millions of pink salmon the seiners would harvest, the canneries retained another fleet of larger tenders. The cannery-owned tender fleet employed professional crews, which included cooks who kept us fed and engineers, who were good problem solvers.

The first trip out is when boats discover any equipment bugs. The canneries wanted the tenders to find those problems before the seine season opened. That week half a dozen seine boats purchased salmon from the gillnetters and transferred their load to the cannery tenders while those boats stayed anchored in the bays and verified all their systems worked. The cannery boats ran the loads of salmon to town.

Jerri, Duane, and the crew on the *Tamnik* unloaded their salmon and enjoyed a weekend off. I spent the night with my skiff tied off the stern of the *Tamnik.* I had survived another week of my crash course in fishing. My days had become easier, but not mistake free. I developed, in addition to several new visible muscle groups, a routine to set and pick the net that worked most of the time.

In the morning, the *Tamnik* towed my skiff to the anchorage at the north end of the pass. Along the way Jerri pulled close to the island offshore from a waterfall. She shifted the *Tamnik* into neutral alongside a buoy. Duane reached over the side with a long boat hook, snagged the buoy, and pulled in the line. Tied to the line was a hose that hung from high on the cliff into the water, and it had a surprising amount of water pressure. Duane grabbed the hose and lifted it to his mouth. After a sizeable sip, he inserted the hose into the boat water tank. The water tumbled down the mountain collecting oxygen, which made the water taste pure and fresh.

"We prefer to drink water from that waterfall and travel out of our way to fill our tanks," Jerri said. "The gillnetters prefer this water too. We installed the hose when we arrived, and at the end of the season, we'll take it home for next year."

Anchored at the north end of the pass, the gillnetters slept throughout the rainy weekend. Monday morning I ran the skiff up Port Wells to College Fjord. The low clouds obstructed landmarks and limited my view to the lowest landscapes of the fjord. I set my net near Coghill Point along with most of the boats. After an hour or two the skippers began their migration south to the warmer weather. By afternoon the sun burned through the fog and the area grew quiet with only about twenty boats spread across the waters high in the fjord. A parade of icebergs drifted down the fjord. A constant breeze flowed off the glaciers and across the water that chilled both the air and water. The difference in air temperature between the north and south end of the district varied ten to twenty degrees. The icy water was less inviting for the dreaded jellies, which may have also kept me at the river.

All the gillnet boats looked larger than mine until I saw one cabin-less skiff in line at the marker that measured eighteen feet long. An elderly woman operated the skiff. I could tell she had years of experience by the way she fished the Coghill Point marker. Her husband fished a cabin skiff and preferred to fish away from the crowd. He returned in the evening and tied to their seine boat, the *Tina,* anchored in the lagoon. Semiretired, the couple parted each morning with a thermos and lunch for a day of fishing. Living in my cramped skiff with a temperamental stove, I thought life would be perfect if I fished days and tied to a roomy seine boat with a hot stove and good company each night.

On Thursday the tender crews relayed the Department of Fish and Game announcement of a Monday seine opener. Most of the gillnetters were also seiners or members of a seine crew, so they made a beeline for town. I followed the skippers from the river, but by the time my skiff reached the south end of the island, the boats were gone. The *Tamnik* and the other seine boat tenders were also gone. I looked around at the few boats that remained but failed to recognize any of them.

Traditionally Coghill closed to the gillnetters when the Sound opened for seining. That year the number of sockeye in Coghill Lake to spawn exceeded the Department of Fish and Game goal. The pink return for the area appeared strong. The Coghill fishery would remain open "until further notice." Vacationing longer was exciting, but I dreaded a solitary life in the wild without any break. I'd been counting the days and was down to thirty hours until Tom thought Coghill would close and I could walk on land and eat someone else's cooking. I longed for a shower, clean clothes, and long conversations with a multitude of people other than myself. Instead, the extension doomed me to live in isolation on that cramped skiff indefinitely.

That night I motored into Island Bay, found a tender, and delivered my catch. I plied around the numerous small islands scattered within the bay until I found a shallow anchorage. Early Friday morning I ran the skiff out of the bay and set my net without any regard for the strength of the tide, one of the largest of the season. The tide raced southeast with a powerful current that swept my net and skiff flying down the island and away from the shore.

Startled at the distance my skiff traveled in the brief time, I began to pick. I saw something big floating against the cork line. When I reached the mass of vegetation, I found two fresh spruce trees. The branches and needles wove into the web when the trunks bounced in the water and snagged the net for more than twenty feet. I struggled to pick them apart, but the current held the heavy load against the cork line. I strained to help the trees get over the net, hoping the current would carry them away, but they extended longer than my skiff with too many branches tangled in the web. Picking them out proved ineffective.

Rummaging through the toolbox and all of the compartments under the bunk, I searched for a hatchet, a saw, or a big knife, anything to cut the branches and trunks into manageable pieces. I found a sharp knife and a rusty hacksaw with teeth that showed a life of abuse. I struggled for about an hour sawing and separating the trees from my net. Stopping for a coffee break, I looked at the world around me. My net raced toward the fishing boundary line, worse yet, a thousand-foot pile of half-submerged rocks lay in my path. I canceled the coffee break, tussled with the trees, and sawed with more haste. To calm down, I told myself, if the net drifted into the rocks, I'd set the net on the reel back in the water, and let the net go into the rocks without me. The drift would damage the web, but Tom felt Bean lost his life because he hesitated to cut his new cork line. Tom made me promise never to let my concern for equipment distort my judgment on safety.

I felt trapped, exhausted, and incompetent. Too frequently in the previous three weeks I'd faced seemingly insurmountable tasks. The cannery tenders stayed anchored; the tendermen weren't going to rescue me.

About half the trees were free of the net and bumped against the side of the skiff. A speedboat headed toward me from the west. Without the fleet of boats to mark the boundary line, I wasn't sure if my net had drifted over the line or not. Were officers from Fish and Game Protection coming to arrest me for illegal fishing? At that point I didn't care. I welcomed them. Maybe after they arrested me they'd help me remove the trees. The speedboat ran past without slowing. The people in the boat were sport fishermen out of Whittier, a town farther west with a small harbor and train access to Anchorage.

I continued to cut and clear branches. I sawed and threw chunks of tree free of the net. By the time I reached the end of the second tree, my skiff may have drifted beyond the boundary line. The net that remained in the water raced toward the rock pile at a good clip. I threw the reel transmission into third gear and yanked in the net. After loading the salmon into my hold, I ran the skiff toward the island while I bailed the water. Without a second thought I continued up the pass to the north end where the close shores of the fjord made me feel more secure.

On the eastern shore near the lagoon, I began to set my net. The kicker bumped bottom and quit. Again I forgot to consider the size of the tide. The extreme tide that swept me away from the island earlier left the water shallower than I'd ever experienced. The skiff sat so shallow that the kicker bumped a gravel bar and wouldn't tilt. The tide was flooding. "Wait for the tide to come in," is what I guessed Willie would say. Situations that seemed disastrous to me didn't seem to alarm him. When the tide rose, the kicker remained stuck in the down position.

The crew on the tender *Florist* noticed me in the shallows. In spite of the seine opener, unlike the other tenders, the *Florist* stayed tendering. The skipper and crew had years of experience switching equipment. They were confident they could stay and buy salmon until the closure that night, run to town, unload their salmon, the auxiliary gas tank, any other tendering equipment, and still have time to load the seine net and be ready for the Monday morning opener. The *Florist* pulled alongside after my skiff drifted down the fjord into deep water. Half my body hung over the stern, but the kicker puzzled me. The engineer glanced at it and noticed the reverse-lock was on.

"This lever prevents the outboard from tilting, which comes in handy when the engine runs in reverse," the engineer said when he released the lock.

Vibration had set the reverse lock sometime that eventful morning. Skiffs from the Flats encounter shallow mudflats often enough that the outboards need to tilt without warning. The reverse locks are always off; some people even remove them, a well-known fact to others, but something Tom forgot to mention to me. I felt dumb but was relieved the kicker tilted.

I had never felt such repeated exasperation, humiliation, and vulnerability. I fished for the three weeks Tom expected, but the gillnet season wasn't going to end that evening like he'd predicted.

CHAPTER SIX

THE FRUSTRATION I felt that morning pushed me to my limit. The thought that I had to stay on the skiff without a break for who knew how long was more than I could tolerate. I requested that the *Florist* call and find out if a seat was available for a ride to town on a floatplane. Reaching town from high in the fjord surrounded by mountains proved difficult, even with the most powerful radios. Through radio relays, the message came that a floatplane on a parts flight would pick me up off my skiff anchored at the north end of Esther Passage.

I delivered my catch and garbage and filled my fuel tanks for the Briggs, the kicker, and the stove. The skiff was ready for the next opener, the unexpected fourth week. I ran the skiff to the pass and anchored, cleaned the cabin, and packed my clothes for the Laundromat. I was accustomed to hearing my voice, because I began talking to myself the first day. Pep talks helped me struggle through the hard lessons I'd learned. While I waited for the plane after three weeks of isolation, I heard myself respond, "Good idea. Why didn't I think of that?"

The minute I heard that question, I knew I was in trouble. My sanity wouldn't last another week. When the plane was late, I worried about surviving another lonely closure. I begged the crew of the *Florist* not to leave without me. If my flight didn't arrive before the *Florist* departed, the skipper assured me I could ride to town with them.

The plane was hours late, but I didn't complain. I was thrilled to hear it and then see it land and skim across the water. Tom Parker, owner of Park Air, a flight service in Cordova, taxied toward me. The plane looked as if it was going to T-bone my skiff. At the last minute, Parker hopped onto one of the floats, ran forward, and with his hands stretched out, stopped the plane before it crashed into my skiff. He passed me a tie-up line, which I secured before I passed him bags with my laundry and everything I needed for the weekend. While he loaded the bags, I stepped onto the other float, climbed in the back door of the empty Cessna, and buckled into a seat. Parker untied the line, climbed into the pilot's seat, and latched the door.

"You're my only passenger. You want the copilot's seat?"

"Sure." I crawled to the front.

He started the engine, checked my seatbelt, and motored off. Parker maneuvered the plane away from my skiff with help from the wind and current. With a clear stretch of water in front of us, he accelerated. The plane skimmed across the water, bounced once, and we were in the air. We would arrive in town in an hour.

Parker flew out of the north end of the pass and turned south above Port Wells. He talked on the radio and relayed messages to the boats high in the fjord. I couldn't hear above the noise of the engine, but I saw him check his clipboard for information. I was more interested in the bird's-eye view of where I'd lived the last three weeks. We cruised low above the water around the island to the south end. Parker flew without effort while he talked on the radio and wrote notes. The radio conversations ended at the edge of the district, when Parker began to spot schools of pink salmon. I never saw the salmon he spotted. My untrained eye couldn't distinguish rocks and shadows from the brown spots that Parker told me were schools of pink salmon.

We flew the same course a boat runs to town until we flew over Hawkins Island and landed on Eyak Lake. Parker tied the plane to a dock secured at the end of a ramp. When I climbed out onto the dock, my legs acted like rubber. They felt weak after not walking more than a few steps at a time for weeks. I felt unsteady and blamed the feeling on the unstable dock because it floated, but even on the ground, I had the sensation that the earth moved. Living on the water had thrown off my equilibrium. The perceived motion felt weird and lasted for hours.

Tom Parker's wife, Stephanie, greeted me in the office. I asked her about a return flight on Sunday. "We haven't scheduled a flight yet, but I'm sure we'll have a parts flight by Monday morning," she reassured me. "Even if none of the boats need parts, someone typically forgets something in town. If it's their Limited Entry Permit, they'll charter a flight to have their license on board for the opener. Check Sunday morning for the flight time."

From the airport the short walk into town felt impossible. I rode a taxi. Without any cash I was pleased the driver charged the fare to a cannery purchase order. Peggy once again invited me to sleep on her couch. A long, hot shower, clean clothes, and someone else's cooking were more pleasurable than any memory I had of them. Talking to someone other than myself was heaven.

In preparation for another week, I washed clothes, replenished my supply of cotter keys and shear pins, and shopped for groceries. I'd struggled writing a grocery list for the prior couple of weeks, but picking food off the shelves was a pleasure. The chore required no thought, just inspiration from well-stocked shelves. To minimize the weight on the plane, the grocery store delivered my boxes of food to the cannery. I loaded my clean clothes in a box and did the same. The beach gang loaded the freight onto a tender headed for Coghill. Sunday Stephanie at Park Air confirmed a parts flight scheduled to depart town at four Monday morning.

"YOU'RE MY ONLY passenger, but my list has numerous stops to deliver parts. Do you want me to drop you off first or last?" Tom Parker asked as he checked my seatbelt.

He knew the ride to town had been my first flight in a floatplane. If he dropped me off first, I would arrive in time for the opener at the river. The clear skies and light winds tempted me to enjoy a sightseeing flight over Prince William Sound in his Cessna 180. "Drop me off last. I'd love to see more."

Parker seemed pleased I wasn't as frantic as the skippers waiting for parts and relieved he could deliver the parts first. The plane flew above the south part of the Sound, where I had never traveled. He landed at different seine boats, some anchored in hidden bays, and others idled at key points and waited in line for a turn to set their net that morning at six.

He delivered parts to one boat with an anxious skipper and crew. The boat had broken down and the crew was desperate to complete repairs before the opener. Others received nonessential parts and were more relaxed when they saw the plane. Soon the piles of parts were gone.

Parker flew northwest, up Esther Passage, and above my anchored skiff. The plane banked around, glided down, and skimmed across the surface of the water until it floated not far from my skiff. He maneuvered closer with the momentum and a set of foot pedals, and then he hopped onto the float, caught my skiff, and secured a line. I climbed aboard and Parker handed me the small box I brought with me. When he was in his seat with the door latched, I untied his line. The plane drifted with the current until it cleared my skiff. Parker started the engine and was back in the air. Late for the opener, I ran my skiff north toward the river, passing boats headed south. I anticipated the afternoon flood tide that promised the arrival of fresh salmon.

Since the tenders *Tamnik* and *Florist* went seining, I delivered my catch to three larger boats. Morpac owned the *Zachary R,* a tuna fishing boat. Danny, the skipper, had gillnetted, but found he enjoyed operating the radio and the wheel with a crew to handle the other jobs on the boat. The *Eyak* and the *Seldovia* were power scows, boats with flat-bottom rectangular hulls with sloping ends, built during WWII to supply the Aleutian Islands. NEFCO owned the *Eyak*; Scott was captain. His crew included a cook, James, who was ready to feed any company gillnetter. The *Seldovia* was unique for its size because the boat was family owned. Peter was the skipper and owner. His younger brother, Michael, and sister Laura were the crew.

The Sound fishery was more relaxing, compared to the Flats. Rock reefs seemed to be the most threatening hazard. Some reefs are on the chart, while many are undiscovered. At the end of the week, hungry and exhausted, I wasn't in the best mood, and I caught my first reef. I panicked. I towed the net and tried to pull it off the reef. The ridge of rocks and my net fought in a tug-of-war. The rocky bottom held my lead line with help from the current. I tugged on the cork line, and neither let go. In a fighting mood and determined to win, I towed my net in spite of hearing "*pop, pop, pop*" when the lightweight web ripped. When the tug-of-war ended, I retrieved my lines and mounds of torn web. The pile no longer resembled a fishing net.

Too late I learned Willie had a saying about fishing on the Sound: If your net looks bad, go to sleep. If things aren't better when you wake, you haven't slept long enough. He was spot-on when catching a reef. The best action is to wait until the tide changes and hope the current switches direction and drifts the net off without too much damage.

I scolded myself because I had panicked and caused the disaster. I pulled the lines and web off my reel, fighting every fathom of the tangled mess. After I coiled the net on top of my fish hold and secured lines around the bundle, Michael lifted the net onto the deck of the *Seldovia*. I anchored my skiff in the pass and rode across the Sound on the tender. In town Michael hoisted the net to a cart on the dock. I pulled the cart to a warehouse where a man who mended nets for his living helped me assess the damage. We pulled the lines and stretched the net. When he saw the ragged web, he shook his head with a pessimistic frown.

A third of the way through the net, he stopped, walked over to pour himself a cup of coffee, and said, "You better find yourself another net. You'll be lucky to see that net mended before next season."

I coiled the lines on the remaining pile of net and moved the pallet down the hall for storage. The Sound was full of pink salmon. The season was open. I needed a net.

Willie was seining but had flown to town for parts. He owned a net he said would work even better for catching pinks and he leased it to me. I loaded his net onto the *Seldovia* and rode with Peter, Michael, and Laura to my skiff. Sunday night I wound Willie's net on my reel, prepared for week five.

The cork line bounced wildly on the opener. A large school of salmon swam past. The fish traveled along the net and a couple of them hit the web and bounced the cork line every few corks. Where the net caught bunches of pinks, the net sank. I cheered with excitement because of how many more pink salmon Willie's net caught than my previous net. The change of a half-inch smaller mesh size made a dramatic difference in the size of salmon the net caught.

A couple days later, my net was full of pinks when my kicker quit working. My spare outboard, an easy engine replacement, had spent three weeks riding around Coghill on a tender. When those tenders went seining, I didn't have room to store my spare outboard, so they delivered it to Park Air.

I pulled in my net when I saw the *Seldovia*. It came alongside, and Laura and Michael tied lines to my skiff. Peter called Park Air and requested the first available parts flight bring my outboard. We transferred the broken kicker to the *Seldovia* for a ride to Johnny Dollar's.

After I delivered my fish and washed the skiff, Peter stepped out of the wheelhouse and passed my fish ticket to me. Wearing a mischievous grin, he said, "Since your skiff is tied alongside, how about if *I* set your net?"

Without a second thought I agreed and dropped my buoy over the stern with a handful of web and lead line. Peter bumped the power scow in and out of gear. Gradually the boat advanced. Michael stood ready to cut my skiff loose in case of a backlash. My reel spun and the net flew through the rollers at record speed. I stood back ready to yell, "Cut her loose." When the net was set, we imagined how funny the *Seldovia* looked setting a net because gillnet boats are small. To someone who watched from the other side, the *Seldovia* looked like an eighty-six-foot gillnetter.

Drifting without power, I stayed south of the icebergs, away from the shore in the middle of the fjord and used the wind to set my net. Not efficient, but my net stayed wet, and I avoided the bugs in the anchorage. Alaskans have good reason to joke that the mosquito is the state bird. In the afternoon Tom Parker landed his plane and tied to my skiff. We wrestled the replacement kicker onto the stern and tightened the two bolts. With a working motor, I ran north near Coghill Point.

I enjoyed fishing until evening, when I proved setting my net near the lagoon at night was pointless. The seals feasted on the salmon before I could pick the fish. I picked seaweed and guts from my net in the fading light and ran to the tender anchored in the lagoon. With fishing slow, the crew members of the *Zachary R* felt challenged to stay busy, with the lack of activity on deck. The captain, Danny, couldn't believe the seals were problem enough to quit fishing.

"Do you want to make a set to see what I mean?" I asked.

"Cut us loose," Danny said as he hopped onto my skiff in his deck slippers.

We set the net and saw a salmon hit. It wiggled the cork line. Within seconds a seal ripped a bite out of that salmon. We buoyed our end and ran to where we saw the seal. It moved to the other end of the net and ate a different salmon. We raced the skiff back to the other end. More than one seal ate the salmon. A whole family enjoyed an easy buffet. The seals saw us not as a threat but as dinner entertainment and were quick to yank another bite from the net. We watched the cork line bounce when a pink hit and then the net sank when a seal pulled the salmon out of the web. The cork line floated to the surface without any wiggle or fish. Danny agreed, fishing was pointless competing with all the seals. They were too numerous and efficient. We picked the net full of heads and guts and joked about cleaning the scraps off the seals' dinner table. We tied to the tender without any of the salmon that we'd seen hit the net.

The tender crew was busy playing poker. I joined in for a few hands before I enjoyed a couple hours of sleep. When I woke I set my net, but I caught my fingers in the web. I tried to pull my hand free of the net, but the tension of the thread tightened. I heard Tom's voice in my head when he warned me, "Never wear a watch, rings, or anything else on your hands or lower arms because of the threat of tangling in the net and going overboard."

Going overboard? Another desperate jerk, and my hand came free. I left skin tangled in the web, but I hadn't gone overboard, and I still had my fingers. I soothed them in ice water. After constant exposure to salt water and fish slime, my fingers were red with infection by the end of the week,

Ralph Pirtle, the Department of Fish and Game manager, announced on Saturday morning that the salmon fishery wouldn't open the next week. The *Zachary R* traveled from town to fuel boats that could run to town and offered a tow to the skiffs that were too small to undertake the trip on their own, including mine. Half a dozen skiffs towed off three different lines behind the *Zachary R* signaled the end of the gillnet season on the Sound.

COHO SEASON WOULD be productive on the Copper River in mid-August, another two weeks. My fingers would have time to heal. I made enough money to fly to Seattle, visit my family, and shop for a survival suit. Cold-water immersion survival suits that prevent hypothermia in icy water were new to the industry. The material used to construct the suit was similar to a wetsuit but thicker and with flotation. The suits were roomy enough that I could don one fully clothed. Sealed properly, the suit covered me head to toe, with my eyes exposed. If forced into the icy water, where people live for minutes, I would stay dry except for my face. The suit's insulation extended my possible survival time to hours, which increased my chances of a rescue.

"The suits are too bulky and cumbersome to wear until going into the water is a threat," the skeptical old-timers argued.

"The suits are good in theory, but no one has enough time to don it. You don't know you're going overboard until you feel the icy water."

"I know you speak the truth because of Bean's accident, but if you feared you might go overboard, you'd be relieved you could slip into the suit," I responded.

The suits were not Coast Guard approved, although to me the suit seemed more valuable for frigid water than the life jackets that wore the USCG stamp of approval.

"The life jackets work to float your body, makes 'em easier to recover." I heard the older fishermen scoff. I wore a float coat, but purchased a survival suit, just in case.

DISCUSSIONS ABOUT SALMON prices in Cordova were unlike the previous fall. August 24, after a short strike, the canneries offered fifty cents a pound for coho. CAMA members accepted the offer. When interest is strong, it's sometimes because few salmon are available. Traditionally gillnetters fished silver season from Monday morning until Saturday morning. That year Ralph Pirtle expected fewer coho and shortened the fishing period. It closed Thursday night.

Tom came with me for the first opener to show me around the inside of Egg Island. He ran the skiff up a long, crescent-shaped channel called Copper Sands. The channel was behind a few sandbars and miles from the currents near the bar entrance. At the top of the crescent, a fishing boundary marker sat on a high sandbar.

"Beyond that marker you can follow the channel to Glacier Slough. It has high sides for protection from the wind, a good spot to hide if a storm catches you before you can run to town," Tom said. He felt some responsibility for Bean's death because Tom encouraged Bean to fish. He was encouraging me but plagued with the fear of losing another friend. He taught me to be overly cautious and be prepared for mistakes.

"Set your net one hour before low water," he instructed me. "Fish the flood until high tide. The flood current pushes your net toward the markers. If you screw up and drift beyond the markers, you'll be in trouble with net snags or Fish and Game Protection. Neither is fatal. When the tide changes from high to low, the ebb current carries your net toward the ocean bar and the breakers. You want to avoid your net washing out the Egg Island Channel and into the surf."

Tom encouraged me to anchor through the ebb. "Drop your anchor above the main anchorage. If your anchor drags, the skiff will likely bump into another boat before you drift out the main channel."

He cautioned me about picking the net. "You know how stubborn and time-consuming the Briggs and Stratton can be when it's cold, time you can't afford if your net is drifting toward danger. Start the Briggs before you set your net, to guarantee the engine starts. The engine is easy to start once it's warm and has fuel."

When we reached town Tom flew south for the winter. The next week I fished on the Flats alone. I survived the four days because of the strict precautions Tom demanded, the favorable weather, and my previous experience on the Sound. I stayed behind Copper Sands, except when I ran the skiff to the main anchorage at Egg Island and delivered my catch. The way the channels ran had no rhyme or reason. Because I was unfamiliar with their course, the skiff bumped most of the sandbars. When the skiff bumped and stuck, I hopped over the low sides and pushed the light skiff off the sand into the channel. I lived in my hip boots.

The boats fished day to day, but with the poor catch, the gillnetters anticipated the Department of Fish and Game closing the season. Before the end of the week, Ralph Pirtle announced the season would close Thursday night. George, skipper of the tender *Teal*, offered to tow my skiff to town at the closure. We headed toward Whitshed on the rising tide. When the *Teal* passed Mummy Island, I rode in the stern for a better vantage point. With the sky blue and winds calm, the sun warmed me. When the sky is clear and the sun shines, the warmth makes me forget the miserable rains and threatening winds I'd endured. My memories of fishing were like those of the weather, filled with the pleasure I experienced. I remembered the beauty, the fresh air, and the wildlife. I forgot the pain and frustration.

I felt like Cinderella. My skiff was going to turn into a pumpkin. The lease was over. My permit would expire and return to Bean's family. I would go back to town, find a normal job, and a place to live. I watched the skiff in tow from the stern of the *Teal* and reflected on the season. The thought of my life without fishing didn't sit well with me. I liked the independent life of hard physical labor, living by the tides, and being at the mercy of Mother Nature. I worked for about a week, winterized the skiff, and stored the fishing gear. The whole time I asked myself, how can I fish again? I never considered flying south with the Bellingham fishing fleet. I didn't know how, but I was determined to buy a permit and skiff and become a gillnetter by spring.

CHAPTER SEVEN

AFTER THE SEASON, I stayed with Peggy until I found a place to rent. Jobs were easy to find in Cordova, full-time, part-time, and temporary, but housing was in short supply. I rented a room in one of Cordova's original boarding houses, a wood building on First Street, half a block from the town center. The room on the second floor measured about ten by twelve and came furnished with a bed and a dresser. The bathroom and shower were in a room at the end of the hall and were shared with the second-floor residents. Yes, I was desperate.

The limited size of my living quarters never bothered me because I only slept there. I served food at one job and drinks at another, seven days a week, and ate at work before and after my shift. The boarding house was clean and comfortable until I came home one evening and found police tape on the first floor of the building. I went across the street to Bill Tiedeman's apartment. If anyone knew answers, he would.

A local Alaskan Native, Bill proudly termed himself *The Iron Indian*. He observed the community while he worked days and people-watched on days he wasn't working. At night he sat in the bars or at his window and viewed the nightlife. He had his finger on the pulse of Cordova. Bill asked how people were and then listened to their responses. Many people poured their soul out to him. He had a way with people that gave them comfort, no matter how dismal their lives.

He worked at the grocery store, delivered groceries, and enjoyed the responsibility of caring for his customers. The older folks who found shopping hard never went hungry when Bill delivered groceries. In a town where males dominate by a large margin, Bill prided himself on the fact that he didn't fish. He stayed in town and cared for the women and the elders. He delivered the groceries to the boats, and when the boats left the harbor, he made deliveries to his customers left behind.

Bill knew the whole story. A suspected murder happened earlier that day in one of the rooms. The resources in town for that type of event were nonexistent.

"The police sealed the room, until people from Anchorage can fly in and investigate. Do you want to stay here?" he asked with concern. "You should. At least until they remove the bodies."

"Yeah, please. I don't want to sleep there."

Investigators flew in from Anchorage and removed all traces of what they concluded was a murder/suicide of the couple living in one of the rooms. I didn't know anyone who lived on the first floor, but the losses still made me sad and wonder why it happened. Alaskan summers stay light practically all night. Winter days offer few hours of daylight. With the darkness, depression can set in. I wished that when people considered suicide, they would remember things change, or as Bean said, "Change is our only guarantee."

Between Bill's job with his hobby of people watching and my working full-time at one job, part-time at another, and picking up odd jobs whenever I could, although I was staying with Bill, we didn't see much of each other. When we did meet, Bill said, "I like you living here. The place isn't so empty. You want to stay and share the apartment?"

The boarding house returned to normal, but I switched my room for a room at Bill's apartment with a kitchen and a bathroom I shared with him, instead of with the entire second floor. He treated me like a younger sister. My first winter in Cordova he became my blood brother, my older, wiser brother. He kept a protective eye on both Peggy and me.

All I wanted in my life was to buy a fishing permit by spring. I told people in town of my interest and listened to a spectrum of their beliefs. They held strong opinions. One night at Bill's the subject came up.

Bill supported Limited Entry, "Since territorial days we've seen more and more salmon fishermen from down south. One of the main reasons for Alaska becoming a state was to gain control of our fisheries management and eliminate the cannery-owned fish traps, but after statehood fishermen from the lower forty-eight continued to flood in." He shrugged. "The state had to do something. Last year they limited permits to those who previously owned a fishing gear license, and this year they adopted Limited Entry, which restricts the number of salmon fishing permits in different areas of the state." He straightened his back and said with pride, "*We* are the *only* state to write sustainable fisheries into our constitution."

"Limited Entry stinks," Carl, another friend weighed in. "Before Limited Entry, a person leased a skiff and a net, paid for a fishing gear permit, and went fishing. For years fathers and mothers have taken their kids fishing; other families live on their boats. After the children grew and learned about tides, nets, and locations, they acquired their own boats. The bad part of Limited Entry is that it excludes those kids who are becoming old enough to fish, threatening our culture and traditions." He leaned forward. "That's why Alaskans hate the new law and have challenged it with a referendum."

"Alaskan voters are going to repeal Limited Entry," an older fishermen cautioned me. "Don't waste your money."

The vote to repeal Limited Entry depended on a vote in the fall after the season. A permit to spend the summer at Coghill, even if valid for one season, was worth something to me. Tom wrote that Bean's family wanted to sell his boat and permit. The *Equinox* would be easy to sell but was worth four times my boat budget. Not knowing the price, I wrote to Bean's brother and told him I wanted to buy the permit. Financing wasn't available for a permit; after all, it might be worthless at the end of the season. I saved every penny I earned that winter to buy Bean's permit. I needed financing to buy a skiff. A loan wasn't available for the *Any Day Now,* because it was too basic to insure. Insurance and financing were for larger vessels with additions I craved. My search for a skiff that could be insured began in earnest.

Nervous about obtaining a loan, I remembered my hesitation when I bought my car. The debt was a scary commitment, but one

I'd make again. I'd started Tom's outboard with a pull rope. I lusted for a turnkey ignition. Larger skiffs came equipped with a key start and a steering wheel. They had a roomier cabin and, I hoped, a more dependable stove. The engines came equipped with alternators that charged twelve-volt batteries. A battery charger meant increased safety and luxury, with possibilities for a bilge pump, a CB radio, and a tape deck. The additions were well worth the extra expense. Determined to own a deluxe skiff by spring, I discounted my apprehension about going into debt.

Bill supported the idea of my buying into gillnetting. With so many people opposed to the idea, I enjoyed his faith and encouragement. He drew a scene of me running a skiff with the mountains in the background. The animals in the water cheered and my face wore a wide smile. He hung the drawing on the wall at the foot of my bed so that I saw the picture before I went to sleep and in the morning when I woke.

"Visualize it, and it will happen," he said with a smile and a magical twinkle in his eyes.

AFTER THE SPRING equinox, people in town talked nonstop about the upcoming herring season. "Have the herring shown up yet?" "How big is the biomass?" "Where were the fish spotted?" "How mature are they?"

One evening at the apartment I said to Bill, "Seems the herring are important."

"Yes, herring have been important to the community since before Seward purchased Alaska." He sat down and continued, "Long before statehood packers moved in and salted the herring in wooden barrels to preserve the fish. When eating pickled and dried fish lost popularity, the packers rendered, processed, the harvest into fishmeal and oil. Peru then captured the world rendering industry, and local herring lost its value." He stood and began to rummage through a closet.

"Local boats had a limited herring harvest, which fishermen sold for bait. Six or seven years ago the herring fishery began to thrive again, when the Japanese developed an interest in herring sac roe and roe on kelp. The newly popular Asian delicacy created demand and a new market for local herring that the natives and locals have enjoyed for centuries."

He sat down again empty handed and looked puzzled, "Two fisheries harvest herring for bait or sac roe. Both fisheries require a large boat and a sizable investment in equipment. A third method, the wild kelp fishery, harvests certain seaweeds after herring cover the leaves with fresh spawn. All that fishery requires is a grappling hook."

"A grappling hook?"

"A grappling hook is a type of rake. I looked for one I thought I had in the closet. It has a foot-long bar with a dozen half-inch round rods that form a V. You throw it overboard, allow it to sink, pull the rope attached to the hook, and rake the bottom. A good toss over a thick bed will fill the tines with kelp. I'll find one for you, if you decide to harvest wild kelp."

Most people used a grappling hook to harvest kelp, but I learned another method of diving to cut the leaves produced a superior product and yielded less impact on the kelp beds. I decided to buy a skiff early enough to harvest wild kelp. George, a friend from college days, loved to dive. I wrote and told him I was going to buy a skiff and go kelping with either a rake or a diver. We might earn some money, or his trip might be an expensive vacation. George wrote that the possibility of diving for money interested him. He'd try to arrange for the time away from work.

I wanted to fish for New England Fish Company, NEFCO. Located a couple of miles north of Cordova, Orca is where a processor has packed fish since the late 1880s, decades before Cordova existed. Hugh, a manager for NEFCO, came to town for herring season. When I saw him, I expressed my interest in a boat and permit.

"NEFCO will back you if you sell us all of your salmon," Hugh assured me. "We have the largest fleet of fishermen, and some years the Orca plant packs more salmon than all the other town canneries combined."

He sent a letter of credit to Bean's brother to secure the permit. When I found a skiff, I called the NEFCO office in Seattle for a loan. The skiff sold before the cannery approved financing.

The following day, Bill came to see me at work. "I heard about a skiff owner waiting for his new bow-picker to arrive on the next barge." He paused for a moment, saw my puzzled look, and whispered, "You don't get it. He hasn't' sold his skiff yet. He's waiting until his new bow-picker arrives."

Most people sell their old boat for a down payment on the new one. At the boatyard I found the skiff before it was on the market. Bill Tiedeman's dad, Skinny, built the hull, and Bud Banta built the cabin a few years earlier at the local marina. Skinny built several hundred boats of his own design. People knew the boats for their quality. After the 1964 earthquake, the government commissioned Skinny to build or repair all the vessels in Chenega, a village on the Sound devastated by a tsunami after the quake.

The skiff measured twenty-four feet long with sides the height of a twenty-six-footer. It came equipped with an inboard/outboard engine, a steering wheel, an electric ignition, a Lankard reel, and a bilge pump. The cabin had two bunks, a mounted compass, a depth sounder, a CB radio, and room for a tape deck and speakers. The skiff had no name. The Fish and Game registration number 00400 identified her.

Most skippers in the area painted their boats gray to blend in with the background of the sandy flats, which made them less noticeable and saved the skippers some embarrassment when their boat sat dry, a temporary monument on a sandbar. The seller of the skiff, John Paul, was one of four brothers who grew up fishing near his parents. He and his brothers, Max, Bob, and Earl began fishing as youngsters, and they painted their skiff cabins bright yellow, which enabled their parents, Hank and Marion, to keep sight of them. I knew the skiff would sell quickly once it was on the market. I went to talk to Johnny Wheeler, the banker, and filled out the paperwork necessary to finance the boat.

"The bank is more interested in a person's intent and ability to pay than in collateral, but you must own something you can include on your application. Maybe a stereo?" Johnny said after he reviewed my application.

"I own a yellow foreign sports car convertible parked in my parents' garage in Seattle."

His eyes opened wider, and he inquired, "What's the make?"

His face dropped when I confessed the car was an older Volkswagen bug. He felt my enthusiasm and was confident his bank would collect its money.

John Paul prepared his seine boat for the herring season. Fishing held a higher priority than selling his skiff. I checked at the bank daily. When Johnny approved the loan, I went in search of John Paul, hoping he hadn't left the harbor. When I found him we went to the bank, completed the paperwork, and the skiff was mine.

THE SEINE FLEET left the harbor for the fishing grounds, where the fishermen waited for the herring roe to mature. The product value is in the sac roe that the market wants ripe, but a few hours separate ripe from spawned. Once spawned, the herring are useless to the seiners, but the eggs are valuable to the wild kelp fishermen if the roe attaches to marketable kelp.

Time was short if I wanted to harvest kelp. I had time to complete the most necessary repairs and changes to the boat. I knew a well-burning stove was invaluable for a heater, coffee maker, cook stove, and, most valuable, drying my clothes. Snow covered the ground, and more was certain to fall while we harvested kelp. The cabin made of plywood, without insulation, demanded a stove that burned hot. John Paul included in the sale the stove he'd removed. Fireclay lines fireboxes of the oil-burning stoves, but flat-bottom skiffs pound on the water and break the clay loose from the walls. My top priority was replacing the fireclay.

George, my diver friend, arrived in town and accepted the stove project. He cleaned it, removed the rust, and installed new clay to the sides of the firebox. He bolted the stove to the base and connected the fuel supply line, but the stovepipe was inches short of reaching the roof. A simple solution of buying a chunk of stovepipe was impossible until the next barge arrived from the lower forty-eight and the hardware store received its shipment. Richey, dad of Ron, the skipper of the *Shirley H*, moored his boat, the *Camelot,* across the float from my skiff. He'd fished the Copper for decades. George expressed his frustration with the stovepipe to Richey.

"Open a coffee can at both ends; it'll fit between the stove and the stovepipe," Richey suggested.

The can did the trick. George lit the firebox, but the stove oil didn't burn. Disappointed, he went to find Richey, who knew all of the stove solutions. George returned with some sand. He sprinkled it on the bottom of the firebox. Another match, and the burn pot glowed. The firebox had been too clean. The fuel needed a wick. The stove warmed the skiff cabin and proved its value.

After I installed a spare twelve-volt battery, a fuse panel, a new CB radio, a tape deck, and speakers, I felt something, or someone, had misled me. I thought connecting power was complicated, but the job was easy. All I needed to know was red is positive and black is negative. The connections were so simple to hook up, that I felt I'd been fooled about my ability. Never again would I blindly believe anything was too hard or complicated before I tried it.

That spring Bill fell in love with Darcy, and I saw even less of him. One afternoon with impeccable timing he arrived unannounced with boxes of supplies.

"I have come to outfit your skiff with all the things essential to a galley." He announced each item aloud when he passed things to me to stow in the cabin: "Coffee cups, coffee thermos, teakettle, paper plates, paper towels, and a holder, salt, pepper, potholders, cast-iron frying pan, and spatula." The look on Bill's face and the twinkle in his eye confirmed the pleasure he enjoyed for his part in my skiff fantasy becoming a reality.

THE FISH AND Game manager watched schools of herring spawn along the beaches in Valdez Arm. The fourth day, the herring spawned in mass. A seine fishery was no longer possible. The seine boats sailed south for the anticipated fishery around Green Island, and the wild kelpers moved in to begin their harvest.

George and I loaded the skiff with fuel, water, food, raingear, clothing, sleeping bags, a couple of charts, George's dive equipment, and Bill's grappling hook. We ran the skiff west halfway across Prince William Sound, where we turned north up Valdez Arm to reach the kelp harvest area.

The best thing about living in the wild for herring season was witnessing the birth of another cycle of life. When I pulled the boat out of storage, the lack of sunshine had kept nature frozen solid for months. When the temperature increased, the thunder of melting snow falling from the trees or rooftops broke the silence. Spring commenced like a song. It began with a whisper that increased in volume when the animals began to converse. The days grew longer, temperatures continued to rise, local animals became even more active, and others migrated into the area. The herring danced on the water while the animals that ate herring chased the numerous schools. The Sound transformed within a few days from a dormant, lifeless scene into a bustle of activity. Except for an occasional barge or ferry, the fishermen shared the Sound with whales, sea lions, seals, and birds. George and I joined the wild party. We all celebrated the birth of spring and the abundance of life.

George brought a dry suit made for diving in frigid waters. A compressor pump, called a hookah, supplied his underwater air through a long hose. He dove, surveyed the area, and cut samples of kelp for us to eat. We tasted the kelp straight out of the water covered with fresh herring eggs. It didn't have much flavor, but the roe supplied a good high-protein snack, if the leaves were clean. If sand or silt covered the leaves before the herring spawned, the eggs trapped the grit. The texture of dirt made it less desirable and hard to sell. Japanese buyers wanted kelp with numerous layers of eggs on the leaf, but the leaves had to be grit free. My experience was selling salmon that we sorted by species and sold for a firm price per pound. Selling kelp was different. We separated it by species, but the Japanese buyers bargained and haggled about what price they would pay.

"So dirty maybe we not even want to buy your kelp," they said.

When I complained to Tom about the buyers, he laughed, "I learned if you eat the kelp, they change their minds."

After that when the buyers were reluctant, we began to eat the kelp, and sure enough, the buyers became eager.

George's air compressor broke a few days into the season. A tender captain called town on his radio and ordered the parts. He reported, "Park Air will deliver your parts when it has a flight, which could be days."

We resorted to the uncivilized method of raking kelp with a grappling hook until the flight arrived. The rake pulled the leaves. Sometimes when we tossed the rake it pulled out the kelp including the roots, which was wasteful but better than the days we spent anchored watching the fierce wind blow snow horizontally.

One morning Willie came by. "I'm headed south. Fish and Game opened another kelp district down there."

We joined the migration of boats and animals. I ran on the inside shore of an island where Tom warned of a dangerous reef. As instructed I lined up two navigational lights, which allowed the skiff to travel in the old steamship channel and avoid the infamous Bligh Reef. We used a chart and navigated the rocky narrows to the shore near the villages of Ellamar and Tatitlek.

I asked George. "Do you think the rock-filled waterway gave the village security before charts?"

"Looking at the chart, I'm sure the hazards did," he said.

"Yeah, I've heard even equipped with a chart, many skippers will sail a longer course to avoid the rocky Tatitlek Narrows."

"Wow! Look at that blue and white church perched on the bluff," George said when we approached Tatitlek.

"It's a Russian Orthodox church. The Russians arrived and influenced the village years before Russia sold the territory to the United States. Many people who live in Tatitlek fish out of Cordova for the Flats season, and most residents are out here harvesting kelp."

George looked interested, so I continued. "They salt the kelp to preserve it, so they can eat it throughout the year. When people keep food for themselves, they call the harvest subsistence, as opposed to commercial. Some residents on the Sound depend on subsistence fishing, hunting, and gathering for survival."

One day the wind blew hard enough that we sought shelter near the shore of Tatitlek. We thought our anchor was secure, and we settled in to wait out the storm. The blizzard intensified. My anchor broke loose. The skiff sailed through the anchorage past the other boats. I burst out of the cabin with my jacket in hand and started the engine. George ran to the bow, pulled the anchor line in, and struggled to clear a thick ball of kelp entangled in the anchor flukes. I drove the boat through the anchorage to another spot. He dropped the anchor overboard. We watched while the line went taut, and then limp, taut, and then limp. The anchor tried to grab, but because of the abundant beds of kelp, the flukes fouled before they gripped the bottom. We repeated the exercise, but each time, the anchor came up thick with kelp, no roe.

An old-timer whose anchor held watched our anchor-drill comedy. The third time the skiff sailed past the *Tom Boy*, the skipper came halfway out of his cabin and pointed to a spot we should try. I drove the skiff to where he pointed. George dropped the anchor. We stood in the blowing snow and watched the line. When we were convinced the anchor held, we scampered, drenched and miserable, into the cabin. We cranked up the stove and watched the snow paint the scenery while the wind swung the skiff and yanked on her anchor line.

The snow fell and the wind blew throughout the night. I hoped the storm was the last battle between winter and spring.

We woke to a gentle breeze. When the sun came up, I knew spring had won. The clouds parted and the sun reflected off the fresh snow. The sky cleared, the air smelled of spring, and the Sound was abundant with wildlife.

Peggy flew to the skiff for the weekend, her first boat outing since we'd lost Bean. She was writing a series of stories about the wild kelp fishery for *The Cordova Times*. She witnessed the harvest on Saturday. On Sunday the Fish and Game manager gave us a day off. He wanted to tally the harvest to date.

After morning coffee, I anchored the skiff and George, Peggy, and I climbed on board the *Sugar* with Tom, Merrie, and Jesse. Tom ferried us across the lower part of Valdez Arm to Columbia Glacier, at the terminus of its forty-one-mile course from the Chugach Mountains. We rounded Glacier Island and saw the face, a solid block of ice 250 feet high and miles wide at the water's edge. Towering behind it were coastal mountains. Farther beyond stood a peak of nearly ten thousand feet.

Some days glaciers are quiet, but that day Columbia was active. Tom picked his way around the icebergs, ever closer to the face. The wall of ice grew taller in front of us, and the mountain range disappeared. Icebergs of various sizes bounced, crackled, and rolled while they drifted past us.

Peggy asked Tom, "How close do you plan to go?" She sounded concerned.

"Looks like we can reach the face," he said enthusiastically.

Peggy rolled her eyes with a look of disapproval. She and George went inside the cabin.

Merrie and I threatened mutiny if Tom didn't reconsider his course to the face. When we voiced our concern, he shifted the boat into neutral and listened. While we drifted at a distance in front of the wall of ice, the glacier rumbled. The thunder ended our conversation. We turned to see a chunk of the glacier the size of a house fall from the face. We heard a loud crash when it hit the water, which caused an impressive splash. Water shot thirty feet in the air. The impact of the gigantic chunk of ice formed a frightful wave.

Merrie and I stood with our mouths wide open in dead silence. We anticipated the enormous wave rolling straight toward the *Sugar*. The sight paralyzed us.

Tom casually shifted the *Sugar* into forward. With a couple of fingers on the wheel, he turned the bow into the oncoming surge, prepared for the impact. The bow of the *Sugar* gracefully lifted and slid over the top of the wave.

Merrie and I breathed a sigh of relief.

"I can't believe you landlubbers. You two must be spirits from the *Titanic* to be so neurotic." Tom roared with laughter. "It's only a little ice."

We harvested kelp a few more days until the Japanese quit buying because the eggs were too mature. The wild kelpers harvested less than half the kelp they sold the previous year. After George and I paid for fuel, groceries, repair parts, and the parts flight, we shared a pocket of change for our profit. The trip was an expensive vacation for George, but with our bills paid, we were ahead of some seiners.

The seiners waited to fish farther south. In early May, the Fish and Game manager announced a one-hour fishing opener. Boats crammed into a limited area and harvested what they could in the short time. The space was congested. Some boats never caught a fish. Some didn't set their nets in time. Others made a set but caught rocks and tore their nets. More than a hundred boats were eager to seine at the beginning of the season, but sixty-six boats delivered less than half of the herring quota. The seine crews prepared boats and nets and waited on the grounds for a month. At the end of the hour-long season, they went home. Those who caught herring paid expenses and put money in their wallets. Others owed for groceries and fuel.

When we arrived in town, I picked up my mail and found a letter from my brother Jon. He reminisced about the salmon I sent the previous spring and enclosed a check in case I wanted to send another box to my parents; he'd pay the air freight. Everyone in town reminisced about the flavor of fresh salmon.

The skiff needed to be ready to gillnet. Having lived on the skiff the previous couple of weeks, I thought it was almost ready.

Another gillnetter and a hoist helped me lower the reel and set it on the mounts in the skiff. He remarked on the poor condition of the tow post, a post next to the reel that people used to hold or tow the net. "One hard jerk on that post, and it is apt to be floating out behind you," he cautioned. "I hope no one is in the way when it goes. Anything anchored in a boat where it's wet should never be wood. It rots."

After more education from the old-timer, I wanted to order an aluminum post and mount. I found Art Gunderson, a metal fabricator who was semiretired but willing to construct a new tow post on a rush order. Art was slow and deliberate in both speech and action. His casual attitude frustrated people in a frantic panic. He didn't care, and he wasn't going to speed up because of someone else's poor planning. He readily accepted my order. My problem began when he looked around his shop and didn't find the piece of aluminum he needed for the mount. He told me what he needed to complete the job. "When you find the piece, bring it by, and I'll get started," Art said in a slow, relaxed voice.

With the season opener days away, I searched the entire town until I found the aluminum cylinder Art needed. Once he began work on the new tow post, I went to work on the skiff. I fastened the reel and tried to start the Briggs and Stratton. I tried every secret I knew, without success.

"Pull the Briggs off and haul it to Vern Johnson's shop," one of the gillnetters said when he walked on the dock past my skiff.

Vern was one of the most respected mechanics in town. He had a shop at APA, the old razor clam cannery. The shop had specialty tools, but even more valuable was Vern's knowledge.

"I don't fish for APA," I pointed out.

"Vern lets noncompany fishermen work in his shop if they don't displace any of his fishermen," the gillnetter assured me.

The following day while holding my engine precariously, I asked Vern, "Will you help me with a tune-up?"

The shop was busy, but he pointed to an empty spot on a bench and told me what to dismantle. I changed the lube oil, checked the magneto, and bought a carburetor rebuild kit from Johnny Dollar. After I replaced a gasket and a few springs on the linkage, I made a few adjustments to the carburetor, and the Briggs ran like new. I returned to my skiff, mounted the engine on the reel, loaded the net, bolted down the new tow post, and resupplied the skiff. All that mattered was the price of salmon.

CHAPTER EIGHT

PRACTICALLY THE ENTIRE fishing fleet attended the spring CAMA meetings and heard the local cannery offers. The CAMA members voiced their opinions and cast their vote on the latest price. Some years negotiations dragged on for weeks into the season, which caused tempers to run hot. That year the processors eventually signed a spring contract that included the minimum price they paid for sockeye, king, keta, and pink salmon. The price agreement for coho waited until August. The fishermen shared their major economic interests. The price war united and pitted the fishermen, both gillnetters and seiners, against the canneries.

Armin was a local gillnetter, seiner, and a fierce advocate for hatcheries. He knew CAMA meetings were an opportunity to speak to a captive audience. For years he talked about hatcheries and their ability to increase and stabilize salmon production. "Hatcheries will create a more viable fishery," he claimed.

Convincing fishermen to invest money in a hatchery was a chore Armin, with his silver tongue, embraced as his life's mission. He sold ocean ranching to the Alaskan legislature and the fishermen hook, line, and sinker. The fishermen were receptive, because the 1964 earthquake had lifted the ground from five to thirty feet around the Sound. The shorelines changed and much of the shallow water habitat used by spawning salmon dried out. Everyone wanted a stable pink fishery.

Pink salmon are two years old when they return to spawn. The scarcity of pink salmon that returned on even-numbered years closed the seine fishery in 1972 and 1974. Instead of fishing, Armin and CAMA members organized the local private nonprofit salmon hatchery and called it The Prince William Sound Aquaculture Corporation, PWSAC, pronounced Piz-whack. The fishermen volunteered to donate a couple of cents for every salmon they caught. The canneries joined in with their support and matched dollar for dollar the fishermen's contributions.

Armin's partner in the aquaculture vision was Wallace H. Noerenberg, a retired Alaska Fish and Game commissioner. Armin was short and round. Wallace was tall and slender. Both had grown up in Germany on opposite sides of the war, but their passion for enhancing salmon created a powerful friendship.

Private land in Alaska is scarce. In 1975 PWSAC leased the San Juan Packing Company, an abandoned NEFCO cannery in the southwestern part of the Sound. Armin and Noerenberg, with help from the fishermen, tendermen, canneries, and townspeople, converted the old cannery buildings into a hatchery. More than a hundred people in town loaded 3,500 sacks with gravel for incubating the salmon. The tenders and fishing boats hauled the gravel and other materials to the site and worked when they arrived. In October an oil company helicopter delivered the hatchery water pipe to the site.

The previous summer Wallace seined some wild pink salmon at Larson Creek and transported them to the old cannery in Port San Juan. Armin, ruthless in his determination, admitted in private that while he was in Juneau securing the permits for his partner's activities, Noerenberg harvested and transferred the pinks. I wondered if the ex-commissioner knew he possibly fished illegally.

"The San Juan Hatchery incubated the eggs from Noerenberg's catch," Armin, with his thick German accent, reported. "The eggs hatched into fry, and the fry swam out of the hatchery."

We found aquaculture interesting, but after a long winter, the gillnetters were out of money and eager to learn what the canneries were willing to pay. The fishermen wanted news about when they were going fishing. After Armin spoke, to move discussions to price, the members voted again to fund Armin and Noerenberg's dream fish.

After CAMA members heard the offers from the local canneries, they instructed Bob Blake to negotiate a better price. When the meeting broke up, half the gillnetters stood around and talked about the market, the predictions, and their expectations for the season. The other half ran to their boats in a panic, still preparing for the season. The market appeared good, and the price offers were close to acceptable.

On Friday Bob Blake presented an offer from one of the local canneries. When one major cannery signed the contract, the others followed. The members accepted the offer. For the first time in decades CAMA settled the spring price contract before the season opened and without a strike. That welcome break in tradition found many gillnetters unprepared. Saturday, May 15, the gillnetters could legally set their nets at midnight for six hours. Those who were ready dashed out of the meeting and were off to catch the tide for a home-pack. Others ran to their boats and prepared for Monday when the canneries would begin to buy salmon.

TOM AND I ran our boats to Outer Paulson's Hole on Sunday. Although close to the ocean, Tom thought Outer Paulson's was the safest place for me to learn to catch sockeye. Copper Sands produced silvers and kings, but few sockeye, which dominated the spring catch. Outer Paulson's was a long, narrow channel that ran sideways behind the major sand island that stretched between Egg Island and Pete Dahl bars. At high water the channel expanded to more than triple its low-water size. Shallow water covered the extensive sands. The trick was to keep the boat floating while the tide ran out. I failed the challenge.

A boat "going dry" is a common part of life on the Flats. Getting stuck in the shallows was the most common hardship of early explorers. The Coast Guard Chart labels the delta as non-navigable waters. When experienced gillnetters become stuck on a sandbar on the ebb, they never admit going dry wasn't intentional.

"I was tired from all the work over the closure and needed some sleep," I've heard them claim on the radio.

At other times fishermen made their skiff go dry. In a monstrous storm the lack of motion throwing and bouncing your body is a relief. Tom told of a night when the wind blew more than 120 knots. "The rough water pounded my skiff and threatened to break it apart. I ran aground on top of a sandbar shortly before high tide. Waves broke over the bow, and each one spilled into the skiff. I secured myself to the tow post with a rope to prevent blowing overboard, sipped Hudson Bay Rum, and bailed water. After high tide I stuck my oar over the side until the water ebbed enough that the boat couldn't sink. I quit bailing, dried off, and collapsed in my bunk while the skiff went dry."

When he woke the wind was silent. His muscles were sore from having bailed water the previous night. With all the energy he could muster, he opened his skiff door. He told how the wind had blown hard against the sands when the tide went out. "The wind sandblasted the paint off my skiff and the fiberglass finish off my kicker cover. Worse yet, my skiff was half buried in a sand drift."

Full of sand, the skiff couldn't float. Tom threw sand overboard any way he could while he watched the tide increase the water depth around his skiff. He dug out enough sand to make the boat float, leaving inches of freeboard, the distance between the level of the water and the upper side of the skiff.

"If the wind had come up, my skiff would have gone down."

Most of the time going dry is uneventful and the skiff floats again in less than twelve hours. If the wind isn't screaming, sleep on a sandbar is quiet, peaceful, and the only time everything stops moving. To sit on a sandbar for a tide was inconvenient and sometimes expensive, because of lost fishing time, but the boats were shallow draft with flat bottoms, and going dry usually wasn't a problem.

Going dry becomes a problem when a boat goes stuck on a falling tide, a tide higher than the following tides. A boat might wait months to float off the highest sand. For that reason everyone takes precautions during the unforgiving highest tide of the month. When the tides are not as extreme and dropping in size, skippers are sometimes not as aware or as cautious.

One such tender drove across the shallows on her way to town with a load of salmon. The skipper misjudged the time or the tide and ran the tender hard aground. The boat became a landmark on the sand. The cannery sent a shallower boat that unloaded the salmon at high water. The tides were falling. The boat wouldn't float for a week, but the skipper refused to leave with the salmon and his crew. If he went to town, he knew he'd hear all the talk about his boat. Watching boats run past in the water that at high tide only lapped at his hull must have tortured him.

The worst time to get stuck is during the first set of the opener. The first few hours of an opener are the most profitable. In Outer Paulson's boats packed the narrow channel on openers. To find space to set a net was a challenge. At six o'clock sharp the scene rivaled a boat race. Everyone drove fast, set their nets, and claimed the water.

One high-water opener, I saw what appeared to be an open spot with plenty of room between two boats. I was proud that I set my entire net. I watched the salmon bob the cork line. My net exploded with splashes. The net drifted a short distance, the salmon stopped hitting, and I began to pick the net. I pulled in about two-thirds of it when the reel stopped bringing in the net. I examined the reel, but couldn't find the problem, until I looked over the stern and saw I was trying to pull my skiff onto a sandbar. One-third of my net sat dry in the sand. In the minutes I took to comprehend the problem, the skiff went dry.

The net had looked promising because the shallow water allowed me to see every fish that hit. I had set my net on top of a shallow spit. The skippers on both sides of me must have chuckled and shaken their heads when they saw me set my net. They knew my location better than I did.

The salmon caught in the last third of my net were also dry on the sandbar. I climbed off the skiff, walked along my net, picked the fish, and carried them back to my fish hold. The birds zeroed in on the meal spread across the sandbar. They reached the salmon at the farthest end of the net before I did. The last fish was missing its eyes. I laid that fish closer to the skiff and away from the net to share with the birds. I watched the eagles devour the fish, which helped pass the hours while I waited for the tide to finish going out before it returned and floated my boat. In my experience the channel was magic. Now you see water; now you don't. I struggled to visualize the location of the main channel, but the water going in and out constantly changed the design of the shoreline.

When fishing began at low water, the space was even more limited. I felt intimidated by the boats with experienced skippers and tried to stay out of their way. On one opener we set our nets, but I hesitated for a moment, and bam! My net wrapped around the propeller. While the other skippers picked bright, shiny salmon out of their nets, I picked a shiny prop out of mine. I spent hours sitting high and dry or hanging over the stern removing my net during every fishing period, which unknown to me at the time earned my skiff the nickname of *Sleepy Hollow.*

Most of the boats deserted Outer Paulson's after the first low water of each period, after they caught the salmon that built up over the closure. About seven boats homesteaded Outer Paulson's, meaning they fished there all season. At that number I found room in the channel to set my net. The area grew quiet except for the surf I heard pound on the ocean side of the sandbar. A couple of gillnetters kept an eye on my skiff without my knowledge. I knew only enough to be dangerous.

One morning while I picked the last of my net, the wind blew my skiff onto a beach. The problem had become routine. The tide was rising. I pulled in my buoy, dropped my anchor, and waited for enough water to float the skiff so I could drive away. Gerry, the honorary mayor of Outer Paulson's, came by and offered to pull me off the beach.

"I'll wait for more water," I replied because I hated to waste his valuable fishing time. "I'm okay."

He knew better. Gerry shook his head and gave a look that said I was dumb enough that he had no choice but to help me. He insisted he pull me off the beach and explained what was obvious to everyone else. When the water level increased, the other side of the channel covered with water. The shoreline became part of the outside beach. The beach I was on would cover with breaking waves. I thanked him for the tow and the knowledge, and I never again fished that far down the channel.

WHILE I WAS bucking the tide from Whitshed to Egg Island one Sunday night, the skiff pounded so hard the stove filter broke off the mount. I shut off the flow of oil. Drenched and without a stove, I dreaded freezing all night in my skiff. At the Egg Island anchorage, I spotted the *Mummy Mist.* Joel kept his boat cabin hot. I pulled alongside and asked if I could tie up. Joel fished on the ocean, but he'd stay anchored until a few hours before the opener.

"You're welcome to sleep in one of my extra bunks, then you can begin fishing warm and dry," Joel said.

I was dry for the first minute of the opener, and then I was miserable. Cold food and no coffee on a wet boat made running to town for parts enticing, but the catch remained steady. When I repaired the stove filter, the task required an education about plumbing with copper tubing and flare fittings. I had no idea what I was doing and could see only the next step, so each step required another trip to the hardware store. The storeowner was patient and happy to educate me; however, the cannery office hated my numerous purchase orders for a couple of dollars or cents.

The time between fishing periods was short. For some closures we anchored the boats on the grounds and spent the entire time eating and sleeping. The closures seemed even shorter when we ran to town because our runs were dependent on the tides. The time spent in town was filled with repairs, maintenance, or mending nets, and of course we celebrated cheating death at the bars into the early hours. Everyone returned to their boats exhausted. A flight to and from town was the most efficient way, because the plane was quick and less tide dependent.

One fishing period closed on the ebb tide. We had to wait six hours for enough water to run our boats the one-hour trip to town. Instead of waiting, Tom and I flew to town. The floatplane lifted off the water, I blinked my eyes, and the plane landed at Kramer's Hole, a small, shallow channel down the outside beach from Outer Paulson's. There, the channel dead ended at low water into a fishing pond that was tiny but productive. The fishermen named the hole after Dean Kramer, who spent seasons fishing there until he perished during the Memorial Day storm of 1971. Patsy, Dean's widow, homesteaded the hole and was the only boat most years.

The plane landed to pick up Wally, Patsy, and her children. That year Wally also fished in Kramer's. The *Blind Faith* ran poorly. Wally needed a new engine but didn't have the money to buy one. With an unreliable engine, he found Kramer's Hole was the one safe channel to fish on the Flats.

None of the tenders could navigate the shallow channel. Neither Patsy nor Wally wanted to run through the breakers to deliver their fish. A cannery flew Patsy and Wally's catch into town. We guessed how many salmon they'd caught by the number of times we saw the floatplane land at Kramer's Hole.

When the plane door opened, Wally, Patsy, and her children filled the empty seats. Dean and Patsy had four children—three boys, and the youngest, a girl named Susie, who I guessed was about ten. The previous July Patsy had given birth to a baby boy and named him David after her new husband, "Sealand Dave" Glasen. Patsy was a delightful, patient woman who felt comfortable with her children on the boat. She wore a smile and carried the youngest. When everyone fastened their seatbelts, the plane lifted off and landed on the lake within minutes. We walked into the office, paid for our fare with a cannery purchase order, and scheduled another flight for our return. Another benefit I found in a flight to town was the pleasure of a day off. I couldn't do maintenance or make repairs with my skiff anchored on the fishing grounds.

My most memorable set that spring season was when I tried to catch my first Copper River king salmon. They are huge, averaging twenty-eight pounds, but a few weigh forty to fifty pounds.

Tom tried to prepare me, but kings are strong and throw their weight around. "Sneak the gaff next to their gills, and in one motion set the hook and bring the salmon on board," Tom instructed me.

A gaff has a round wooden handle with a hook on the end. I followed Tom's instructions, but when I tried to set the hook and pull the king salmon in, he woke from his nap. The net hadn't caught him; he was resting against the web waiting for it to move out of his way. The king was strong, free to swim, and full of energy. Before I pulled him over my stern, he lifted me off the bottom of my skiff. He tried to pull me into the water. With my feet in the air and my arm overextended, I released my grip, dropped back into the skiff, and watched the king salmon swim away with my gaff. After that encounter I developed my own method to bring kings on board. I wrapped the net around the king, shifted the reel transmission into third gear, and jerked the king in, lightning fast. I didn't give them a chance to wake. Wrapping a king consumed time, and a few of the kings swam away, but losing a king felt better than the threat of those royal beauties pulling me out of my skiff.

That spring the Copper River Sockeye returned strong. Most of the gillnetters harvested a good season, with money in the bank when Coghill opened. I hadn't paid my bills or made my skiff payment, but I gained a wealth of knowledge about fishing. To restore my confidence I reassured myself that I'd earn money fishing on the Sound, and if I was broke at the end of the season, I could sell my skiff to pay the bank.

AT COGHILL THE scenery, the sunshine, and the crisp clean air picked up my spirits, but compared to my memories and expectations, fishing was disastrous. The frustration of not being able to catch salmon felt similar to fishing the Flats. Unlike the Flats, my skiff floated, and my net stayed wet, but I caught fewer sockeye that week than I'd caught my first week fishing when I knew nothing. By the end of the week I felt discouraged and feared I failed as a gillnetter. The catch wasn't meeting the Fish and Game manager's prediction. All the fishermen caught fewer salmon than the previous season, but after two weeks I found the boats around me caught more sockeye than I did.

"No one wants that net except to strip it for the cork and lead lines," was Tom's response the previous fall when he looked at Bean's net that I had destroyed on the reef. "You can buy the net for the value of the lines."

I bought the net, but instead of stripping it, cutting all the knots and throwing out the web, I learned how to mend and repaired the web. The net went on and off the reel, but I learned mending involved more than connecting the knots. The mended net's ability to catch salmon was pathetic; the geometry was wrong. I wished I had thrown away the web instead of mending it.

I didn't have money to buy a new net with new lines, but without changing my net, my catch would continue to suffer. Plenty of people would quit gillnetting to go seining and want to sell a net. When fishing closed, I flew to town and found Kenny Quinn at Orca. Kenny, a gillnetter and net salesman, owned a store in Bellingham that sold fishing gear. In a warehouse at Orca he filled an oversized locker with supplies from his store. His passion for fishing and solving fishing gear problems made him a natural salesman; he thrived on solving gear problems. Kenny, with a clean-shaven smile and short hair, was a jovial person who was excited to write orders and always on top of his game, even in the bars at closing time. He offered me a net with new web on used lines, ready to fish, and he charged it to the cannery.

I loaded the net on a tender that hauled it to my boat. On Sunday night I switched nets. Monday morning the cork line wiggled the minute the new net hit the water, and in the first twelve hours, I exceeded my catch of the previous week. That week all of the remaining gillnetters caught more salmon because of less competition. Some skippers went seining, and the Washington gillnetters ran their boats south to gillnet in Puget Sound.

At the end of the week I wanted to celebrate. The closest town, Whittier, was located ten miles down Port Wells and another ten miles up Passage Canal. To visit Whittier, I needed some cash. The cannery tenders gave fishermen a fish ticket. The cannery credited the boat's account. If fishermen wanted money, they went to the office in town and requested a draw. Living without money wasn't a problem, because we lived in a cashless society and charged everything to the cannery. Whittier didn't accept cannery purchase orders or have a bank. The bar wouldn't cash our out-of-town checks; however, the bartender cashed checks from Whitney Fidalgo, a seafood company with an operation in Whittier.

Lyle and his wife, Marge, owned the *Sprite* and purchased salmon for Whitney Fidalgo. Marge gave gillnetters a check with their fish ticket. All day Friday, the *Sprite* drifted on the route to Whittier out of the sight of the cannery tenders. The boats headed to Whittier saved the last of their catch for the *Sprite* and weekend spending money. The gillnetters termed the sale as being a chippy, being unfaithful to their processor, which added excitement to the cash. Friday morning I sold my salmon to NEFCO. At the closure I found the *Sprite* at the entrance to Passage Canal and sold my catch. After Marge wrote my check, I pulled out my chart and then cruised into unknown waters.

As I neared Whittier, constant flocks of kittiwakes flew from the rock cliffs on the shore ahead. When the boat reached the rookery, I saw their nests built in the crevasses and crannies of the sheer rock face. Hundreds or maybe thousands of blacklegged kittiwakes flew above me. A mile and a half across the fjord from the rookery sat the town of Whittier, about a square mile of flat area surrounded by mountains. The chart showed the tank farm at the head of the bay, but nothing prepared me for the two cement skyscrapers that dominated the skyline of the town.

I tied the boat to the transient float and walked out of the harbor. In front of me was a bunch of railroad tracks laid from a tunnel to the wharf. After I crossed the numerous rails, a lengthy covered stairway led me to a cinderblock building. There I found the opportunity for a hot shower, clean laundry, groceries, and a restaurant. I walked a few feet farther, and saw what I really desired, a place to socialize with people and have a party on Saturday night. I went into the bar and found a local, Harry, who loved to talk. I asked him about the cement buildings.

"In its time the taller building held the record of the tallest skyscraper in Alaska," he said with pride. "During World War II the military built those towers as barracks for the troops." He waved a hand in the general direction of the mountain. "They also blasted two and a half miles through that mountain range and laid railroad tracks to Anchorage and the Interior."

Harry sipped his beer and went on for an hour, telling me all about his town. He lived there when the city purchased the site from the federal government in 1969. The population, fewer than a hundred, either fished or worked for the railroad, the barge company, the seafood processor, or the government. The tallest building remained vacant, but in the other tower, he told me, residents were renovating two of the fourteen floors for condominiums.

The fishing boats tied up at the transient float five and six boats deep. A few of us spent the weekend doing laundry and buying groceries. Most fishermen caught the train to Anchorage to pick up parts or spend a night in the city. The problem with the train, the one land route out of Whittier, was its infrequent schedule.

A NEFCO fisherman told me, "One night I ran my boat into town to catch the train to Anchorage, but I arrived after the last train. Desperate for boat parts, I walked more than two miles into the darkness." He slapped his thigh with a chuckle. "I almost messed my pants when I saw the silhouette of a bear in the light at the other end of the tunnel. I arrived in Anchorage the next day, exhausted from my land-speed-record run."

The skippers hurried back from Anchorage on Sunday. They usually cruised to the fishing district, anchored, and waited for the morning opener. That night the fishermen headed out of Portage Canal, but when the boats turned north, the seas tossed them wildly. The wind blew down Port Wells with the force of a freight train. Many of the skippers turned back to a bay protected from the wind. In front of my skiff I saw a log and tried to avoid it. The wind, current, and wild water controlled my skiff more than my engine did. I turned back, anchored with the other boats, and waited for the wind to calm down.

We fished a couple more weeks before Coghill closed, but the seiners continued to fish in other districts. Traveling across the Sound without another boat in sight was common, but that day's trip was quite different, with seine boats fishing along the way. When they fished at a point close to my route, I stopped and watched. I saw how different seining is when compared to gillnetting. Seiners are always active.

Gillnetters set their nets and wait a few minutes to a couple of hours for the salmon to hit and then gillnetters pick the fish out of the net one by one. The crew on the seine boat laid its net in a circle around the fish and closed the net. The crew pulled a purse line to gather the bottom of the net. With the salmon captured, the crew members brought the net on board and spilled the fish into the hold. The boat and crew were ready to set the net again. I looked at my clock. The time had been less than an hour. I might spend an hour picking my net, in addition to the time the net drifted and caught the salmon. I saw that seining was more efficient for large catches.

After I tied the skiff in the harbor, I walked to Bill's and my new house. Bill had rented a two-bedroom house while I was fishing on the Sound. He moved us out of the apartment and gave me a tour when I returned to town. I enjoyed the additional space and loved having a yard.

CAMA SETTLED THE price for the silvers before we lost any fishing time. The size of the gillnet fleet for the fall fishery was smaller. Schoolteachers and students were back in school, and because harsh weather is typical for September, many gillnetters choose to miss silver season.

The predominant storm winds blow from the southeast. My skiff bucked into the wind when I traveled from Point Whitshed across the sand flats. My flat-bottom skiff navigated well in shallow water, but it didn't slice into the water; it belly flopped. The swells slapped my bow. Water sprayed up the sides of the skiff and splashed over the cabin. The salt water drenched my face and gushed through the opening at the top of my raincoat. Buckets of salt water flushed the inside of my raingear and filled my boots. By the time the skiff reached Egg Island, the water had soaked me, salty and icy cold, clear to my underwear. After a couple of those trips, I decided that before next season, a wheel-house was essential to protect myself from the saltwater spray.

Two noticeable differences exist between the spring and fall seasons on the Flats: the duration of foul weather and the contrast in the hours of light. The spring season begins a month before summer solstice when dusk and dawn are minutes apart. We begin silver season two months after the solstice, and some years it continues past the fall equinox, when dusk and dawn are hours apart, and every night the darkness increases in length. The sky, without a moon or the northern lights, was black. The area is flat, and lights with any height were visible from a distance. Two landmarks at Egg Island, the Cordova airport to the north and a White Alice Site to the west, guided me. I judged my location by those lights on the horizon, the water depth, and the lay of the channel.

Anchored one Sunday night before an opener, I woke to a frantic conversation on my CB radio from a new gillnetter whose anchor dragged. He had no idea where he was. He said the thunderous noise he heard let him know he was close to the breakers. Daylight was hours away, long after the tide changed the water around him. Where was he? More importantly, would the breakers pound on his boat soon? I'm glad it wasn't me.

Terry Robinson, a longtime gillnetter, was calm, patient, and knowledgeable about the area. He talked to the lost sailor and guided him back to a safe anchorage. People listening to the radio sighed with relief, checked their anchors, and went back to sleep.

After a couple of weeks of fishing at Egg Island, Tom offered me a tow to Softuk. With the *Sugar* he towed his, Floyd's, and my skiff to the farthest eastern inside channels in the Copper River district. The tides were high enough to have plenty of water to allow us to travel inside of the sand islands. The week at Softuk was wonderful. The channels were well-defined without the shallows that made Outer Paulson's hard to navigate. Amazing to me, I fished from Monday to Thursday without getting stuck, even once.

Tom anchored the *Sugar* and fished his skiff. Tom, Floyd, and I tied to the *Sugar* and shared meals and conversation. They disappeared in the dark to fish the change of tide. I was unfamiliar with the area in the daylight, and that far east, no lights were visible in any direction. My skiff stayed tied to the *Sugar* through the dark nights. The next week, ready to tie up for the night, I delivered my catch to the tender.

"The weather forecast predicts a storm warning," the captain cautioned me.

Not far past the fishing closed markers was the Martin River Slough, where skiffs ran to hide from the brunt of storms. Tom and Floyd stayed at the anchorage with the *Sugar*. I chose to run up the slough before the wind blew any harder. The slough was east and north of the marker, with acres of water covering the channel and the shallows.

"Stay to one side of the channel, and you'll know which way to turn when you run out of water," Tom said.

The skiff crept up the south side of the channel. Every time the prop began to dig sand, I turned the wheel north toward the deeper water. My eyes stayed glued to the depth sounder. An engine noise made me look around. On the other side of the channel, Brian King's engine idled at the entrance of the slough. My skiff was on the wrong side of the channel. If the noise hadn't alerted me, I might have missed the entrance.

I navigated across the channel and past numerous skiffs already anchored in the slough. I ran beyond the boats, until my skiff was almost out of water. I dropped my anchor off the bow, and to set the anchor, I powered the boat in reverse. A storm can be cozy if I was warm and hidden in my bunk. Life was miserable if my anchor dragged in a storm. I'd have to battle the wind and rain to secure my skiff while it banged into other boats or blew against the shore.

The sides of the slough were high, and at low water, much of the wind blew above us. After dinner I felt secure with the anchor but went to bed dressed and ready for an anchor drill. The wind picked up in the night, and my skiff danced wildly on the end of its anchor line. I found the noise unbearable for sleep. I couldn't hear the music from my tape deck, even at full volume, because of the deafening howl of the wind.

At first light I peeked out my skiff window to the shore of the slough and saw smoke, which made me look closer, knowing nothing could burn under those soggy conditions. Where the streams of water drained into the slough, the wind blew the water hard enough it defied gravity. Volumes of water resembling smoke blew into the air.

Eating and reading consumed most of my day while I waited for the storm to blow over. The skiffs I could see out of my cabin window, like mine, lurched and jerked on their anchors and shuddered with the stronger gusts. Again the wind gusted above us through the night, but by morning, the wind grew quiet. When the tide flooded across enough of the sand, the boats trickled back to the fishing area. I followed them and paid more attention to the lay of the visible sand around me. The security of that slough gave me comfort, and I wanted to become familiar with the channel to the entrance.

When the wind died down, Tom and Floyd were in prime position for fishing. Most of the boats anchored up the slough, and the tide forced the skippers to miss low water and wait to travel on the incoming tide. Tom and Floyd suffered the brunt of the storm. Their misery paid off when they fished without competition during the low water that morning. I was miserable while up the slough. At the anchorage I would have been puking.

The rest of the week, still following Tom's precautions, I fished low water, the flood tide, and then anchored and waited for the ebb to slow toward low water. On the weekend I anchored the skiff up the slough and flew to town. Tom and Floyd ran their boats to Morpac. Floyd sold his skiff because he planned to build a new bow-picker that winter. The canneries told the gillnetters they would quit buying silvers at the end of the next week. News came that another low-pressure system was imminent.

"You should ask Floyd to go out, fish your skiff, and run it to town for you," Tom suggested.

Floyd had years of experience fishing the area and hated to miss any opener. I dreaded crossing the Flats during a blow and agreed without a second thought. Monday night was stormy and dark when Floyd returned to town. We met near the harbor at the Reluctant Fisherman, and I bought him a hot drink.

"The wind never stopped. I headed in after a few sets. The wind blew me home in record time." Floyd reported. He was cold and wet. He told of the unusual course he'd run because the storm surge pushed deeper water onto the tide flats. I didn't mind missing that experience.

NEWS CAME FROM the Bering River, the fishing district east of the Copper River. The storm trapped Willie, along with a fleet of boats. The surf was so violent they were unable to run from the river out the Bering River Bar to the gulf. Anchored inside at Pete's Point, the skippers waited for the weather to pass. When the ocean calmed, the ocean bar would open a passage for their journey home.

A boat stocked with plenty of food, water, and stove oil can turn a storm into a relaxed, forced vacation after a hard fishing season. Willie's new love, Linda, was on board, so we knew he was in no rush to head for town. Other boats tied together and shared an anchor and a game of cards, or they ran a skiff up the river to hunt. The fishermen had experienced equinox storms, and they were prepared to wait out the weather.

For Cal, skipper of the tender *Stardust,* his time trapped was quite a different story. He worried about the quality of the salmon he'd purchased and felt obligated to deliver them to the cannery. Cal, in his early sixties, was born in Oregon, but had lived in Cordova since his twenties. He'd fished a seine boat he named after his two children the *Emily Scott,* but purchased a new larger boat, the *Stardust.* Cal tendered his new boat for Alaska Packers that fall.

Cal and another skipper were having a contest. Which of them could eat, without a tear in his eye, the hottest pepper? The two men each had a selection of peppers that ranged from hot to fire. Each day the two ate another, even hotter, pepper. Cal couldn't stay anchored and taste peppers. His salmon were going to spoil. With the size of the seas, if the ocean bar opened a passage, the time would be at high water. Cal ran the *Stardust* to the ocean bar every tide before the high to look at the breakers. He watched and waited, but each time, he returned to the anchorage.

After a couple of days of that routine, on Wednesday's tide, Cal didn't return. A boat heard a call on the radio. The message wasn't clear, but the few skippers who heard the call knew something was wrong. Gillnetters who had their boats tied alongside an anchored boat cut loose and sped to the ocean bar. The two rescue vessels had two men on each boat.

Minutes after the call, the rescue boats reached the bar. They saw the *Stardust* caught in a whirlpool. Debris hurled off the boat and into the breakers. Another powerful wave knocked Cal's lifeless body into the water. Together Jerry and Marty pulled Cal out of the water. Soot covered his limp body. While Marty tried to resuscitate Cal, Jerry ran his boat to a tender anchored at Pete's Point. While he traveled, he radioed to the tender and requested that someone call a plane. When the plane arrived, the gillnetters were still trying to resuscitate Cal, but his body didn't respond. Unwilling to give up hope, they transferred him to the plane. We later learned Cal had suffered a fatal blow to the head. The gillnetters guessed that when the *Stardust* disintegrated, the stove broke loose and delivered the skull-crushing injury.

Did Cal run too close to the breakers before he decided against running the bar? Maybe a rogue wave found him before he could react. Did concern about the salmon cloud his judgment? The skippers considered countless ideas of what might have happened. They tried to explain their loss, but no one would ever know the real story. I search for reasons to explain why, to learn how to stay alive, so it wouldn't happen to me.

The fishermen respected Cal. Relationships with tendermen were special and Cal Aiken was a special man, a tender man the fishermen loved and hated to lose. He left a widow and his children Emily and Scott in Cordova. I didn't know Cal but knew from the townspeople and fishermen mourning his loss that he was important to the fishing fleet and loved by a town full of people.

CHAPTER NINE

THE EQUINOX STORMS continued to blow. People can sleep, read, and play cards for only so long. Supplies on the boats ran low and the fishermen felt restless. Friday the *Rawhide* and the *Kuana* made their way out the ocean bar in a break for town. Once in the gulf they sought shelter because of violent seas. With the bar entrances closed, the boats bucked into the wind until they found marginal protection in the lee of the Martin Islands.

The anchor on the *Rawhide* held, but the *Kuana*'s anchor continued to drag. The captain of the *Rawhide* threw a line to the drifting boat. The *Rawhide*'s anchor held both boats into the night. The way the wind and waves pounded against the skiffs, the fishermen feared their wooden boats were going to break apart. The *Kuana* leaked. Before that bitter night ended, a Coast Guard helicopter lifted the two men off in fifty-knot winds. Later when the skippers flew to their boats. Only the *Rawhide* remained.

On Sunday the wind diminished, but the seas were still violent. A fleet of boats, including the *Phillip L,* made a break for town. The swells were enormous and the struggle to power through the walls of water slowed their progress. The skippers pushed on. They wanted to cross the ocean bar on the flood tide.

At Egg Island the breakers climbed out of the fierce ocean and slammed down for miles off the beach. Angry waves broke all the way across the main channel. No entrance existed. The skippers waited outside the breakers and searched for a gap in the wall of surf. A temporary passage opened at high water, and a parade of boats fled the ocean.

Two boats reached Egg Island later than the *Phillip L*, after high water, after the temporary bar entrance closed. The skippers had flown to their anchored boats that day. In the brief time the men had spent in town the days had lost an hour of light. The voyage, longer than planned, used much more fuel than anticipated. The seas were more powerful than the skippers had imagined. Low on fuel, the pair drifted in the dark.

The *Commando,* a research vessel from the University of Washington, sighted the lights of the fishing boats. The crew pulled the skippers aboard and transferred them to the Coast Guard Cutter *Sweetbriar*, which delivered the skippers to town. Days later, one of the boats washed up on the outside beach of Montague Island, the other boat was never found.

The town sighed with relief when the rest of the boats returned to the harbor. The fishing fleet lost a respected seiner, tenderman, and longtime Cordovan. Newcomers, including me, developed more respect for the fall equinox storms.

IN TOWN THE gillnetters winterized their equipment and stored gear for the winter. The outsiders yearned for home and their families. Locals traded fishing for hunting.

All summer the cannery filled the waterside warehouse at Orca with cans of salmon stacked high on pallets and stored for shipping. Once the salmon shipped to Seattle, the beach gang packed boats into the warehouse for the precious inside storage. The boat hoist at the end of the dock was accessible only at high tide. The earthquake had lifted the land and reduced the water level six to eight feet below the docks. The hoist used a cable attached to an I-beam frame, which suspended two long wide straps that lifted boats out of the water.

The beach boss, Harold Larson, lowered the frame of the hoist. I drove the skiff into the U the straps created and positioned them at the balance points under the bow and the stern. Harold turned on the switch. The cable pulled the straps tight, cradled my skiff, and lifted it a few feet above the water. Most people rode to the top of the dock in their boats. I hated that ride. A boat is unnatural out of the water. When the hoist lifted my skiff and it swung in the air, the motion scared me, not just the height, but the thought it of dropping. Harold understood. After he surveyed the balance of the load and gave me the okay, I climbed the ladder onto the dock.

At the top of the lift the hoist moved sideways and hung above the dock. Harold lowered my skiff onto an old wooden cradle with steel wheels. A forklift rolled the cradle into the expansive warehouse and parked inches from another boat. The beach gang moved heavy wooden blocks under the skiff, removed the cradle, and rolled it out to move the next boat in.

The second floor of the storage warehouse held lockers. Nets on pallets lined the sides of the long, wide halls. One hallway opened into the net loft, a room with a smooth wood floor that extended a hundred feet in one direction and fifty in the other. People stretched and repaired nets on the snag-free floor. In the oversize locker on the side of the loft, Kenny operated a store full of gear supplies.

I unloaded and lugged my gear up to my locker. Way up. Because I was a new fisherman, my locker was located in the attic. Getting there involved a long climb, but I never complained, because locker storage was a valuable commodity.

Another year had ended. I knew fishing was dangerous, but I survived. Seattle had a serial killer running wild, eventually identified as Ted Bundy. I told myself I was in control, and I'd prefer to die in nature than at the hands of some crazy killer. I continued to reassure myself that the danger existed outside in the gulf, but just in case, I made sure to wear a pretty pair of underwear for Hollis, a friend and the local mortician.

With all I had learned, I wondered how I survived the previous season; however, I was thankful I risked the money and bought Bean's permit. I had lived for five months on the water, and it felt good, and catching enough silver salmon to make my boat payment felt encouraging. Before the next season I wanted a new engine with more power, a wheelhouse to protect me from the saltwater spray, and if time allowed, a paint job.

Willie prepared the *Philip L* to spend the winter in the harbor. He'd fallen in love with Linda and planned to follow her south. He needed a winter watchman, someone spending the winter in Cordova to care for the *Philip L*. The job involved checking the pumps, batteries, and tie-up lines and shoveling snow. The job was risky. A check on the boat was a pleasant stroll in the harbor, but snow changed the pleasure into a laborious job. The gamble was how much snow would fall.

Living in Alaska was expensive. Peggy and I were both staying the winter, and to me the extra income sounded attractive.

Peggy received a letter from the top boss in Fairbanks complimenting her on the series she'd written about the wild kelp fishery. Even so, she wasn't satisfied at the newspaper and devoted more time to her independent writing. After she sold stories to various publications, she quit her full-time job and found a part-time job that ironically involved writing an article each week for *The Cordova Times*.

"Do you want to share the risk?" she sounded eager. "We can substitute for each other when the snowfall is light or one of us is out of town, and we can help each other shovel when the snow refuses to stop."

I agreed. I knew I could use the extra money.

Tom parked the *Sugar* on the same float, a few slips from the *Philip L*. He also needed a winter watchman. "A second boat, the *Sugar*, requires no additional work for *twice* the money," He made the job sound easy. "Because the *Philip L* obligates you to frequent trips to the harbor, you should include the *Sugar* in your watch."

We agreed.

Peggy mentioned hunting a deer for our winter meat. The idea of saving money on food sounded good to me. We discussed going to the shooting range and learning to shoot accurately. We planned our trip across the bay to Hawkins Island after snowfall brought the deer to the lower elevations, to the beach, if we were lucky. We'd borrow a skiff and anchor it near Wally's cabin. The adventure sounded exciting while we planned our hike to find a deer. Then we imagined shooting it. We realized neither of us could shoot Bambi. We dropped the idea before we ever went to the shooting range.

We never shoveled snow that fall, but we walked the harbor daily. We checked and retied lines. The wind blew for a solid month. The boats danced in the harbor, and the wind shredded the tarp on the *Sugar*.

I wanted to visit my family for Thanksgiving, and because of the high cost of travel, decided to stay until Christmas. Before I left town, Peggy and I met and secured a new tarp on the flying bridge of the *Sugar*. The tarp would help Peggy remove snow and ice. We retied the lines we had doubled as a precaution during the earlier storms. When we left the harbor I think Peggy prayed she wouldn't shovel feet of snow without me.

That fall, while Peggy and I worried about snow and tarps, the majority of Alaskans cast their ballot and endorsed Limited Entry. Many Alaskans objected to the law, but when a decision by Judge Boldt, a federal judge, jeopardized the commercial salmon fishermen in Washington, Alaskans feared an invasion of boats and voted to limit the number of salmon permits in areas of the state. My fishing permit to harvest and sell salmon in Area E remained valid.

AFTER CHRISTMAS I returned and found Peggy survived without snow entombing the boats. I arrived in time to celebrate the community New Year's Eve celebration. The party continued the next day. One of the owners of The Club Bar, Bob Sherman, celebrated his birthday New Year's Day. He offered a drink to everyone who came to wish him many more birthdays. Nothing happened in Cordova on January 2, either.

Without a skiff payment until after the next season, I cut back on work to five days a week and enjoyed more of the winter leisure time. Before Cordova owned any televisions, before the internet and video games, people had to entertain themselves for months of long, dark nights. When the weather permitted, people ice skated on Eyak Lake, cross-country skied on various trails, or skied downhill on Mount Eyak. On rainy nights the town offered pool tables, shuffleboard, and music in the bars; a bowling alley with leagues; and games at home or at a friend's house. On my evenings off, I played games with friends: dominoes, cribbage, pinochle, Monopoly, and Scrabble. We weren't competitive at Scrabble. Rick Bray, Red, RJ, and I played with an open dictionary. We played as a team against the game for the highest score. We learned unfamiliar words and built scandalously high scores that we found entertained us more than an individual win.

MY NIECE DESIREE called and asked, "If I visit, may I stay with you?"

On my visit to Washington I talked nonstop about my adventures in Alaska and my love for Cordova and the people who live there. Desiree was seven years younger than I was and enticed by my stories. Bill had gone south with Darcy to meet her family in Eastern Washington.

"Yes, you can stay in Bill's room," I told her.

The next month, Desiree moved in, fell in love with Cordova, and found a job. She arrived in time to join the community when it celebrated the Iceworm Festival, an annual multiday event held in Cordova in early February. Residents had survived cold nights with nineteen hours of darkness. The whole community suffered from a severe case of cabin fever. In 1961 the town began the festival because everyone knew they needed to leave their house and socialize. Mentally everybody was ready to say goodbye to winter and celebrate the days growing longer. Many long nights were ahead, but the community's attitude changed when people witnessed the daylight increase four or five minutes every day.

For the festival Cordovans organized art and quilt displays, talent shows, craft fairs, a food-tasting contest, basketball competitions, and on Saturday, a parade with an appearance of the Iceworm. The previous Iceworm had appeared scary, similar to a Chinese dragon with a large head and a gaping mouth that revealed long, sharp teeth. After the head burned in a warehouse fire, volunteers scrambled and replaced the Iceworm in time for the festival. They constructed a friendlier round head with a big smile. More than eighty children's legs powered the 150-foot tail of the worm. The townspeople invited friends and relatives for the festival, because everyone was too busy to entertain during the fishing season. The energy in the town continued to build after Iceworm, when the fishermen prepared for the various spring fisheries.

Kenny Quinn came to town for Iceworm because he knew the upcoming fishing season monopolized every fisherman's mind, a perfect time to sell new fishing gear. Kenny offered fair prices and went out of his way to keep his customers happy. I needed a new gillnet and wanted to buy it from him. He charged the web to the cannery and promised to have the bundle delivered to Cordova by April. If time wasn't available for gillnetters to hang their gear, Kenny arranged for net hangers to work in the loft. In case of an emergency, he sat at a bench and tied knots. His needle turned into a blur. He could hang a net with machine precision in record time, although rarely because he was too busy picking salmon. His unmistakable ability to catch salmon made people say, "Kenny Quinn makes fish."

The festival was also a wake-up call that the time had arrived to prepare the boats. After Iceworm, I worked with Tabor on the *Sky River*. He'd come north on a kelp processing ship a couple of years earlier. He tendered for salmon and the previous fall bought the *Sky River*. His girlfriend, Jeanie, came for a visit the previous season and stayed. Tabor accepted an offer to live at the Morpac Cannery in exchange for the job of winter watchman. He and Jeanie moved to the watchman's house high on the hill, where she transformed the sparsely furnished house into a cozy home. The windows overlooked the cannery with a panoramic view of Orca inlet. A big advantage of the job was that Tabor had the winter inside a warehouse where he rebuilt the *Sky River*. He wanted to make the boat more suitable for fishing, but with the fishermen arriving, he felt pressured to finish his projects. We worked days, and each evening Jeanie fed us a delicious meal. After dinner we relaxed with three-handed games of pinochle.

The previous season I had longed for a more powerful engine. Hugh at NEFCO agreed to order a new larger engine at a much lower cost with its cannery discount and charge it to my account. The cannery charged purchase orders to each fisherman's account at no interest and due when the fisherman delivered salmon. A common term, P.A.F., meant "pay after fishing." The cannery made dependence easy and attractive.

When the snow and ice melted on the road to Orca, I spent my days at the cannery. I mended nets, stripped the reef net, and made improvements to my skiff. When I received confirmation the cannery shipped my new engine, I pulled the old engine and worked on my wheelhouse. I designed it with windows in the two sides, and in front; the fourth side, a piece of plywood became part of the door. The shelter would allow me to run my skiff while I stood inside and looked through the windows. From there I could reach the steering wheel on the back wall of the cabin and watch the water hit my window instead of my face. After I cut the first window, I knew I had made a mistake.

Ralph Petersen, an ingenious man, was working in the same warehouse with his son Tim on their boats. Ralph looked at my cut and thought of a solution that made the error appear intentional. He became Mr. Wizard to me, and many times that spring, I ran through the warehouse crying out, "Mr. Wizard, Mr. Wizard." Ralph strengthened his reputation with brilliant solutions.

Those of us who worked in the cannery warehouse celebrated when the mess hall opened in the spring. The canneries in town employed local residents and operated the plants year-round, processing whatever seasonal seafood the fishermen caught. Orca ran a seasonal operation, which housed and fed a migratory crew. Everything necessary to process the salmon had to be on hand at the beginning of the season, including the people to keep the plant functioning. Port engineers, machinists, an electrician, carpenters, and the most valuable, the cook, lived and worked on site and kept the plant in operation. The cannery workers and fishermen lived in bunkhouses.

When the pre-season crew arrived, the cook opened the mess hall and catered coffee breaks began. Before hundreds of cannery workers arrived, the mess hall fed the fishermen. The kitchen workers served an ample supply of tasty food, family style on service plates and in large bowls. We sat at long tables with attached individual seats on both sides. Various groups of workers sat at specific dining tables. The machinists gathered at theirs, the beach gang sat at another, and the office shared the table near the door. The fishermen sat at any remaining tables. In the evening the cannery provided a mug-up, which included desserts, coffee, and cookhouse leftovers that made nourishing sandwiches.

For me the mess hall opening meant eating more often. The morning and afternoon coffee breaks included fresh pastries, cookies, and muffins. The mess hall served me dinner for signing my name. The cannery charged the cost P.A.F. The meal supplied a hardy lunch, and because I worked into the evening, mug-up provided my dinner.

Interesting conversations accompanied the meals. Many times the talk included a discussion and solution to a problem a fisherman experienced. Ralph thought of the most inventive solutions.

At other times small talk dominated. "Did you hear 160 new bow-pickers have arrived in town?"

One evening when more of the office staff arrived and came in for dinner, a new arrival, Sewall, caught my eye. My interest grew during the season. The arrival of my engine was late, which gave me a good excuse to pester him. Chris, the winter watchman, checked on the shipment, and found the engine buried behind a load of cannery supplies.

The 225-horse engine had fresh shiny paint, more horsepower, and no trace of overheating or saltwater abuse. It fit into the limited space of the old engine. The manufacturer hadn't included installation instructions, but I had confidence I could connect everything if I looked at the old engine and leaned on the collective wisdom of the fishing fleet.

"A gillnetter with a skiff in the harbor installed the same engine as yours," a fisherman told me one evening at dinner.

The next morning, I went to the harbor to see the engine like mine. A good-sized metal cylinder that my engine lacked sat on the top front of his engine. I questioned him about the cylinder.

"That's my freshwater cooling system." My face must have displayed a lack of understanding, because he continued, "Without it your engine pumps raw salt water through the engine block. That'd be okay on a freshwater lake, but in silty, salty waters it'll cut your engine's life short."

My engine block needed one of those tanks that supplied freshwater and antifreeze. I ran to a payphone with a roll of quarters and called the cannery office in Seattle. That year May 15, the date in the regulations for the Copper District season opener, fell on a Sunday, and we might fish Monday. The office ordered and air freighted the heat exchanger. My stress began to build. My skiff wasn't ready for the opener. While I waited for the part to arrive, I painted the hull a navy blue. I appreciated the yellow cabin, especially when I wanted a plane or tender to locate me.

When the heat exchanger arrived I installed it, but it consumed more of my limited space. The old custom engine box no longer fit. I could build another box, but the skiff lacked the space, and I lacked the time.

"Mr. Wizard, Mr. Wizard," I called.

True to form, Ralph looked at the conflicting space, thought for a moment, and suggested the solution. "Cut two holes on the front of the engine box. For a form, stuff a roll of paper towels in one hole and a bowl in the other, and then fiberglass over them."

The fiberglass hardened. I removed the paper towels and bowl. The old engine box with the custom modifications fit like a glove.

The gillnetters, without a price agreement, stayed on the beach the first period. I worked at a frantic pace. CAMA could settle the price at any time. On Wednesday afternoon I missed the CAMA meeting. At the end of it, or when the gillnetters knew the vote results, word traveled fast. The warehouse came alive. I heard excitement in the voices of the fishermen, and I knew CAMA had settled the price. We would set our nets in slightly more than twenty-four hours. I worked through dinner. At high water the beach gang lowered my skiff to the water.

I ran the skiff up and down Orca Inlet and varied the engine speed for the break in. Thursday morning I continued the engine break in. Dark clouds moved in from behind the mountain range. The wind continued to strengthen. When the wind blew enough to cause sizeable whitecaps in the inlet, I returned to the harbor. The wind blew through the night and woke me from a sound sleep. I was disappointed to miss the opener, but with the wind and the forecast, I preferred to have my skiff tied to the dock.

When the boats returned from fishing, the gillnetters looked like they had fought a war. The skippers told stories about how hard the wind had blown.

The first salmon opener is a shakedown cruise for the boats, when the captains find that things no longer work. "But it worked last fall," were the most familiar words heard that period.

The high winds accentuated the lack of preparedness. When the wind blew across the Flats Thursday night, a couple of gillnetters lost their nets. Friday the skippers searched for the nets from floatplanes. The gillnetters from Puget Sound fished boats equipped with larger reels, which held a net twice the length. Those boats retrieved the lost nets. The skippers then found the owners and returned the nets in exchange for the salmon the finder had picked. I heard their stories and no longer regretted that I missed the opener.

My new engine ran perfectly. The additional horsepower was overkill. The reserve of power was a comfort. My new wheelhouse kept me dry and provided the one spot inside my cabin where I could stand.

In the harbor I bumped into Tom. He ran his new boat, *Brown Sugar*, up the coast with Merrie and their son, Jesse, on board. They crossed the Gulf of Alaska and arrived ahead of the storm the night CAMA settled the price. Tom also missed the first opener.

With a break in the rain, Tom unloaded the supplies he'd brought in his fish hold and hauled them to his locker. I offered help with a load, because I knew he'd entertain me with one of his stories. Most years, he drove the Alcan Highway to avoid flying. He dreaded the way airplanes made him feel. He told me about their fretful trip across the gulf with nowhere to hide and the raging storm that threatened them from behind.

"Flying may be preferable to crossing the Gulf of Alaska in a slow boat," he admitted with a laugh. "I'm short on time to make the next opener, but the *Brown Sugar* will be ready," he insisted.

We met outside of the breakwater at four Monday morning and tried to navigate the inside entrance to Outer Paulson's. The channel proved too shallow. I fished at Egg Island. Tom, desperate to fish inside

Outer Paulson's, ran to the outside entrance. Fishing remained slow for both of us.

The next morning, we ran our boats to Softuk. The small tides forced us to travel outside in the gulf. The calm wind we had enjoyed for a couple of days made the ocean swell nonexistent. The power of my new engine thrilled me when we shot in between the rows of breakers and through the bar at Softuk. We found the catch wasn't any better at the east end of the Flats. We dashed to town at the closure while the weather permitted safe travel in the ocean.

On the closure, I sent a seventy-pound box of salmon to my parents. The next period the price went up a dime to ninety-five cents a pound. Competition increased among the buyers because of the low catch, which brought higher prices to the fishermen. The buyers were beginning to sell more salmon fresh and frozen, instead of canning the entire pack. The fresh market resulted in a new group of buyers we called cash buyers, those without canneries.

Fred Pettingill owned Bayside Cold Storage on the shore of the Cordova harbor. His oldest son, Jeff, ran Fred's boat, the *Gandil*, and bought salmon on the fishing grounds. Fred, an independent man and a trailblazer, sent the first planeload of fresh Copper River sockeye to Japan that spring. The successful reception created a new "fresh" market. The increased number of buyers fueled the competition, which also resulted in better prices for the fishermen.

During the next period, the lack of salmon in Outer Paulson's frustrated Tom. He pulled his skiff alongside mine. "We might find more sockeye at Grass Island. You want to go?"

"No, I fished there with Dick, but don't remember much about the channel. The way the buyers are bidding up the price, I'm guessing the salmon are scarce everywhere."

I stayed and saved the fuel the run to Grass Island would have cost me. At fifty cents a gallon gas wasn't a big expense, but the salmon that paid expenses were harder and harder to catch. Tom wasn't alone when he deserted Outer Paulson's. Half the homestead boats moved out in search of salmon. The processors were desperate for more sockeye and bumped the price up another nickel to one dollar a pound.

Outer Paulson's remained shallow at high tide, which made navigation inside a challenge. Enough water for a boat to anchor and stay afloat at low water was hard to find. Bob Bernard tendered the *Scamp* in Outer Paulson's. Gerry, who homesteaded there with his wife, two sons, and a brother, each with a boat, owned the tender. If the *Scamp* didn't fill up with the homesteaders' salmon, I sold my catch to that tender. When it was full, Bob had me follow him to Egg Island or Steamboat where I delivered my catch. The run was on the flood, valuable fishing time for me. When half the boats left Outer Paulson's, I delivered to the *Scamp* and fished the entire flood tide.

Friday night had the largest tide until September. The good catch tempted me to fish through high water. I questioned what setting my net could cost me in money and embarrassment if my skiff sat on a sandbar for three months. The talent I had for getting stuck, and the thought of missing fishing on the Sound made me drop my anchor in deep water for the last of the flood tide. My boat had gone dry or wrapped my net in the wheel once a week instead of a few times every period, but I yearned for the magical world at Coghill with deep tranquil water, beautiful scenery, and a fishery that was forgiving.

MY BROTHER JON, who lent me the money when I leased Bean's permit, wanted to visit Cordova and go fishing. He flew to town in time to fish with me at Coghill. He returned the wet-lock box, a sturdy cardboard box impregnated with wax, that I had sent south full of salmon. He'd packed the box with garden ripened fruits and vegetables that we shared with friends.

"I hope I can take the box home full of salmon," he said.

Another gillnetter, Richard, offered to tow my skiff behind his boat, the *Nordic Traveler*. Richard enjoyed company for the long voyage. His comfortable boat offered us sightseeing in luxury. The excursion provided Jon a captivating way to see the sights in Prince William Sound. The vastness, the beauty, and the wildlife dazzled him.

My letters had given him a hint, but the experience impressed him more than my words could convey.

Photo by Jon Halgren

Jon joked about the floating homes we lived in and praised the meals we prepared without a kitchen. We set the net near Coghill Lagoon. When I picked a good catch, Jon became more enthusiastic and wanted to pick the net. The catch dropped off after a few hours. Jon watched other boats travel south. More skippers than usual stopped at my skiff to say hello. I found out that the skippers all stopped to see how a man six-foot-four, 280-pounds was managing on my little skiff. Jon's size caused chatter on the radio, and the skippers all found the sight humorous.

When the majority of the boats disappeared, Jon became concerned that we were missing big catches wherever the other boats went. His curiosity made us run the skiff south on Wednesday. There we found we weren't missing anything. Jon felt fine the days we drifted in the protected waters of the fjord, but at the south end of the island, we encountered more of a swell. Well known by my fellow skippers, I become sick with the slightest provocation from sea or air. My brother was even more sensitive to movement. After a day of drifting in rougher water, he was desperate for the boat to stop moving. He watched the tide book and our catch and noticed we caught the most salmon at the change of the tide.

"I can't stand drifting, because of the way the motion makes me feel. We aren't catching much mid-tide," Jon said, looking pale.

My memory of feeling seasick and the desperate desire for everything to hold still made me run the skiff into the bay and anchor.

Photo by Jon Halgren

Before the tide changed, we buoyed the anchor, ran out of the bay, and set the net. After we picked, we went to the buoyed anchor. For the rest of that day and the next we ran back and forth, fishing the change of tide. Jon departed at the end of the week with a wet-lock box full of salmon.

The next week, Willie arrived at Coghill on the *Philip L* with a seine net and crew. I didn't see much of him during the spring season because he fished outside in the ocean. I waited to fish near him at Coghill. I depended on him for a thought-provoking conversation and a bold, sometimes to the extreme, cup of coffee. He often expressed a strong opinion or a philosophy that kept me in deep thought at least through my next set. At Coghill Willie gillnetted by the river or by the pass, but with the *Philip L* outfitted with his seine net, he concentrated on a few popular points along the south shore of Esther Island, where I saw him in line. His crew included Linda, who ran the hydraulics when the crew hauled in the net. She kept count of the weight of the salmon when the crew delivered to the tender, and she cooked. One crew member drove the seine skiff and another helped Willie on deck. Four people living on the *Philip L* made my skiff seem roomy.

I visited long enough for a cup of Willie's cowboy coffee before I went out deep and made a set. The Briggs's loud exhaust blasted while I picked salmon and tossed seaweed, kelp, and an occasional stick. I drifted deep in a daydream, contemplating something Willie had said. My boat shifted with a strong jerk. I regained my balance, flipped around, and saw strangers dressed in uniforms and wearing guns.

"Permission to come aboard," the man hollered from the bow.

I hadn't noticed the Coast Guard ship anchored outside the fishing boundary. Smaller vessels drove around and inspected the fishing boats. Without any boats other than a tender alongside, I stood paralyzed and speechless. Two of the coastguardsmen tied their boat to my skiff and came on board to check my safety equipment. My survival suit wasn't a certified flotation device and my float coat, a jacket with a float vest for a lining, something I wore religiously, wasn't Coast Guard approved either. I showed them the orange life jacket that met their requirement, but it would be my last choice for survival.

AFTER A COUPLE of weeks at Coghill, Jeannine Buller, nicknamed Red, a friend and winter Scrabble player, wanted a break from town. She asked if she could join me on my skiff. She possessed a cheerful outlook and a marvelous sense of humor. I welcomed her on board.

When Red flew out, she brought news of a fishing opener at Eshamy, a district about an hour's run south. Eshamy opened for one season every four years, so I hadn't fished there. We looked at the chart, pulled our anchor, and headed south.

In the Eshamy district another group of fishermen used set gillnets. Fish & Game limited the anchored nets to specific spots on the beach. The set netters anchored their nets from the shore and waited for the salmon. The drift gillnetters spread out and set their nets throughout the entire district. About twenty drift and ten set gillnetters fished the opener. No one found the mother lode, but everyone enjoyed plenty of space with the limited number of nets.

In the afternoon, Red pointed to a sea lion on top of a rock. His body was huge and completely out of the water.

"You want to have a better look?" I hooked the buoy on the end of the net and tossed it into the water.

We knew the enormous animal would slither into the water when we approached. The skiff, slow and quiet, advanced toward the rock. The sea lion didn't move. To our surprise, when the bow of the skiff kissed the rock, he moved to the inland side. We were shocked and looked around for a reason for the unpredicted behavior.

Red pointed offshore to a pod of hunting killer whales. "Look, the orcas chased the sea lion onto the rock. He must have figured we posed less of a threat than those hungry whales."

Humpbacks and orcas dominated the marine life at Eshamy much more than at Coghill. We delighted when we watched those massive beings swim through the area. The whales swam around the net. We never experienced any interaction with them. Old-timers told me the whale's sonar tells them where the nets are, and they avoid them.

I also heard a story about an old-timer who had caught a whale. It had pulled his skiff backwards threatening to swamp it. The gillnetter cut his cork line. The whale dove deep and when it broke through the web, the net resurfaced. The corks reappeared distorted and flat from the extreme pressure of the deep water. The story never identified the gillnetter. I'm not certain if the story was true, or one of the fables the fishermen tell new gullible gillnetters.

When we saw the killer whales hunt in the area, we unhooked the net from the tow post and fastened a buoy on the end. The wind was slight, and the weight of the buoy held it over our stern, but if a whale struck the net, the line and buoy would pull free. We sat on top of the skiff cabin, played cards, and watched the whales without fear. The pod intended to eat that sea lion but was also aware of our net and stayed clear. Hours passed before the orcas left. We lost interest before we ever saw the sea lion budge from that rock. Those whales caused the one and only time I ever saw a sea lion with any humility. Most of the time sea lions are monstrous bullies.

All week Red and I delivered our catch to Mike on the *New St Joseph*. Friday night we anchored the skiff and caught a ride with Mike and his crew into town. The boat traveled through the night while we slept to the hum of the diesel engines. In the morning we woke in the harbor and made reservations for a flight back to the skiff on Sunday. We delivered boxes with our fresh laundry and groceries to the *New St. Joseph* on Saturday night, before the party began.

Red and I flew to the anchored skiff with a few necessities Sunday night. Mike on the *New St Joseph* delivered our boxes on Monday. Red, an enthusiastic cook, fed us well and more often. Our replenished supply of food would sustain us for another week.

Tony, another gillnetter, came to visit after he heard Red talk on the radio. He picked wildflowers on the beach and brought her a bouquet. Flowers are uncommon on a boat, a special treat for Red. Tony, a faithfully married man more than twenty years Red's senior, constantly professed his timeless love for her. Red saw Tony as ancient but acknowledged his confessions in good humor.

"I have loved you for centuries. The sight of you makes my heart flutter. If my wife ever leaves me, I'll come for you," he told her in his thick Czech accent.

He asked us, "Are you running your gear?" Tony's eyebrows went up anticipating an answer, but before we could say a word, he excitedly continued, "The sun is bright, and the salmon are leading around our nets. I'll show you."

We moved to the bow of Tony's bow-picker. He ran his boat along the side of my net where he suspected the salmon traveled. When we passed a school of salmon that swam close to the surface, his boat scared the fish, and we saw them hit the web. The sockeye splashed and wiggled the cork line, which made our blood pump faster and brought a new excitement to the afternoon. When Tony left us, Red crouched in front of the cabin and peered into the water off the bow. We cruised along the net.

"Hit it!" Red called out when she saw a school of salmon.

She held on and I pushed the throttle up. The skiff chased the salmon into the net. The boat ran close to the cork line, which added to the threat of wrapping web in my propellor. When the skiff traveled too close or couldn't navigate a sharp turn, I shut off the engine and lifted the lower unit before the prop caught the cork line or web. The momentum of the skiff pushed it sailing across and free of the net.

At week's end I'd caught enough salmon to break even with the cannery. Red and I ran the skiff into Whittier for a celebration. The weather continued sunny, and life at Eshamy turned into a vacation. We competed with few boats, and an abundance of marine life entertained us. A breeze kept the skiff off the net and the bugs away.

Too soon the Fish and Game manager closed the district and we ran the boat to Cordova.

CHAPTER TEN

SILVER SEASON ON the Flats is cold, dark, and stormy. The distinct advantage was the crab pot buoys. The round, red floats marked the pots fishing Dungeness crab in the deepest waters of the inlet from town to Whitshed. Sometimes the crab buoys popped up in unexpected locations, because of a blinding fog. Travel in fog adds an extra element of uncertainty. I followed the channels with my compass, depth sounder, and my memory of the lay of the channel. Not being able to see, I couldn't always tell how much time I'd spent traveling. When the fog rolled in thick, verification of my skiff location other than my depth was impossible. When the skiff ran out of water, I tried to visualize the channel and locate the deeper water. Sometimes more than a few tense minutes passed before I found any. If I lost my confidence, I anchored in enough water to float at low tide and waited until I could see.

Limited visibility feels weird. My eyes struggled for sight through the white cloud that engulfed me. I heard more than I saw. When the mist lifted, I saw a boat or two caught in the shallows. Those boats sat high and dry for the tide. My lack of ability to see in the fog was comical, especially when I anchored in a certain spot but surprised myself with my location when the fog lifted. With simply a depth sounder for electronics, all the boats were hopeless when navigating in thick surface clouds.

ONE NIGHT IN September the *Cowboy,* a shallow draft tender, and two deep-draft floating processors, the *Indian* and the *Scout,* traveled south from the Yukon River where the crew had bought and froze salmon. The skipper of the *Scout,* the lead boat, knew a low was intensifying in the gulf. For the safety of his crew and valuable cargo, he planned to duck inside Prince William Sound for shelter. The *Scout* led the *Indian* with the *Cowboy* in tow to conserve fuel. Maybe the gusty wind and strong currents pushed the boats off course. We suspected the skipper of the *Scout* had confused the navigational lights and mistook the light at Egg Island for the light at Hinchinbrook Entrance. Off the Egg Island light, the sandy ocean bottom measures thirty feet. Miles west at Hinchinbrook Entrance the rocky bottom is hundreds of fathoms. The dramatic difference in the depth of the water at the two lights should have signaled the mistake, but the skippers must have had no idea, because the boats traveled without a depth sounder. In the stormy darkness, with poor visibility, the captains navigated toward the light, relieved by its sighting while they anticipated their warm bunks, believing a safe anchorage waited minutes ahead. The *Indian,* with her steel hull plunging thirteen feet into the water, bumped bottom. We heard that the captain thought the boats were at the entrance. The chart told him the boat should be in seventy fathoms of water. He reported he hit a rock.

"Just get around the corner," the skipper of the *Scout* urged the *Indian* on the radio.

The *Scout* raced toward the mistaken anchorage, but a mile ahead the eight-foot-deep hull of the *Scout* ran out of water and sat hard aground. The tall waves pounded against the sides of the vessels, both grounded on Egg Island's outside beach. The wind blew a steady eighty knots, and the seas were twenty feet. The *Indian* towed the *Cowboy* at the end of five hundred feet of cable. With less than a three-foot draft, the *Cowboy* still floated but had no bolt cutters. Someone called the Coast Guard. The buoy tender *Sweetbrier* departed Cordova, but the ship's deep draft forced it to run fifteen hours around Hinchinbrook Island. The *Sweetbrier* radioed Kodiak Search and Rescue.

In the dark the wind screamed. The violent water picked up the *Indian* and slammed her hard on the sand, which split her open at the keel. The *Cowboy* maneuvered alongside the *Indian*. The boats slammed together. To avoid crushing the *Indian* crew members between the boats, the *Cowboy's* skipper spent hours timing the transfers and picking the nine crew members off one at a time. When the Coast Guard helicopter arrived, the crew lowered a pair of bolt cutters to detach the cable that tethered the *Cowboy* to the *Indian*. Once loose, the *Cowboy* ran the rescued crew of the *Indian* into Cordova, a short trip past Point Whitshed for the shallow draft vessel.

The breakers beat against the side of the *Indian*. It bounced on the sandbar, broke apart, and spewed frozen salmon fillets onto the front of the Flats. The *Scout* sat hard aground, but her steel hull held together. The crew of eight stayed on board and operated the freezers that held about half a million pounds of salmon fillets. If the hull held together, other boats stood a chance of pulling the *Scout* off the beach.

Tom Madsen demonstrated his excellent flying ability when he banked his Beaver ninety degrees and dropped a 340-pound towline from fifty feet in thirty-knot winds. It landed squarely behind the bulkhead of the *Scout*.

The tug *Kustika* ran out and attempted to tow the beached *Scout* into deeper water. The towline snapped.

Ralph Petersen, Mr. Wizard to me, heard about the drama on the beach he homesteaded. He forgot about fishing. For him the tragedy wasn't about the loss of a boat with a valuable load of frozen salmon. The shipwreck would destroy nets on the beach he fished. The net snag would last for his lifetime. The *Indian* on the beach in pieces caused him enough nightmares. He wanted to make certain the boats pulled the *Scout* off "his beach." He ran his boat, the *Forty-Mile*, to the *Kustika* with two additional lengths of twelve-hundred-foot towline. He secured another line between the *Scout* and the *Kustika*. The *Forty-Mile* and the *Kustika* pulled for about a week until the tug *Trojan* arrived. Ralph secured a towline between the *Scout* and the *Trojan*.

Together the *Kustika* and the *Trojan* pulled on the *Scout* to prevent it from blowing farther onto the beach.

The boats called for another tug and waited for the *George S*. While it traveled from the other side of the gulf, Ralph rigged an intricate scheme of anchors and winches. He secured a cable to the *George S* when it arrived. The skippers waited for the peak of the flood. The water wasn't deep enough to float the *Scout* at high tide, but the three boats tugged. The tow boats dragged the *Scout* a hundred feet across the sand. The strain of the tow burned out the reduction gear on the *George S*. While it ran out to sea for repairs, Ralph ran his boat to town and loaded it on the last cannery tender for a ride south. He borrowed a more powerful gillnetter, the diesel powered *Never Ready*. He ran back, connected a tag line on the towline of the *George S,* stood by with the three tow boats, and waited for water. At high tide, the highest of the cycle, the boats tugged with their combined horsepower. The *Scout* shot off the sand. No one pulled back on the throttle. The skippers towed until the boats were in deep water. The *Never Ready* and the *Kustika* turned to Cordova and the *George S* to Hoonah. The *Trojan* towed the *Scout* to Whittier for repairs.

Jokes told about the three boats and their cargo circulated for weeks. The gillnetters joked about a catch of fresh coho along with previously frozen keta and king salmon fillets. Gillnetters laughed at the jokes, which released their stress. Everyone was amazed, relieved, and thankful no one had lost their life.

DESIREE DIDN'T LIKE living alone, so a friend moved in with her. I returned from fishing and found the house full. After I pulled my skiff and stored my equipment, I flew south to visit Kris and Jym in Bellingham. The two were my closest friends in college. I lived with them before I left for Cordova and when I returned that fall. I missed both of them and looked forward to spending time with them.

After the holidays I returned to Cordova and found a job. The winter crab harvest in Cordova, better than average, kept a dozen boats busy.

The Iceworm Festival woke the town from hibernation. The fishermen geared up and the businesses that supported the fisheries increased their hours. As the population grew, the hardware store, grocery store, and restaurants all hired more workers. The economic benefit of the anticipated harvest breathed new life through the community.

Seeing old friends return to town was reminiscent of the joy and excitement of greeting friends when school opened, except that after about two weeks, I wanted them to go home. Winter spoiled me with plenty of space. All the faces on the street were familiar, and I enjoyed good service at the stores and restaurants. When the outsiders flooded into Cordova, I no longer knew everyone, a spot to park wasn't easy to find, and I waited in lines. I knew how the increased population made *me* feel and imagined how the influx made the locals feel. I began to understand some of the locals' resentment of outsiders. The invasion rewarded Cordovans with the economic stimulation the fishing fleet provided.

The number of herring seiners increased, but the opposite held true of the wild kelp permits. New rules outlawed grappling hooks. Fishermen needed to cut the kelp, which involved diving. Few Cordovans swam and even fewer were divers. The change eliminated many locals, but no one complained, because everyone knew that cutting the stems benefitted the kelp resource. The kelp fishermen had been predominately gillnetters, warming their skiffs for the salmon season. Without hooks, most of the gillnet boats sat out the kelp season. The outside fishermen delayed their arrival, and the local gillnetters had a reason to procrastinate.

An influx of divers arrived, many from California. They flew into town and departed on the kelp barges. None of them launched skiffs that they prepared, repaired, moored, or fueled. The divers didn't buy groceries, raingear, charts, or other supplies from the town merchants like the local kelp fishermen had done. The merchants noticed the lack of business.

Peggy cooked on one of the kelp barges that housed and supplied a group of divers. She wrote and complained about the fifteen-hour days she worked feeding the divers while they lounged around waiting for the kelp season to begin. She celebrated when the season opened, and she could enjoy a moment of silence.

Processors bought kelp for ten days. The eggs ripened and the fishery closed. Cordova missed the flurry of money the merchants anticipated when the kelp divers returned, because they flew away before they spent a dime. Despite the loss of the wild kelp fishermen, the energy of the community continued to build.

TOM AND MERRIE drove the Alcan Highway and arrived on the ferry one evening in late April. They planned to set up their tent, but over the winter the tarp they used to protect the tent from the rain had deteriorated while stored in the locker. Tom ordered a new tarp from down south. Desiree had moved in with friends, so Tom and Merrie moved into Bill's room. They prepared the *Sugar* to live on and waited for Willie to bring the new tarp. Tom waited for the boat transporting his new skiff, the *Resin Detra,* more eagerly than the tarp. After fishing the *Brown Sugar,* he decided he needed a bow-picker. He hated how the *Brown Sugar* performed on the Flats. "It needs too much water."

After the fall season Tom sold the *Brown Sugar* to one of the local doctors for a sport fishing boat. He liked how his old Larson skiff maneuvered in shallow water. Over the winter he, Willie, and Max built three hulls. They used remnant fiberglass and a twenty-one-foot Larson skiff for a mold. Willie and Max built the *Jalapeño* and the *Comic Relief* as seine skiffs. Tom intended the *Resin Detra* for a seine skiff on the Sound and a gillnetter on the Flats. The afternoon the boat builders arranged the layup of Willie's hull, Linda went into labor. So much for schedules. The baby came early and the skiff was late. When he and Linda arrived in Cordova, they paraded Clifford, their two-month-old boy, around the cannery. Linda moved into the bunkhouse. The old-timers who had lived there for decades wondered how life was going to change, not with a baby living in the bunkhouse, but a woman.

The men were a generation that spent a week or two in the spring running a boat to Alaska. The skippers went south when the season ended and after five or six months, reunited with their families. They lived their summers and winters in two separate worlds, the way they had for decades. The old-timers were skeptical about Willie's family living in the bunkhouse, but no one uttered a word.

AT A CAMA meeting Armin announced, "The State will build six hatcheries throughout Alaska, one of them in Prince William Sound."

He went on to explain the state planned to build a hatchery at a deserted cannery site at the northern end of Unakwik Inlet. The fishermen shared an interest in fish that might exist in the future, but not with the sense of urgency they felt about settling a price and going fishing. Everyone knew Armin's passion for hatcheries could keep him talking for hours. Eager to move the discussion to price, the CAMA members voted to support the voluntary assessment for aquaculture.

Bob Blake gave a presentation about the salmon inventory but presented no offers. After hearing comments and opinions about the market, CAMA asked $1.26 for reds and $1.64 for kings. The night before the opener, the major processors offered CAMA $1.15 for reds and $1.25 for kings, less than asking, but members settled. We were going fishing on the season opener.

Sunday afternoon I ran with Tom to Outer Paulson's Hole. The Flats are slightly different each spring because of sediment from the river and the brutal winter winds. With the calm water and clear skies I explored, which means my skiff bumped sandbars along the way. Following Tom became a challenge, because he equipped the *Resin Detra* with a jet pump, which propelled the skiff with a water pump instead of a propeller. His skiff no longer had an outdrive that hung two feet in the water the way my skiff did.

The evening was tranquil, and we saw a salmon jump. We dreamt through the night about loading our boats. In the morning when we dropped our nets in the water, most of the salmon were gone. The fish swam up the river on the high flood tide in the middle of the night. The salmon were up the river for our future, and everyone caught a fish to eat during the closure. We set our nets, caught the stragglers, and waited for the next wave of salmon.

Thirty-six hours after our arrival, the sky grew dark, the wind picked up, and rain pelted me. My stove went out, which made life miserable. I anchored, changed into dry clothes, and crawled into my bunk. Safe on the anchor and warming in my sleeping bag, I listened to conversations on my CB radio. A forty-foot tender, *Rainbow* had lost its steering. The boat bounced in the twelve-foot surf on the outside beach between Softuk and Kokenhenik. The powerful surf forced the boat farther onto the sandbar. Dramatic chatter went on for hours. The skipper and crew member were desperate to save the boat, but their situation worsened when the *Rainbow* laid over. The captain and crewman knew their peril but refused to abandon ship. They half donned their survival suits. Angry breakers fifteen to eighteen feet tall slammed down on the *Rainbow.* A huge wave broke out the cabin windows. The flying glass cut the skipper, and the impact knocked him out for about half an hour. I'll bet that half hour lasted an eternity for the crew member, alone with his bloody and unconscious skipper, trying to save the boat, the captain's life, and his own.

A floatplane and a helicopter stood by. The aircrafts lacked rescue equipment, but the pilots could assist if the men made their way to the beach. After three hours, having tried everything, the captain decided he and his crewman needed to abandon ship. On the radio I heard the life raft reached the beach with only the crewman. The breakers had caught the weak and injured skipper. He faced certain death.

Gary Raymond raced his boat into the breakers and pulled the skipper from the water. He ran his bow-picker through the bar and delivered the bloody, semiconscious captain to the inside beach. The helicopter landed, picked the injured skipper off the sandbar, and rushed him to the hospital, where the doctor closed the wound that stretched seven inches across his head. A state trooper picked up the uninjured crewman and flew him to town. I relaxed and slept, knowing the rest of the boats were safe and anchored for the night.

The wind calmed in the morning. I ran my boat to town when enough water covered the Hump. In the harbor I tied my skiff next to the *Sugar* and cleaned the dozen sockeye and a king salmon heavy enough that I struggled lifting it out of the fish hold. The box of fish Dick and I sent south my first season began a tradition. I boxed the fish and delivered them to the Airporter. It guaranteed air shipment that day for a fee. I called my parents with the air bill number. After a hot shower, I went back to the boat where I tackled the dreaded stove project.

A dependable stove is essential. Becoming wet and miserable was bearable if my stove worked. The thumping when the skiff pounded in rough water damaged the tight fit between the brass fittings and the rigid copper tubing that fed fuel to the stove. I was tired of fighting and repairing the stove and freezing without it. I replaced the copper tubing with a flexible neoprene hose that the Coast Guard had approved for fuel. Richey, my stove expert, suggested another inline filter because of the water in our fuel. I followed his advice.

In the harbor during the closure I heard a constant buzz about the gillnetters who broke lead lines after their nets snagged remnants of the *Indian*. All winter pieces of the *Indian's* hull burrowed into the sand. Hidden underwater, the numerous protrusions in the sand caught the nets of unsuspecting gillnetters. The net menders and hangers stayed busy, and the *Indian* became a famous net snag.

Thursday I woke to the noise of the wind. That night's opener was at six, but the tide demanded we run our boats out in the morning. The weather forecast called for the wind to diminish to ten knots by afternoon. In my skiff I met Tom outside the breakwater. The engine in the *Resin Detra* gave him trouble, so he turned back before we reached Whitshed. I ran my skiff to Outer Paulson's and dropped my anchor. At six I wished I had never left the harbor. The wind blew harder. The new weather forecast no longer called for the winds to diminish. I watched three of the homestead boats leave the anchorage for the opener. After a brief time when I peeked through my window, the boats were back.

The next day the boats bounced and swayed on their anchors. The experienced homestead boats braved the storm and fished at low water. The skippers were never gone long. With the anchorage shallow,

I let out anchor line on the rising tide and shortened the line for low water. The wind woke me Saturday morning at two o'clock. I checked my depth and shortened my anchor line. At four o'clock, I woke to a strange quiet. The wind was silent, and the rain had stopped. The sun rose from behind the mountains, and the clouds changed from black to white and began to disappear.

The anchorage was empty except for two boats that sat dry. I felt proud I wasn't one of them. The other boats had gone fishing when the wind quit. The skippers hoped everyone else remained asleep. To avoid noise, sly skippers pull their anchors and drift away from the anchorage before they start their engine. I pulled my anchor and set my net before the closure. That morning's catch more than paid for my fuel and my days of bouncing.

On the last leg of my run to town I turned north early and navigated a shallow shortcut. About four miles shy of the harbor, my engine quit. Without coughing or hesitation, it went from purring to dead. I pulled the throttle down, shifted to neutral, and turned the ignition key. The engine cranked and sounded strong but didn't start. My skiff died in the middle of a shallow shortcut where not a single tender traveled. I dropped my anchor and looked at the engine.

Jack Hopkins, another gillnetter whom I had never met, stopped his skiff. "Throw me a line; you can look at it in town," he called to me.

I jerked in my anchor, passed him a line, and accepted a ride on his skiff. While he ran his skiff to town with my skiff in tow, we talked. Jack grew up in Cordova and fished since childhood. He was excited to reach town and celebrate his birthday. Jack gillnetted and seined. His gillnet boat needed a part scheduled to arrive during the fishing period. Instead of missing the opener, he resorted to using his seine skiff. Shorter than mine, his skiff was open without a cabin or shelter of any kind. I'm sure he must have tied to a tender for protection through the worst of the storm.

"Thanks for delaying your birthday celebration for my tow," I told him.

"Watching out for each other is part of being in the fleet," he replied. "We need to keep an eye on each other and help whenever one of us needs assistance. You'll probably never be in a position to rescue me, but someone else will. You can assist someone you see. We'll pass it around."

Jack docked my skiff in the harbor at the float and tossed my line. I leaped onto the wooden dock, thanked him, wished him a happy birthday, and secured my skiff.

After I warmed in a hot shower and ate a huge breakfast, I returned to the skiff. The engine started. I ran the skiff up the inlet to Orca and back to town. The engine purred. Shy of the harbor, she quit. Another skiff stopped and towed me to the dock. I tried to diagnose the problem. The fishermen were helpful with suggestions of things I might check. After I tried their suggestions, I ran out of possible answers for the breakdowns.

The next morning the engine started without any sign of difficulty. In desperation I ran the skiff to Orca and consulted with the port engineer at coffee break. I told him everything I knew about the trouble and the solutions I'd proven were wrong. The problem wasn't constant, which drove me crazy.

His assistant, Neal, heard the discussion and voiced an interest in the puzzle. A genius, Neal considered working a summer at Orca as a vacation, and he loved a challenge. "May I look at your engine?" he sounded excited.

"Yes, you can look at it. I'd be grateful, but it's working."

"Even if it runs now, you can't go fishing with an undependable engine. Let me look at it."

Who is this person? He was even ready to look at the engine before the coffee break ended. We walked out the long dock and down the ramp to the float where the fishing boats tied. Neal asked more questions. We stepped onto the skiff. I pulled the engine box off, turned the key, and she started. She purred, and he listened.

"When did you last change your ignition points?" he asked after he'd checked a few things.

"Ten days? Maybe two weeks? Before the opener."

"And you never experienced the problem last year?"

"Never."

"Do you have an extra set of points?"

I opened a can of parts from under the bunk and handed him a set, factory wrapped. Neal installed them. He cut the plastic that wrapped the thin strip of metal. He held the strip in his hand and tugged on one end.

"Your problem is solved," he said with pride as he showed me a hairline break. "When the fracture parted, the electrical system lost contact, which caused your engine to die. The crack isn't common, but I've seen the problem before," he admitted.

Thanks to the visiting assistant port engineer, my engine ran. Neal found the intermittent trouble, an inexpensive fix. The best part was that he'd already made the repair. With the closures short, I could have missed an opener while I tried to solve the mystery. Instead my skiff had a dependable engine and was ready for the morning opener.

When I walked from the harbor, I saw Rick Bray, a winter Scrabble player. He sold his boat and fishing permit but stayed and showed the buyer around the Flats for a week. "When are you leaving town?" I asked.

"I want to catch a few more salmon before I catch the ferry."

"Do you want to come with me for the opener?" I enjoyed his company and knew I would learn something about fishing from him. Rick grew up fishing with his father, and like his two brothers, he'd fished his own boat for years.

He showed me a channel that I never knew existed. It led into a tiny waterway at Egg Island. The water was shallow and net snags covered the bottom. "Low water is the one safe time to set a net, after the current has stopped. We need to pick up the net before the current begins to move," Rick explained.

We set the net, turned off the engine, and lifted the outdrive. Sheltered by the high sands around us and without wind or current, the channel felt like a lake. A salmon hit. I fastened a buoy on the end of the net and dropped the buoy overboard. Rick leaned over the side and grabbed the cork line. We propelled the skiff along the net with a hand-over-hand grip on the cork line and picked the salmon. After each fish hit, we picked it out of the net. We wanted to have the net empty, so we could quickly pull it out of the water. If we pulled the net in fast, we could leave it in the water longer and maximize our catch. When the current began, we pulled the net in before it tangled in the snags. Once the tide changed, we had to wait twelve hours before that set was again safe to make.

"Let's go outside the ocean bar, to the point east of the *Indian,* and set the net," Rick suggested. "The skiff will drift in through the main channel of Egg Island."

The steering cable broke just as we reached the point. The skiff drifted up the channel with the tide while Rick fastened a hose clamp to hold the steering arm. We stayed inside and fished with the temporary repair until we lost our patience the third time the hose clamp broke. Rick's brother, Russell towed my skiff to the tender and whisked Rick off to fish with him. Tied on the end of a line behind the tender, I listened to the CB radio and read.

That night the *Wildfire* burned. From its deck Larry, the skipper, emptied three fire extinguishers. The flames didn't back down. Stove oil fueled the burning fiberglass. Mike Roberts, on the *Pearl,* ran down the slough minutes behind the *Wildfire.* When he saw the boat in flames, he rushed alongside. Larry leaped onto the *Pearl.* People reported on the radio that the powerful fire was a frightening sight even at a distance. The fiberglass burned for hours before the final remnants washed up on the grass banks in Walhalla slough.

On Wednesday a tender towed my skiff to town, where I replaced the steering cable.

Word spread through the harbor that we would have a period off. Ralph Pirtle was disappointed with the catch compared to what he'd predicted. The gillnetters hoped the calm weather kept the salmon from moving, but no one wanted to risk another opener if the run was weak.

Most years we were busy and too exhausted to celebrate Red's birthday with much enthusiasm. With a closure, we dined and danced through the night. A new restaurant and bar, the Black Sheep, opened six miles out of town. What existed at six-mile to warrant a restaurant? It was outside the city limits. The owner, a previous mayor, built the bar and applied to the state for the permits including a liquor license, which wasn't available in Cordova. The Black Sheep, complete with a stainless-steel dance floor, was a modern and unique addition to Cordova. Everyone loved the new night spot except the bar owners in town. When Diane Ujioka cooked, the dinners were delicious and the seats were full. The nights that the Black Sheep offered live music, room on the dance floor was scarce.

The next period, the Memorial Day opener, memories of Bean flooded through my mind. The Copper River Sockeye run was at the peak after a five-day closure. The gillnetters expected the period to produce the best catch of the season. The opener was at high tide. I risked going dry and set my net. The current ebbed. In the excitement of picking salmon, greed took over. I set my net a second time. Instead of catching a load, the *Sleepy Hollow* sat dry on the sandbar, stranded until the tide rose.

I listened to the radio and heard the tendermen warn of the latest forecast, another blow. The gillnetters at Egg Island planned to run to town when enough water covered the Hump. I would have run with them if my skiff could, but hours would pass before it floated. The wind continued to pick up speed. When my skiff did float, the water was too rough to travel. I ran the skiff to the anchorage, delivered my catch, threw my anchor, and waited for the wind to calm. Tom quit fishing and came past in time to see my rollers blow off the stern of my skiff. He pulled them out of the water, kept them on board, and threw his anchor. The wind blew forty-five knots with gusts to sixty by low water.

A skiff anchored at Pete Dahl swamped while the skipper slept. The water awakened him in his bunk. He tried to call a Mayday, but his batteries were underwater. Within minutes the skiff sank. Another boat close by rescued the skipper.

A floatplane pilot reported, "Two people frantically waved from the top of the cabin.".

The boat was underwater in heavy seas near Strawberry Bar. A helicopter flew above the *Western Sea*, which by that time lay on its side, submerged. The pilot searched the water. He saw an empty life raft on the shore, and then he spotted the two missing men down the beach. The chopper landed and flew the pair to town unharmed.

That evening a pilot flew the skipper to the *Western Sea* that sat dry on the beach at low water. On his return trip to town, the pilot noticed the thirty-two-foot *Dragnet* capsized and dry on the beach. He called town and reported the sighting. A search began. The chopper landed. The two men climbed on board the *Dragnet*. They found no sign of Glen. The next morning, searchers found Glen's survival suit in the sand five hundred feet from his boat. The search continued but hope for his survival without his suit faded.

The *Rainbow* went down, the *Wildfire* burned, and we lost three boats during the Memorial Day period. We were two and a half weeks into the season and had lost five boats. The loss of Glen Behymer, a veteran gillnetter and lifelong Cordovan made the Memorial Day period tragic once again. Why the *Dragnet* capsized, we never discovered. The loss of Glen reminded the gillnetters how quickly and quietly the Copper River Delta claims the lives of even the most experienced fishermen. Memories of Bean continued to flow through my thoughts. Over the years, from the loss of John *Bean* Scott, Glen Behymer, Dean Kramer, and of others, I concluded the Memorial Day period was the deadliest.

CHAPTER ELEVEN

THE TIDE LIMITED the time boats traveled in or out of Outer Paulson's Hole. That year the weather lengthened the time the water trapped the boats. I misjudged the tide one morning and left too early. The channel that runs parallel between the breakers lacked enough depth for a smooth passage. The skiff ran too shallow. The propeller touched the sandy bottom. A breaker curled toward the skiff. I turned the bow into the wave. It broke over or the bow broke through, and the skiff raced along on the deeper backside of the wave. Again the prop bumped bottom. I turned the bow and grabbed another wave, rode the backside, and repeated the routine until I reached the main channel at Egg Island. The description of the run sounds like fun, but at the time, the trip terrified me. After that scare, I explored other channels to fish where I didn't travel near the breakers.

Bow-pickers like Bean's increased in popularity. My net hung off my stern picker skiff and acted like a sea anchor. When I brought in my net, the reel pulled the skiff into the wind stern first. The wind slapped the rough water against the flat transom. When the wind blew hard, the two forces collided and caused water to surge over the stern. When too much water flooded into my skiff, I quit fishing and anchored until the wind speed came down.

While I sat in the anchorage with most of the stern pickers because of powerful winds, I watched a bow-picker fish in the main channel. The boat maneuvered gracefully in the swell. The skipper threw the buoy off the bow, and the boat blew away from the shore. The cork line pulled hard, and the wind caught the web and flew it dancing into the air until the lines pulled the web into the water. The bow-picker hung on the net in the channel and bounced less than my skiff sitting in the anchorage. When the reel pulled the net on board, the bow-picker charged into the wind slicing the surface with her sharp V-bow. The rough seas slapped the side of the boat, but the chop wasn't even noticeable to the skipper who picked salmon while the stern-picker skiffs sat anchored and empty. The reason more gillnetters switched to bow-pickers became obvious.

Another benefit of the bow-picker design is the distance between the propeller and the net. The span of a boat length allowed people maneuverability while they picked their net. In my skiff I lifted the lower unit out of the water and hid it under a metal frame, which prevented the propeller from snagging the net. The ability to tow while picking was revolutionary.

I watched the bow-picker and remembered my difficulty when my net caught the trees while my skiff drifted toward the rocks. With a bow-picker, I could have towed my net away from the trees and picked without much trouble. The more I saw bow-pickers in action, the more I fell in love.

The next announcement closed fishing on the Flats because of poor escapement. That spring the Department of Fish and Game installed a sonar counter fifty miles out the Copper River Highway, near the Million Dollar Bridge at river-mile thirty. That location was the first where the numerous channels and sloughs of the Copper River Delta converged into a single waterway. The department brought the sonar counter from Cook Inlet to count the salmon that escaped the fishery. The fishermen questioned the sonar's ability and were skeptical. The management goal was to maximize the commercial catch but have enough salmon escape our fishery to satisfy those who fish upriver, including the bears, and have plenty of excess salmon to spawn the next generation.

"Why will the sonar counter work on the Copper, when it didn't work on the Kenai?" people clamored.

When I visited Tom on the *Sugar* I asked, "Do you have more confidence in the counter or Ralph Pirtle?"

"Ralph. He has managed the Bering and Copper Rivers and Prince William Sound fisheries since the territory became a state and established the Department of Fish and Game."

"I've noticed the fishermen all seem to trust him."

"Yes, Ralph Pirtle watches the tide, the weather, the ice conditions, the number of boats fishing, and most important, the catch. He predicts the catch for each fishing period. When the catch isn't within the range, he looks for reasons to explain why."

Tom paused when Willie climbed on board and then continued, "On the Copper the problem with Ralph Pirtle's method is that no one knows how successful his management method is until after the season. From the time the salmon swim in the fishery until they reach the sonar counter varies from days to weeks. From there the fish need time to swim to their spawning grounds. Months into the season the department counts the salmon after they have spawned in the lakes and rivers. Then we find out how close Ralph's theory was to reality, but any changes were impossible."

"The future of our fishery depends on good escapement," Willie said. "The fishermen understand when Ralph Pirtle is conservative and wants the fishery closed for some reassurance. We understand how Ralph makes his decisions and often predict his decision by what we know about the weather, the tides, and what we and the rest of the boats have caught."

At the cannery I also heard fishermen voice more faith in Ralph Pirtle's opinion than in the new sonar and its reported escapement. The department believed the sonar counter's numbers were gospel. The gillnetters became critical of how Fish and Game used the data because the counter lacked history to verify or dispute any management theory. The fishermen argued for a short fishing opener to test the theory. The closure lasted another two weeks.

The Bering and Coghill River Districts historically opened a week apart. With the Flats closed, Ralph Pirtle thought the entire gillnet fleet fishing at Bering River was unwise. He decided on a compromise to spread out the boats. He split the week and announced both districts opened June fifteenth. The timing was early for Coghill. The best bet for a profitable period was going east to the Bering River, which required a long voyage on the open waters of the Gulf of Alaska. I followed my heart and headed west into the Sound.

I ran to Coghill River for the opener. It was the first time I had set my net in two weeks, and my muscles noticed. I fished the morning at the river and then headed south. Fishing at the south end of the island was warmer, but by mid-week I felt frustrated. My net with sixty meshes, about twenty-five feet, competed with nets three times deeper. The boats from Puget Sound fished larger reels with nets two or three times deeper than mine. The boats had a real advantage over the local skiffs with undersized reels and shallow nets. My net competed better at the river; so I turned the skiff and headed north.

Fishing became a love-hate experience. The weather, tides, length of the fishing period, and the catch made life different from day to day. The experience ranged from panic to boredom, with pure pleasure and contentedness in between. For me to fish five days straight, I needed food or sleep. Being without both, life was a disaster. Because sleep was scarce, a low food supply influenced my attitude more than the tides, weather, and catch combined. The tenders sold meat, bread, and beer, but for a well-stocked galley, I needed to go to Whittier and resupply. Dick had mentioned us running into Whittier together. He'd switched from the *Pagan Queen* to a bow-picker, the *Copper King II*. A hot meal sounded sensational after living on a boat for a week, and radio suggestions can be hypnotic. Once anyone talked on the radio about town, not going was a challenge.

I tempted Dick on the radio, "Do you want to run at the closure or quit early and reach Babb's Burgers before she closes?"

"Oh, just the words 'Babb's Burgers' made my mouth water," he responded. "I'm ready. I'm not catching much, and I'm famished."

Everyone used a CB radio to talk when fishing was slow and to call the tenders when fishing was good. On Mondays not much came across on the radio, but people filled the airwaves with more conversations as the week progressed. One gillnetter, Bud, was the extreme example of the need to talk. On Monday after a party through the weekend, he was quiet, maybe catching up on his sleep. We might hear him call for a tender, but not much more. While the week progressed, the fishermen heard Bud talk more often. He was a starving social wreck by Friday. We heard him call everyone and anyone. If he heard someone talk, he called them when their original conversation ended. He never said much, he was simply desperate to say something. Everyone understood, and in need of conversation themselves, people answered back for a chat. The rest of us listened. Listening to people talk entertained us, especially on rarely used channels where the talkers thought no one else heard.

The size of the fishing fleet was the main topic of radio conversations. Everyone felt crowded because of the extra nets. More than a hundred additional boats ran across the Sound. The closure of the Copper River district was hard on the gillnetters who homesteaded a favorite spot on the Flats. Those skippers fished one location and fished only in that location. Those gillnetters had two choices: move or sit in town. A few stayed in town, but most traveled to Coghill. The Sound with deep water and sharp rocks made some feel out of their element. Their stay was brief. Others fished different areas until the skippers found a beach at Coghill to homestead.

Toward the end of our week of isolation, gillnetters complained on the radio about poor fishing and threatened to quit early. The fishermen who complained the earliest and loudest were the last to quit. Those fishermen planted thoughts of going to town early in the minds of other fishermen, hoping to lessen the competition. Dick had heard conversations about town all day. He was more than ready for a hot meal. We picked our nets and delivered our catch to the *Sprite*. On the entire run to Whittier our stomachs growled in anticipation of hot food. When we saw the harbor, we called Babbs on the CB radio and ordered cheeseburgers.

After we ate, I found a pay phone at the harbor and called Red in Cordova. "Will you send my mail on a tender?"

"Do you want some help? I can bring your mail with me."

"I haven't been catching enough salmon to need help, but you're welcome for a vacation. I enjoy your company and your cooking. You won't earn much money, but I'll pay your airfare out here."

"Anything you want me to bring with your mail?"

"Buy more groceries, send them on a tender."

"I'll send plenty of food and fly out Sunday night."

Dick and I walked back to our boats for a good night's sleep. The next morning, we slept late, enjoyed showers, and began laundry while we ate breakfast in Whittier's one restaurant. Drying our clothes made a good excuse to sit around, drink another cup of coffee, and hear news from Cordova. That morning we heard someone had salvaged the *Western Sea* off Egg Island and towed her into Cordova.

In the afternoon, Dick and I talked to the harbormaster about parking in a boat slip. The harbor rented the empty slips to us when the recreational boaters planned to return after we were gone. We pulled our net onto the float and mended the web in the warm afternoon sunshine. I treasured weekends in Whittier, but the area is a blowhole where rain is more common than in Cordova. I cherished the rare sunny days with calm winds in Portage Canal.

On Sunday, with our weekend chores finished, Dick and I decided to become tourists for the morning. We rode with Willie, Linda, and Clifford on the train through the mountains to Portage. When the five of us disembarked, we found the train stop had nothing more than a sign. We hiked down the highway toward Seward until we found a restaurant. The server was thrilled with customers who ordered food as though they didn't know when they would eat again. The weather began to change, but we reached the train stop before the rain began. In Whittier after I purchased more food, I headed out. The weather deteriorated and grounded the floatplanes before Red arrived.

The rain stopped Monday afternoon, and visibility improved. Before we saw blue sky, we saw floatplanes fly overhead delivering frantic gillnetters. The fishermen missed the opener after the weather trapped them in town. The water in Port Wells was too choppy to land a plane. The pilot delivered Red to a tender anchored in the north end of the pass. She called me on the radio, and I ran my boat to the passage and picked her up.

Tony, the gillnetter who picked flowers for Red at Eshamy, came for a visit after he heard her on the radio. "I came empty handed. I don't know where the wildflowers grow around here," he said apologetically.

Tony talked about building a new boat. We talked about hulls we thought might be best for fishing area E. When Tony found out I'd never picked a net with a bow-picker, he delighted in the thought of giving me the thrill. He set his net off the end of ours. Red and I tied my skiff to Tony's net and climbed aboard his bow-picker. I began to pick my net with Tony's boat. The main engine drove Tony's reel hydraulically. The lack of noise and exhaust fumes from my Briggs was a welcome pleasure. The additional space in his bow allowed me to spread out the web, which made the job of finding the salmon easier. Guidance of the net onto the reel manually is a bona fide physical workout. Tony had a *level wind*, two vertical rollers on a rail attached to the front of the reel that guided the net and wound it evenly across the spool. The aluminum rail also knocked the jellyfish out of the net. In my skiff I squeezed the jellyfish while I pushed and pulled back and forth and struggled to wind the net onto the reel. His decks were self-bailing. Scuppers, holes in the side of the hull at deck level, allowed the water and jellies to wash off the deck. Without decks the jellies and water collected in my skiff until the depth around my legs became intolerable. Working Tony's bow-picker was effortless. I touched my net when I picked a salmon, stick, or weed from the web. I never touched a jellyfish. I would never again be satisfied fishing my skiff.

By the end of the week news confirmed both the catch and the escapement at Coghill River were below Ralph Pirtle's projections. He closed the district indefinitely. Red and I rode on a tender that towed my skiff to town. The *Eyak,* with three other skiffs in tow, was active with the skippers in the wheelhouse and around the galley table. After a satisfying meal, everyone outside the wheelhouse fell asleep. In the morning Rockum, the skipper, cut the engines of the *Eyak* not far from town.

Rockum resumed cruising speed and said, "The change in engine noise will startle the other skippers awake. They need time for a cup of coffee before they board their boats."

As he predicted, one by one, the skippers stumbled into the wheelhouse with their hands wrapped around a coffee cup. They squinted and searched the shoreline through the wheelhouse windows to gain their bearings. In front of Orca, we boarded our skiffs. Rockum cut us loose before he pulled the *Eyak* to the dock to unload his salmon. The other skippers lived in the bunkhouse. They tied their boats to the float at the cannery. Red and I ran my skiff to the harbor and walked to our homes.

Most years, the fishermen fished on the Fourth of July, but Fish and Game had closed all of the salmon districts; something everyone tried to forget for one day. Cordova celebrated with a Kelp Box Derby and parade.

EACH YEAR AT Coghill River, Fish and Game installs a weir, similar to a gate, fixed across a narrow spot in the river. A technician camps near the weir. A few times a day he opens the gate and counts the salmon when they enter the lake. The technician radios the information to the Fish and Game office in town. Late that week, after high tides and hard rain, half of the desired escapement swam past the weir in a single day. More sockeye swam up the river than the department desired. Ralph Pirtle announced Bering River, Coghill River, and seining throughout Prince William Sound would open Monday July 10. By the calendar most of the sockeye were up the river. The escapement in the lake was more than the goal, but we hoped to catch a few stragglers.

Not fishing, I missed life on the water. I arranged to run my skiff across the Sound Saturday morning with Willie's parents, Tom and Marion. They fished a bow-picker, the *Ada Marion*. The trip was smooth except in front of Knowles Head, where the water is typically choppy. Water splashed up but fell off to the sides instead of into the *Ada Marion*. I followed close behind in her wake and avoided most of the chop. Watching her perform fed my growing desire for a bow-picker. We ran up Esther Passage and anchored together at the north end.

During the season the long hours fishing limits our sleep. Days spent doing chores and completing projects consumed my time in town during the closures. Waking on Sunday knowing I was ready for the opener twenty-four relaxing hours away made me close my eyes again. I was anchored in the pass, ten miles from where we planned to make the opener, so the day lacked the usual stress. The tension and panic to be ready were missing.

Midmorning, Marion cooked a delicious omelet for us. While we ate Tom talked nonstop about the *Ada Marion*. She was new that spring, and he beamed with pride when he talked about her. After breakfast he showed me the features he liked and disliked about her design. I was designing my fantasy bow-picker and interested in every inch, including the bilge.

I napped in my bunk and listened to the gusty winds blow through the trees on the peaks above us. The prediction called for the weather to deteriorate. The high hills protected the anchorage and kept the wind from bouncing our boats more than a gentle rock. At four in the morning, I went north. The sockeye catch dropped after a few sets, but the keta run remained strong, and the pink run continued to build.

Red worked at the hardware store but found town empty with the fishermen out on the Sound. She had joined me for another week. "Red, while I pick the net, will you empty the Jerry Jug of stove oil into the tank? We'll fill the jug when we see the tender."

With the net picked, we went into the north end of Esther Pass and anchored. After a couple of hours of sleep, we went fishing. Prepared to meet the tender, I emptied the gas jug into the tank on the Briggs but found only a few drops. I thought of different scenarios of what might have happened to the gas. I asked Red.

She looked at the jug and her eyes opened wide. "No wonder the stove burned my toes last night. We're burning a really hot mixture."

She'd mistakenly poured the remaining gas into the stove oil tank. The tank was almost full and the jug had been practically empty, or we could have blown up. We emptied the jug with the stove oil into the tank to lower the temperature in the firebox.

I teased her after our concern about the hot mixture had passed. "I know you love Tony's boat, but you mustn't blow up the skiff. I need to sell it to buy a bow-picker,"

The keta run remained strong, with our best catch at the change of light. We picked the salmon from the net and were excited until the fish wiggled and threw jellyfish slime on us. Toward the end of the season, the catch was down to pinks. The net came in slimier with jellies than shining with salmon. After a few days with a poor catch in our shallow net, Red and I felt discouraged and ready to quit. We watched Jeanie and Tabor haul in pink salmon like clusters of grapes and felt worse.

Tabor equipped the *Sky River* with a reel that held a deep net. A powerful pump washed his net. He built a deck across the hull, which made the boat self-bailing. The pump washed the slime from his net and the jellies from his deck. Jeanie and Tabor were at the stern, and despite the wind and rain, they smiled. They rushed to pick the net, reset it, and catch more. When the salmon were too numerous on the deck, the fish obstructed the jellyfish and water from flowing overboard. Jeanie moved to the fish hold and loaded salmon. Soon she was back picking. After Tabor laid their net, we buoyed ours, cut loose, and cruised to the *Sky River* for coffee. I knew Willie for his hot black coffee and Jeanie for rich gourmet coffee.

Tabor heard we fished a shallow net and wasn't surprised to hear of our poor catch. "My net is a hundred and fifty meshes deep and catches all but an occasional stray in the bottom half."

When our net came in with fewer than a dozen salmon, we quit, went to the tender, and played poker. The following morning Fish and Game closed Coghill and the seine districts because of the sparse number of pink salmon in the Sound. The pinks failed to show with much strength anywhere, except in Jeanie and Tabor's net.

When we arrived in town, we heard about Peggy's office warming scheduled for that evening. Her writing and consulting jobs increased, but she needed a telephone. She lived at Eccles Lagoon, a few miles south of town, where telephones weren't a luxury; phones were impossible without a physical phone line. She rented an apartment in town for the privilege of a telephone hookup.

At the party Tom told of his disastrous seine season. All the seiners whined about their two-week season with few pinks. With fishing on the Sound closed, and desperate to earn some money, Tom told us he ran his skiff to the Flats for the opener. "I was back in town in time for dinner with a total catch of ten salmon. They paid for my fuel."

Red went back to work at the hardware store for the rush of gillnetters preparing for coho season. Silver salmon are twice the size of pink salmon. I switched to a net with a larger mesh. I reflected on the season, but more often fantasized about fishing a bow-picker. A new boat was a fantasy. I owed a loan payment to the bank in a month, rent was due in two weeks, and I lacked money for either. NEFCO stopped buying salmon, and the cannery workers left town. I heard Bill Tiedeman's words of encouragement, "Visualize it, and make it happen." Before the week ended, I found a job until silvers came in. If someone bought silvers, I could work in town during the closures.

A couple of seiners switched their seine gear for a gillnet. Those from Washington went south to fish Puget Sound, but most seiners waited for another opener. The first week in August, Fish and Game opened seining for two days. The seiners caught more pink salmon than they'd caught during the earlier two-week season. The next week, the seiners fished again. The late-run pinks were plentiful. Before the seine season closed, the gillnetters, without a strike, were on the Flats harvesting silvers.

Sunday night I ran my skiff out with Mick, another Mummy Island banya builder. We were thrilled with our opening sets. We hoped our silver catch was plentiful because of a strong return and not the lack of competition. More seiners switched gear and gillnetted the next week, but our catch remained strong, and the price held. The silver harvest saved the gillnetters' season. I paid off the bank, paid rent, and rent for the next month was in my pocket. Buyers continued to buy, escapement appeared promising, and the season stayed open.

Dave Kurrent, a friend I'd met while I lived a few months in San Francisco, called. He was looking at a job in Anchorage. Dave had grown up on a farm in the Midwest and worked a few years with computers on the West Coast. I was certain fishing in Alaska would be a new experience for him. I expected his telephone call and once again invited him to visit.

"Your timing is perfect to join me for silver salmon season."

I didn't own a car to meet him at the airport, so I described where my house was located. Cordova named a few streets, but without house mail delivery, houses weren't numbered. People used landmarks or descriptive names.

"What's your address?" he asked.

"We don't have addresses. Tell the shuttle you want to go to Home Plate. With that name, the driver will deliver you to my doorstep," I reassured him.

Someone named the house before my time. Even when the city improved the ballfield and moved home plate, the name never changed. I planned to meet him at the house, but if something unexpected came up, he'd find the door unlocked. The door didn't lock.

Once Dave arrived, he was impressed with the grandeur of Alaska. While fishing he saw the vast difference in the efficiency of the bow-pickers, but more important, he thought the boats appeared safer for fishing. The last day of the opener, the wind picked up with predictions for the weather to worsen. The wind and water changed the motion of the skiff from a gentle rock to abrupt directional movements. Dave felt seasick. We returned to the harbor on the early tide.

After Dave went home he called and offered to buy a bow-picker. He'd lease the boat to me and use tax breaks on the investment. There are few people I would ever consider doing business with, but I trusted him. He was a stable, levelheaded person who was honest and would allow me to finish the boat how I saw best. He'd be a silent partner in the construction of a new bow-picker, one equipped with self-bailing decks, a hydraulic reel with a level wind, and a propeller twenty-six feet from my net. We weren't romantically involved, so I didn't need to worry about a breakup. I didn't need tax breaks, and I wanted nothing more than to fish a bow-picker. I agreed to the offer.

I continued fishing, but on the closures, I made phone calls and requested information about two hulls. I inquired about construction, previous use, and performance before I decided on the hull the Navy used as an officer personnel transport vessel on shallow rivers. The same hull as the *Ada Marion*.

"THE SWELL ON the ocean is growing," Ron on the *Shirley H* said when he stopped at my skiff. "I'm going to anchor in the slough for the night."

I told him, "I need to deliver my catch before I join you."

While I picked my net I watched his boat travel east up the channel beyond the markers. His stern disappeared when he turned north toward the grass banks. I went to the tender where another Morpac gillnetter, Bob Martinson, was delivering his catch.

"Are you going up the slough or making a fast break for town?" he asked while he continued to wash his fish hold.

"I think I'm going to follow Ron to Glacier Slough." I looked toward Whitshed, feeling ambivalent.

"By morning the wind should be down, and we can fish the rest of the week. I'll wait, and you can follow me," he said.

As I followed Bob, I thought about how much I enjoyed friends on the fishing grounds. Ron and Bob were friends from Morpac Cannery I'd known before I began fishing. They and the men who knew me from when I worked in town treated me differently than men I met after I began fishing. I'm not sure why. I noticed if I knew a man's wife, he was friendlier.

The slough wasn't far from the closed fishing markers. The elevated sides of the grass banks gave the boats some protection at low water. When our skiffs entered the slough, Ron, wrapped in raingear, came out of his cabin onto the back deck. He hung buoys off both sides of his boat and motioned for us to tie up. His anchor wouldn't notice our little skiffs. We tied to the *Shirley H* and dashed out of the rain into Ron's spacious warm cabin. We shared a feast with food from all three boats. When we were ready for our bunks, Bob and I dropped our own anchors, because the new forecast predicted the wind to blow harder through the night.

The storm intensified. The weather grounded air traffic. That night the wind blew harder. My anchor line jerked tight, then went limp, and then yanked again when the line pulled tight. Even though I was anchored in the slough, the wind whipped my skiff and tossed me around in my bunk. For another day and night the pitching, jerking motion of the boat and the noise from the wind made sleep impossible. I knew I was safe in the slough, but I wished my skiff was in town tied to the dock.

After the last low water, we decided to run to town. When two boats departed the previous day, the skippers drove away with their survival suits pulled to their waists. The wind speed was down, and we knew the ride wouldn't be pleasant, but we never feared we needed to don our survival suits for the ride. The inside waters were lumpier than I had ever seen. The wind hit us at our sterns and with the tide pushed us toward Whitshed. The skiff rode the swells. The momentum of the swell felt similar to the power of the back of a wave.

We reached the harbor and learned the wind had created havoc in town throughout the night. A gust had toppled a Sealand van and a trailer home. We then heard we had missed the distress call that David Butler, Jr., and Mark Foode made at two in the morning. The *Steelhead,* a tender, heard the Mayday. The caller reported the boat was going aground in the breakers and taking on water. The *Steelhead* lost contact. People reported twenty-foot seas and winds blowing a constant sixty-five knots with gusts of more than a hundred.

The Coast Guard dispatched a cutter in the area and a helicopter from Kodiak. The chopper arrived about seven and found the boat capsized, and no sign of either teen. Throughout the day the Coast Guard and private planes searched the beach and the surrounding water for the two young men. Both were young but experienced fishermen. That season was the first Mark and David gillnetted together. I heard one of them owned the permit and the other the boat. I had known one of the boys, David, and his parents and sister since I arrived in Cordova. He was a child I had watched grow into a teenager.

The Coast Guard suspended the search late in the afternoon and presumed the two were dead. People refused to give up hope and searched from planes, but without any sighting. Mark's dad, a pilot, couldn't stop flying in search of his son. When the families lost hope of recovering David and Mark, planes flew above the area and scattered flowers. The whole town felt the loss of David Michael Butler, Jr., nineteen, and Mark Thomas Foode, almost twenty, because they were two of Cordova's kids.

CHAPTER TWELVE

SEPTEMBER 15 WAS the end of silver season for me. The last storm and the loss of Mark Foode and David Butler, Jr., gave me no desire to return to the Flats. The threat of the equinox storms and knowing the nights increased in length and darkness made me ignore the catch and the price. When I heard the grim weather forecast, I was satisfied with my decision.

While storing my skiff, I worked for a couple of weeks at the Black Sheep. Customers inquired about the rumors of me building a new boat, and they encouraged me. Some left a larger than normal tip, which I translated to express their hopes for me. The love I received from Cordovans felt heartwarming.

When I flew south, Sewall, who had transferred to Kodiak, picked me up at the Seattle airport and drove me to my parents' house. After a short visit with my family, I drove my VW bug to Bellingham. Kris and Jym invited me to stay with them while three brothers in Mt. Vernon turned my empty hull into a fishing boat. When I met people who knew me from Kris talking about her friend who fished in Alaska and was coming to build a boat, they expressed surprise because I didn't fit their image. I thought about women mariners and the one I could remember was Tugboat Annie from a movie and old cartoons. She had the physique to pull in a net by hand, which explained to me their misconception of what I'd be like. Jobs that used to require brute strength are more achievable to women because of mechanization.

I ordered a new hull and flew to San Francisco to finalize the boat project. Dave and I visited his tax attorney, who concluded that investing in a boat wasn't a big tax advantage for Dave. We tossed around different options and possibilities. Dave found his involvement in the construction of an Alaskan fishing vessel excited him. He liked the idea of replacing the skiff with a bow-picker and was more committed to a safer boat than a tax break. He offered to finance the boat with an interest-bearing note. As a computer wizard, he also enjoyed sharing adventures he wouldn't experience working in the financial district of San Francisco.

"Helping you isn't the first time I've helped someone long on dreams and short on cash. I financed a man with a gold mine and a woman who won two Grammy nominations. People with passion and good business sense seldom fail," he assured me. "I consider my help an investment, not a risk."

I hired three brothers to transform the fiberglass hull into a bow-picker. Jon, Paul, and Joel Petrzelka had grown up fishing in Cordova. They spent winters in Washington building boats. The three of them, each with his own talent, proved they knew how to design and equip my hull to make it into a successful boat for fishing the Flats and the Sound. The brothers hauled the bare hull to their shop in October.

The cabin on my skiff felt like a cave. My tiny wheelhouse was the one spot I could stand. The bow-picker cabins were tall enough to stand, but the favored design was to build a fish hold the width of the boat across the front of the cabin. The remaining limited space allowed for a short door above the wide box. People crawled across the hold to pass in and out of the cabin. I was adamant about a cabin with a walk-through door. The brothers would split my fish hold, which most fishermen thought wasted valuable capacity. I was willing to trade voluminous space in my hold for the ease of passing in and out of my cabin on my feet instead of my knees.

Dick's sister-in-law built a new boat, the *Surfer Girl*, with the same hull as mine. I wanted to see any unique ideas she might have incorporated. While I looked around the Blaine Harbor, a man noticed me looking lost. He helped me find the *Surfer Girl*. I explained the boat belonged to my friend's sister-in-law who fished the Copper River. My story lit a firecracker in the previously soft-spoken man. He told me that he believed women don't belong on boats. They should stay in the kitchen. That attitude wasn't new. I'd heard those feelings, "barefoot and pregnant" plenty of times. I didn't admit to him that I was building a boat or that I fished, for fear he might throw me off the dock.

In January my boat's empty hull began to turn into a fishing boat. I delivered the accessories I wanted: a truck heater, a hot water tank, a stainless-steel sink, a freshwater pump, and a stove with an oven large enough to cook a Thanksgiving turkey. Construction came to a screeching halt when snow in Chicago stalled delivery of the engine. When it arrived in mid-February, construction resumed.

At the end of March Paul drove the truck towing the trailer that held my boat to La Conner. He stopped on the way at a gas station and fueled the boat gas tanks.

My mother and a sister drove from Seattle and met me and a friend at the Swinomish Slough below the Rainbow Bridge, where Paul backed the trailer into the water. My mother christened my boat the fishing vessel *Luna Sea*. The moon and water were romantic, but the name when spoken, "lunacy," described the uncertainties of fishing, and my reputation—"Oh, that's just Kathy."

Jon turned the ignition key while Joel visually checked the engine and the thru-hull fittings. When they were satisfied that she floated and everything worked, they presented me with the boat. She was beautiful. The powerful 454 engine and shiny fiberglass reminded me of a Corvette fresh off the showroom floor. I climbed on board. Jon and Joel gave the *Luna Sea* a push. She floated off the trailer. I lifted the throttle and cruised down the slough. I tied the boat to the dock at a restaurant in La Conner where my mother; Fern, my sister; Maryann, and a friend, Jude, helped me celebrate the launch.

After lunch we loaded the survival suits, an anchor, and cushions for the bunk. One downside of a bow-picker is the noise of the engine in the cabin. Maryann constructed extra-thick foam cushions covered with a multicolored striped material that made a comfortable bed and muffled the noise of the engine. She beamed with pride when she admired the fit because she only had the measurements of the bunk. After seeing the boat, she made matching curtains to block out the midnight sun and potholders with the leftover scraps. When we had the boat loaded, my mom and Maryann drove to Seattle, and Jude rode with me for the maiden voyage to Bellingham. The engine lifted the hull and pushed her across the water with ease. I had room inside the cabin to stand and a helm with the luxury of a seat. The ability to walk out to the deck and back in through my tall door was ideal.

The amp gauge didn't show a charge on the trip. I replaced the gauge the next morning, but the new one didn't work either. "She's a girl. Someone go see what she messed up," I imagined the men thought.

Kirk, a mechanic from the shop where I'd purchased the engine, came to fix the problem. I had to suppress a smile after he switched components and scratched his head for two days until he discovered the factory hadn't stripped the insulation off the wire to the alternator before a worker crimped it. The insulation on that wire told me the factory assembled my engine on an off day. Because of the uncertainty of what else would go wrong, I changed my mind about running the boat up the uninhabited West Coast and made a reservation to ship the *Luna Sea* to Cordova.

In Bellingham I loaded a spare anchor, more tie up lines, flares, flashlights, buoys, and tools, and I installed a CB radio and antenna. Parts and repairs are more accessible in Washington. I ran the *Luna Sea* around Bellingham Bay to break in the engine before shipping her. After ten days I was ready with my chart for the run to Seattle, where a crane would load the *Luna Sea* onto a barge. Kris couldn't resist a boat ride on a sunny, spring day. The *Luna Sea* traveled the coast between the mainland and multiple islands in Puget Sound. After a few hours we saw Seattle and ran the *Luna Sea* through the locks into Lake Union. We found Seattle's Fishermen's Terminal, a large area with multiple docks to park boats, which was questionable when we departed, because I was unfamiliar with Puget Sound. We tied the *Luna Sea* to the transient float. Kris took a bus back to Bellingham, and I stayed with my parents in Seattle.

My father, Sven, who emigrated from Sweden, loved the salmon I sent to him every spring, but he was uncomfortable with me gillnetting in Alaska. Before I was born he'd fished one season in Bristol Bay, which is farther west than Cordova. In the 1940s, gillnetters also pulled their nets by hand, but in Bristol Bay, they fished sailboats without propulsion. The boat my dad fished on washed out to sea with the tide. Another vessel rescued the boat he was on, but he knew one season was enough for him. After that scare, he refused to face the risk again. When he saw the *Luna Sea*, he stared with admiration and disbelief. He saw the drastic difference between his former vessel and mine and was impressed with the powerful gas engine and the hydraulically operated reel. Self-bailing decks underscored the fundamental difference in safety, which made the thought of me fishing safely easier for him to imagine.

I wanted to put more hours on my engine and offered rides to everyone. One day, after a spin around the lake, I returned to the terminal and was feet from the dock when the engine died. I reached out, grabbed a line from another boat, and tied the *Luna Sea* at the transient float. When the engine wouldn't start, I called the brothers. They came to the boat the next day.

"The transmission must have been in gear when you tried to start the engine," the brothers said after the engine started right up.

I didn't know much about engines, but I knew it quit while in gear. With my limited knowledge, I couldn't debate them. I invited Red, who was passing through town, to go for a ride. When we reached the locks, the engine died. It wouldn't start, even after I made darn sure the transmission was in neutral. We flagged a boat and were surprised to find it skippered by Tony, Red's admirer from Cordova. He came alongside in the bow-picker he'd built. He also had an engine to break in before he ran north. The *Lisa* towed the *Luna Sea* to the transient float.

"The power of love brought me to you, an opportunity for me to have sight of you during your brief visit," Tony said to Red. "I'm certain my chance encounter with you was in the stars."

I tied to the dock, looked at the engine, and found the cylinders full of water. The barge company wanted the *Luna Sea* for shipment within forty-eight hours, but she wasn't running. Joel came to Seattle and diagnosed the engine with a cracked manifold. He replaced it the next day. We ran the boat around the lake for a test run. With minutes to spare, Joel ran the *Luna Sea* to her appointment with the crane. It lifted her out of the water, set her onto a cradle, and then loaded it onto a barge. Once the barge with the *Luna Sea* on board set sail, I flew to Cordova and waited for her arrival.

My house felt like home, and I enjoyed seeing familiar faces and old friends, but that year, I became part of the spring crowd of invading outsiders. Spring is my favorite season, when the world around me changes from a snowbank to blossoms, a time to watch the birds migrate north and the local animals, including the humans, wake after a long winter. Plenty of skiffs were for sale. When I had purchased my skiff, John Paul bought a bow-picker, and ever since, more of the gillnetters switched to bow-pickers. Wooden skiffs were becoming obsolete. I prepared the skiff to fish while I waited for the *Luna Sea* to arrive. If an immediate need for a boat arose, my skiff would be available and ready to launch.

The *Luna Sea* arrived in late April, and I prepared her to fish. My nephew Bob gave me an industrial hose with a brass nozzle. The high-pressure hose would wash my nets and the jellies off my deck. Tom gave me speakers for my tape deck. I installed them in the cabin along with two waterproof speakers on the front deck. The engine was quiet enough that I could listen to music while I worked my net. My favorite change was the knob I pulled to engage the reel, a welcome switch from warming spark plugs and yanking on the pull cord of the Briggs.

With spare clothes loaded along with spare parts and nonperishable groceries, including those little chocolate cakes that stay fresh all season, the *Luna Sea* was ready. I ran the boat up Orca Inlet beyond the canneries. She ran fine, and even with the weight of the net on board, she was fast. Before the opener I wanted to find and fix any problems and understand the new systems so I could think about fish, not how to make something work. I also needed to learn to maneuver the boat without thought. One wire supplied power to both the stove oil and freshwater pump. The idea was never to run out of either. The possibility of sitting out a storm shivering cold and soaking wet, but unable to operate the stove because I'd run out of water, made me install an independent wire and switch. The opportunity to refine systems before the season was a gift.

The CAMA membership agreed to ask two dollars a pound for the sockeye and $1.85 for the kings. May 15, not a single buyer matched the asking price. The gillnetters went on strike. I was eager to fish the *Luna Sea*, but the wind blew a steady thirty knots with higher gusts. She wasn't leaving the harbor with or without the strike. Before the second period, CAMA rejected an offer of $1.40 for reds and $1.60 for kings. We spent two additional agonizing periods with ideal weather, on strike. CAMA held a meeting Thursday morning. The major processors didn't budge in their offer. The gillnetters were starving. They imagined the salmon flooding up the river. The fishermen were desperate to have some cash and taste their first bite of spring salmon. Members considered the cash buyers' offer of two cents more for kings. The membership voted.

When Bob Blake announced the members accepted the offer, the mob raced out the doors to the harbor. With the opener hours away, a steady stream of boats blasted out past the breakwater, across the inlet, and then turned toward Mummy Island. Time was tight to catch the tide for the opener at six that evening. The *Luna Sea* plied into the gusty wind and reassured me the boat was a pleasure to travel in, and safer. I sat at the helm in my captain's chair and looked through the window. The water splashed off to the sides of the bow, a wiper cleared the rain from the windshield, and not a drop of moisture touched me. In my skiff I would have missed the opener because of the wind. The rough water didn't threaten me in my larger boat.

The powerful reel pulled my net in faster and the level wind guided the wraps, which made pulling in the net require less physical effort. The most dramatic change was my maneuverability while I picked. I was no longer at the mercy of the wind and current when my net was in the water. The big downside of my new boat was the fear of winding anything in the propeller. The brothers built a tiny step to stand on the stern of the *Luna Sea*. From there I would lean over the water to reach the propeller. Even if I didn't fall in, I knew I would never be dry after that job. The thought of web in the wheel sent chills of terror through my body. My foremost priority was to keep my prop and my net a safe distance apart.

After the first few sets of the fishing period, more boats moved outside the sandbars. The skippers worked in groups on the radio and searched the gulf for salmon. When the boats found the sockeye, the gillnetters stayed with the schools until the closure. The nets that fished in the ocean caught most of the sockeye before the fish swam inside the ocean bars, which caused more of the boats to move outside and fish in the gulf. To avoid seasickness, I stayed on the inside of the islands and concentrated on catching the king salmon that were most likely to escape the nets and swim through the ocean bar. I'd been concerned because the bow of the *Luna Sea* measured twice as high from the water than the stern of my skiff; but I had no problem and landed plenty of king salmon.

I thought with my plentiful catch and the exceptional price, the gillnetters were going to harvest a lucrative season. Fish and Game reported a tremendous king run, but everyone cried about their poor catch of sockeye. At the end of the second opener, gillnetters knew their red catch was poor, and everyone worried. When the processors tallied and reported the catch numbers to the department on Wednesday, Ralph Pirtle announced a closure. No one was surprised, because everyone knew the sockeye catch hadn't been good. We knew the manager used a closure for a period or two to ensure escapement, but after a few days, when Fish and Game closed the season "until further notice," a shockwave rippled through the town.

Fish and Game closed the district because of the low fish count at the new sonar. The previous spring, Fish and Game installed a transducer on one side of the river, and that May, the department added a second on the opposite side. The gillnetters were still skeptical about the sonar's ability to count the escapement. Was the counter missing salmon we could be catching?

During the closure, I rode with Guy Beedle, Sr., to see the sonar counter at the Million Dollar Bridge. I had known Guy, a retired gillnetter, seiner, tenderman, logger, freight mover, heavy equipment operator, and excavation expert since my first winter in Cordova. His most prized occupation was his service during World War II in Hawaii. He fell in love and married while in Hawaii. After the war he purchased the *Mahina Ho*, a landing craft, from military surplus. He packed his wife, Gladys, and their daughter, Betty Jean, along with fifteen others, including moms, dads, and children, for a cruise to Alaska. In Everett, Washington, the boat picked up three more men, two with families. Guy told me about the twenty-six of them living together on the boat. His gaze drifted off to his memory of the picture he kept in his head. After a chuckle he readjusted his focus back to me, and described the numerous makeshift tents pitched on the front deck.

"Oh, what a sight. The *Mahina Ho* sailed into Orca Inlet on July 4, 1946. Half of Cordova met the boat at the dock, ready to catch her lines."

"Why did you choose Alaska?"

"I didn't want my wife and my daughter to suffer prejudice in the lower forty-eight."

For a couple of years Guy, with his family on board, logged in the Sound and towed the logs to Whittier with the *Mahina Ho*. He told me about one of those winters, when he experienced an avalanche that buried his equipment. He dug until he cleared a machine that could help him dig. Later with Gladys, Betty Jean, and a new son living on the *Mahina Ho,* Guy delivered fuel and freight to remote sites along the Gulf of Alaska and throughout Prince William Sound. He was familiar with the beaches, and people respected his ability to ride the surf onto the shore. When the tide receded, the boat sat dry, which made fifty-five-gallon drums of fuel easier to unload. The barrels were an essential for those who live in the bush.

One calm day in August 1950, Guy beached the *Mahina Ho* at Cape Suckling. A local storm blew out of Icy Bay. The wind blasted the shore at 135 knots. Within hours the raging surf washed the beach clean of sand. A rocky reef remained. When the *Mahina Ho* floated, the wind blew her parallel to the beach. The violent surf pounded her broadside. Water flushed across her decks to the shoreside. When Guy accepted he couldn't save his boat, he knew his family needed to abandon her. His crew member, Les Meyers, helped him move Gladys and Betty Jean to shore. The water flooded in and forced Guy to toss his sixteen-month-old son, nicknamed Skipper, into the waiting hands of Les. Guy called a Mayday heard in Ketchikan. After a relay to Cordova, a plane flew out and picked up Gladys and the two children.

Les and Guy stayed on the beach. The wind stopped and the tide receded. Guy saw the surf had pounded the *Mahina* on the reef and destroyed all but one dry compartment. He and Les spent eleven days salvaging what they could. Later Guy operated other boats, but none he loved with the intensity he felt for the *Mahina Ho*, the boat that brought him to Alaska.

Guy rescued me with transportation many times. The most prized times were those when I flew into Cordova with boxes of excess baggage. He drove to the airport and met me without any previous request or arrangement.

He teased me about the excessive amount of stuff I had. "Do you own it, or does it own you?" he joked, but I knew he was serious.

One morning having coffee at the Reluctant Guy said, "Well, what do you think? Are you interested in a ride out the highway? We can check out the new sonar that's calling the shots."

The Copper River Highway is the sole highway out of town. The road stretches fifty miles with only the first thirteen paved. Along the way, Guy, an avid sports fisherman, pointed to the various fishing holes he planned to visit during the season. At mile twenty-six we reached the Copper River and crossed a cement bridge to Long Island.

"Twenty-six mile is as far as I'll drive after the tenth of October," Guy said. "The drifts can be forty feet deep out here. No place for human beings after the tenth. The conditions on the Copper change in a heartbeat. The Copper River winds are brutal in the winter. You want some trouble? Come on out here in the winter; chances are you won't return. If you are ever found, it won't be until after the spring thaw."

Off the side of the road were sand bowls and dunes dotted with alder and expanses of snow. At thirty-six mile we crossed another bridge back to the mainland. Past mile forty-nine Guy drove to the Million Dollar Bridge approach and stopped. Next to it, in the middle of the wilderness, stood a large sign posted from the Federal Court in San Francisco. The sign stated a lawsuit brought by the Sierra Club of California forbid any work on the road beyond that point. The highway ended where the bridge crossed the Copper River.

"The road ends here. For years I have wanted to drive to Anchorage," Guy said. "The federal government appropriated money to build a highway on top of the deserted railroad bed to meet the Alaska Highway system. Then I'd be able to drive anywhere. The road stretched from Cordova to seventy-mile when the 1964 earthquake hit. The quake destroyed my dreams along with the bridges on the delta. With the court involved because of environmental issues, the state doesn't maintain the road beyond the bridge."

The outside influence made half the residents in Cordova angry, including Guy. He resented the interference from outsiders who wanted to stop progress. I sided with the other fifty percent in town who were against ending the priceless isolation.

Guy parked his truck, and we walked on a trail through the woods. At the shore of the river we saw Childs Glacier on the opposite side. The massive river of ice reached from the mountains to a three-hundred-foot-tall face on the bank of the Copper.

Guy warned me, "Occasionally the glacier calves a chunk of ice large enough to send a wave across the river. If the piece is massive, the resulting enormous wave washes onto the shore. When the salmon run up the river, the force of the miniature tsunami throws salmon onto the beach." He laughed when he said, "Fish and Game Protection considers taking the stranded salmon an illegal form of harvest. The bystanders want to help the fish back into the river. Watch out! The volume of the roar when the glacier calves depends on the size of the falling chunk. Bears are smart; they recognize the extreme volume as a dinner bell. Within minutes they'll reach the shore and eat the salmon and you too, if you aren't careful."

Near the bridge stood a wooden shack with the sonar equipment that counted the salmon when the fish traveled past. The river is about four football fields wide there. The transducers emitted a beam sixty feet from each shore. People questioned the accuracy of the sonar with ninety percent of the channel not covered by the transducers. The gillnetters feared Fish and Game didn't count the salmon that swam beyond the range of the hydroacoustic equipment. Everyone in town questioned the accuracy and benefit of the counter. The impact of the technology resulted in disaster for the gillnetters' livelihood.

A tremendous run of kings returned, but we feared the lack of sockeye might close the Copper River District for the rest of the spring. I was thankful I had already sent salmon to my parents. The next week, Fish and Game announced it couldn't conduct a sockeye season on the Copper River the following spring. The news stunned the gillnetters and alarmed the whole community. Biologists read scale samples from the catch, which told them the age composition of the salmon run. Siblings of the younger sockeye would be the main run the next year. Those salmon appeared to have suffered worse ocean survival. The lack of a spring salmon season spelled disaster for the gillnetters and the Cordova economy.

Other than the strike, my season began with hopes of a money-making year. In two periods fishing for king salmon I made one-fourth of the value of the seasons I fished a skiff. The strong king return and prices helped, but the boat made a dramatic difference too. One announcement closed the Flats and changed my outlook. I had no income and owned two fishing vessels, both tied to the dock. When someone called with an interest in buying my skiff, I met him with a copy of the survey, similar to a house appraisal, but for a boat.

The buyer harvested halibut and liked the high sides. "I'll be back with the rest in a couple of weeks," he promised when he handed me a check for earnest money.

When he returned he paid me and sailed away. I never saw the skiff again. I heard it went west to Homer. The sale of the skiff was a relief because the season was a bust. The main moneymaking month was past. The Flats closed in June, for the second year in a row. Ralph Pirtle again opened both the Bering and Coghill River Districts simultaneously. The opener would last fourteen hours. I stayed in town because my mother and my fourteen-year-old nephew, Kurt planned to arrive on Friday.

The beach gang hoisted the *Luna Sea* and set her on the dock. I scrubbed the bottom while Kurt and Fern loaded clothes and enough groceries to feed the three of us for a week. We headed across the Sound Sunday morning. I slowed the boat at the navigational buoys, and we stared at the sea lions sunbathing on the base of the bell buoys. Kurt gasped when he saw the whales and cheered when the porpoise swam with the boat.

When we arrived in the fishing district, I ran the *Luna Sea* up Esther Passage to the north end. There we saw Harry Richards, "the Candy Man" on the *Caprice,* anchored with James Edward "Ed" King, on the *Chinook.* Both old-timers were knowledgeable. They fished for decades and knew more than I could imagine about how to catch salmon. The *Caprice* was Harry's boat name, but he'd fished the *Candy Man* for so many years that he kept that name for a radio handle. He refused to rename the boat. Ed and Harry both owned homes in town, well-maintained vessels, and a supply of spare nets all paid for. They were my mentors because I struggled with the debt of my boat and acquiring nets and knowledge. When we pulled into the anchorage, Ed and Harry came out on deck and invited us to tie up with them. They were both outgoing and interesting to talk with. We shared some of the fresh fruit that Fern and Kurt brought in the wet-lock box they hoped to take home full of salmon.

Ed shared a secret about their radio messages with me. "Whenever you hear us talk on the radio about 'candy,' it means we're into salmon. Pay attention and go to the boat with the candy," Ed said during the evening conversation.

Acceptance by other gillnetters felt good. I noticed with my new boat, the skippers had a more positive attitude toward the hippy girl. I was no longer a Johnny-come-lately.

The *Luna Sea* felt crowded on the first night. Fern and I shared the bunk and Kurt made a bed with cushions on the floor. Early Monday morning, the three boats drove away in different directions. The *Luna Sea* traveled north toward the river. Another change in the rules cut the area we could fish before July. The new boundary was miles south of Coghill point. Once we began fishing, we continued nonstop for four days. We traded turns in the bunk. Two of us could sleep, while one of us kept an eye on the net. The season was early for a plentiful catch of sockeye, but drifting on the Sound with the gentle motion felt utopian. The *Luna Sea* was still new to me and at times unfamiliar. I worked my net harder yet with less effort. Mid-week we heard Ed call Harry on the radio. Ed slurred a word or two and blamed his garbled speech on the red candies he was sucking. The secret code meant Ed picked a good set of reds in Barry Arm.

"The water's clean, but I'm not finding many salmon," he said.

When the fishermen talked on the radio, they never admitted to a good catch. They whined even when they passed secret codes. If a fishermen mentioned a good catch, a crowd of boats would swarm them. We picked my net and cruised to Ed's skiff. He stood on deck anticipating our arrival. I shifted the *Luna Sea* out of gear.

"We came when we heard you were catching reds."

"Set your net inside or outside of mine. The salmon are swimming all the way across the arm."

Before we picked our first set, Harry joined us. Ed had alerted Harry and me in time to fish a whole tide of sockeye. Except for those few sets, fishing that week was slow. Late Thursday afternoon thoughts of a hot dinner in Whittier tempted us. Prepared to quit early, I made a set and then cleaned the web with the wash-down pump while I picked. The salmon began to hit the end of the net. I made another set to verify the salmon were flooding in. They were. We picked salmon until the closure.

Jeanie and Tabor flew into Cordova and left the *Sky River* anchored in Island Bay. They offered us the use of their boat and their bunk. We tied the two boats together and doubled our living space. We slept well that night. In the morning after breakfast, we ran the *Luna Sea* into Whittier. My mom gave Kurt and me money for a motel room.

"I want the bunk all to myself," she said. "I love the gentle rocking sensation of the *Luna Sea*. I sleep better in that bunk than in any bed."

Kurt and I were delighted to oblige her and rented a room in Whittier's cinderblock building. After hot showers we enjoyed lunch while our laundry cycled. The cafe overlooked Passage Canal where vessels paraded up and down the channel. The commercial boats ran to town and the recreational boats ran toward the wilderness. When our clothes were dry, we returned to the harbor.

I repaired my net on the dock in the sunshine. Fern talked to everyone who walked past us on the float. After her weeklong visit, she understood my love for the quiet beauty of fishing and the people of Alaska. She bought some jumbo shrimp from a boat when it pulled into the harbor on Sunday. The skipper wrapped the jumbos with an icepack for her to carry home and enjoy with my father in Seattle. She caught the train into Anchorage and flew south that afternoon.

Kurt enjoyed life on the boat and stayed for another week. We ran the *Luna Sea* to the pass and anchored for the night. When fishing began, Kurt, who moved from the floor to the bunk, continued sleeping. Most people consider sleep on top of a loud Chevy engine a challenge, but not growing teenagers. When Kurt woke he saw me picking salmon. He dressed in his raingear and helped. Kurt's energy and good sense of humor were welcome and valuable qualities for a crew. We ran the boat to Cordova at the end of the week, and Kurt flew home with two boxes full of salmon.

The next period opened in July, which meant the point by the river and the fjord beyond were open. I ran the *Luna Sea* to the pass Sunday night, and Monday morning I fished the opener near the lagoon. That week I faced my worst fear. I set my net, but the web tangled around a cork and caused a backlash. I shifted the boat out of reverse, and I cleared the snarl. The gearshift handle appeared to be in the neutral position, but the transmission slipped into forward and inched into the net before I noticed. The engine died and my stomach sank into my boots. I hollered every ugly word at the top of my lungs. I then gathered the tools for the dreaded task of clearing the web. I was about to walk out onto the stern when Harry, on the *Caprice*, pulled up.

My situation was obvious even if he hadn't heard my rant, but he acted unaware of my situation. "How are you doing?"

"I wrapped my net in the wheel. I was about to clear it."

"Don't let me interrupt you. I'll stand by."

I was grateful. The thought of landing in the water was easier to handle knowing someone was close and would pull me out. I hung off the stern with the prop raised, but even tilted all the way up never quite cleared the surface. A boat wake slapped against my stern and made me soggier and even more appreciative of the Candyman's presence. I cleared the net, tightened the prop, and crawled back on board. "Thanks for standing by," I told him. "I appreciate the fishing time you lost to help me."

"You'd do the same for me."

I scampered into my cabin and heard Tabor on the radio, "I'm headed your direction to try a set."

When the *Sky River* arrived, Jeanie was on board and offered to share the dinner she'd prepared. We set our nets next to each other for the dinner hour. Tabor picked me up off the *Luna Sea* in his boat. A life in isolation makes a visit with others an indescribable pleasure. The *Sky River* with Jeanie and Tabor was a pleasant sight. Usually Jeanie had a meal cooked and ready to share, along with her gourmet coffee plus some much-needed conversation. She also understood my caution and reluctance to fish in a storm. She lovingly called me a "Whoosie."

Tabor knew mechanics and was invaluable when a boat had problems. He found a solution, even if the fix was good enough only to run the boat to town for repairs. Jeanie and Tabor loved pinochle, and we found time for at least one game before we picked our nets.

The fleet of boats caught half the number of sockeye harvested most years at Coghill. The number of sockeye in the lake for escapement was twice what Fish and Game desired. We picked pinks at half the weight and half the value per pound.

On the weekend closure, I pulled into Whittier to meet Dave. He had flown to Anchorage and ridden the train to Whittier. He wanted to see the difference between the Flats and the Sound and how well the new boat worked.

At Coghill Dave saw the advantage of the improved equipment and my change from struggle to ease. Midweek a floatplane flew Dave to Cordova in time for the afternoon jet.

Chapter Twelve

The following morning I woke with a bug bite on one of my eyelids. My body sometimes overreacts to bug bites. The bite continued to grow, and within an hour my eyelid swelled shut.

Mick and his wife, Karen, came by in their skiff. "Can I clean my net with your wash-down?" Mick held out the end of his filthy net, "A night set left the web thick with algae and glacial silt."

While Mick washed his net, he voiced concern. "Your eyelashes are no longer visible."

Karen looked closer and shook her head. "The puffiness is creeping across your nose. Maybe you have more than one bite."

The swelling threatened to seal my other eye shut. The thought of struggling alone and blind on the boat gave me chills. When Mick finished cleaning his net, I delivered my catch to a tender and requested the skipper call for a flight to town for me. I anchored before losing vision in my other eye.

When the plane landed on the lake in Cordova, the pilot and I walked into the air service office. People gasped in horror at the sight of my deformed face. A woman rushed to the back and grabbed a bag of ice. "Here, put this on your face," she said.

The ice soothed the hot lump. I walked home and spent the next few days hidden behind icepacks until the swelling went down. When I flew back to my boat, the season on the Sound was winding down. Most of the gillnetters were unenthusiastic with the poor catch of low-value pink salmon except Jeanie and Tabor, who with their extra-deep net were loading the *Sky River*. They hauled in pink salmon by the ton.

The seine fleet was also becoming rich harvesting tons of fish. The pink salmon returned double the numbers of the best season in the previous fifteen years. Earlier in the spring, Willie had bought a larger seine boat, and that season, fish hold volume paid dividends. The majority of the boats were small and like the *Sugar*, were forced to quit fishing to deliver their catch while the boats with large fish holds continued to fish. Most of the seiners had never seen so many pink salmon.

Farrell, Tom's father, offered me a job seining on the *Dancing Bear*. He needed a crew member for one week. Fishing silvers on the Flats wouldn't be profitable for a week or two, so I accepted the job.

Tom Copeland Photo

As skiff-man, I sat alone in the skiff attached to one end of the seine net. When the time came for our turn to set the net on the point, I attached the skiff to the outside end of the lead, a net anchored on the beach that led the pink salmon away from the shallows and rocks. The deck crew pulled a pin that released the skiff towline from the boat. The boat drove away while the seine net, still attached to the skiff, flew off the back deck of the *Dancing Bear* into the water. The net stretched in between the boat and the skiff like a nine-hundred-foot wall.

Farrell held the net in a semicircle while the salmon swimming past the point accumulated in the hook that he made with his end of the net. After about twenty minutes he towed his end toward me. I dropped the lead and towed toward him until the wall of web floated in a circle around the salmon. With the two ends together, the deck crew gathered the purse line threaded through rings at the bottom of the heavy web and captured the salmon. The reason the net is called a purse seine became obvious. The crew pulled the purse full of salmon on board. Working with a team was different from fishing alone and a pleasure after a summer of isolation.

After the week seining, I returned to town and worked in the harbor on my coho net. The gillnetters returned to the Flats without the usual fight over price. The silver run returned strong, and the boats fished for eight weeks. After all the earlier closures, the coho harvest allowed me to pay my bills and begin to earn money.

At the end of the season with the boat in storage, I found a job. In my spare time I worked on mending my nets at Orca before the temperatures dropped too low. Bill Tiedeman called one night; he'd moved to Anchorage after a divorce. He told me about the auto/diesel school at the college and encouraged me to come to Anchorage and learn how to troubleshoot my boat engine. "I have an extra bedroom, so you can stay here. I'll call and request the college send you information on its program."

Desiree had married and lived in a cabin near Peggy at the lagoon south of town without power or running water. She was expecting a baby and wanted to move into town for the winter. She and her husband, Joe, moved into my house in Cordova. After I spent the holidays with my family, I moved into Bill's place in Anchorage, not far from the college. I was excited about going to school and learning more about how to keep my equipment working.

CHAPTER THIRTEEN

BEFORE CLASSES BEGAN, I attended the Board of Fisheries meetings at the Anchorage Hilton. Fish and Game predicted so few sockeye returning to the Copper River the next spring that managers couldn't conduct a fishery targeting red salmon. Without a spring gillnet fishery, Cordova would suffer economic disaster. The department proposed a restricted harvest of king salmon for the 1980 season. To avoid catching the sockeye, the regulation required a large mesh net, six-hour openers with a weekly quota, and the last but most important safeguard, if we caught too many sockeye, the manager would close the fishery. The season would begin May 19. A perfect year to finish my classes and arrive late.

In school from eight o'clock until four thirty, I saw daylight only at lunchtime. The snow added reflective light to the dark mornings and evenings of travel, and the best nights included the northern lights. The classes and instructors at the college were informative and made me aware of how little I knew. I guessed the students would be all men and was surprised and pleased to see another woman taking some of the same classes. The male students accepted us as equals, at least to our faces. I studied engines, twelve-volt electrical systems, the mysteries of the universe, and a new language.

The engines class instructor, Tony, professed engines are simple: "Suck, squeeze, blow, wheeze; that's it."

Tony had a passion for Chevy 454 engines, from his time in the car-racing industry. He was thrilled when he passed me information specific to my boat engine. Tony learned his secrets because of his years of devotion to that Chevy engine.

The most excitement that semester was when the electrical teacher, Frank, demonstrated a "dead short." The freshly charged battery emitted explosive hydrogen gas. One spark, and the battery blew. We all wore safety glasses and laughed while we cleaned the mess. No one from that class will ever forget how explosive gases are from a freshly charged battery.

On Fridays I met Bill at his job in downtown Anchorage. Terry, a silversmith who rented a shop in the same complex, joined us for dinner. We celebrated that we had survived the week. Bill was outgoing and enjoyed living in Anchorage. He knew everyone. I recognized no one and hated city life. I yearned for the secure community of Cordova.

In early April Bill and I flew to Cordova for the weekend and celebrated his birthday. Back in Anchorage, Bill found a VW bus for sale, dirt cheap. The back window was missing, but otherwise the van looked in good condition. After I bought it Bill sealed the missing rear window with heavy transparent plastic and duct tape. I loaded the van for the trip to Cordova.

The date was too early for the ferry schedule to include a stop in Whittier. I planned to sail from Seward. Snow covered the road there, without many cars after the road cutoff the main highway. Bill was concerned the VW might break down in the middle of nowhere. He wouldn't know how to fix it but could give me a ride to find help. Bill borrowed Terry's Jeep and followed me on the highway until close to Seward, where numerous cars traveled. From there I had an easy drive to Seward, where I parked in line at the ferry dock excited to be closer to home.

I drove onto the ferry, which was hours late, and began to feel the warmth of Cordova when I saw John Allen, a friend who had grown up in Tatitlek. He'd fished out of Cordova during the Flats season and had fished his skiff near mine behind Copper Sands years earlier. John and I spent the trip to Valdez talking about what we and the people we knew in common had been doing since he quit fishing and was last in Cordova.

John departed at Valdez, where more familiar faces boarded, including Terry Grainger and his son Todd. Terry's dad was one of the unfortunate longshoremen the 1964 earthquake washed off the Valdez dock. Over the years Terry brought his son to fish with him when school was out. That year, Todd, a teenager, would fish on his own boat.

For me to see recognizable faces and feel the warmth of friendship was a joy after living in Anchorage, a city of strangers. We sat at the bar and told stories about our winters, and our expectations for the season. When the bar closed we fell asleep in the passenger lounge. We woke when the ferry docked at Cordova fifteen hours late, but the trip across the Sound was smooth and no one complained. Many things can happen to delay a trip in remote Alaska, and arrival can be days late. Most Alaskans feel lucky to have arrived.

Earlier in the spring, Desiree gave birth to a son, Joey. The family moved back to their cabin in the lagoon when he was six weeks old. I moved into the house knowing I needed to move out in a month. The landlord had sold the property. I considered buying it, but I wanted to return to school in the fall. I gained a wealth of knowledge at the college and felt a strong thirst for more.

Many times while fishing, I had asked questions over the CB radio. Sometimes the skippers were slow to respond with an answer. I thought the delay was because of the difficulty of my questions. That winter I learned more about engines and realized the gillnetters weren't taking time to ponder an answer; they had been rolling in their bunks, laughing so hard they were unable to talk. I concluded the gillnetters tolerated me because of my ignorance. I was superb radio entertainment. With my new knowledge I remembered some of the ridiculous questions I had asked, and I laughed too. I continued to question how I ever survived previous years.

The annual spring influx of gillnetters didn't happen. The lack of activity on the streets, in the harbor, and at the stores was obvious. With the spring harvest restricted to a limited catch of king salmon, most gillnetters who lived outside never came to town. The fishermen calculated going fishing might cost more than they expected to earn. Everyone knew from memories of the previous season how expensive fishing was with so few hours allowed for catching. The reality convinced most of the out-of-towners to stay home and keep their wage-earning jobs. The gillnetters who lived in town didn't have that option. The economy of the community was dependent on fishing. The town relied on the local fishermen to create jobs.

For the first six-hour opener, which I missed, fewer than a hundred boats were ready. The harvest shocked the area manager when the few gillnetters caught sixty-seven kings shy of the week's total quota. He announced he wouldn't schedule a second opener that week. The manager was new to the area. I'll bet he consulted with Ralph Pirtle, who retired earlier that year after decades on the job. The new manager scheduled the remaining openers for three hours before until three hours after high water.

The second week, I was ready in addition to fifty other boats but was disappointed with my catch. When the manager implemented Ralph Pirtle's strategy to cut the efficiency of the gillnetters, all hundred and fifty boats were disappointed. The skippers caught less than half the quota for the week. We fished a second period but failed to catch that week's remaining quota. The uncaught salmon would contribute to upriver fishing, bear food, or add to the escapement.

Most of the six-hour openers required twenty-four hours to execute because of the tides. The best time to travel on the Flats is on the flood tide. I ran out with the boats before high water and waited nine hours for the opener. With six hours of fishing, every minute my net was wet counted. The boats fished and then waited hours for the incoming tide for the trip to town.

Tom, along with about four hundred other gillnetters, didn't own a king net and bet the investment wouldn't pay. Instead he worked on the *Sugar* anticipating another profitable seine season. The previous year, pink salmon returned to the San Juan Hatchery, and wild pinks returned to the Sound in the millions. Unlike the previous two years, Tom planned to be ready when the season opened. Imagining a tremendous seine season didn't curtail his need for a home-pack of king salmon. He arranged for some time away from his boat work to go fishing with me. He brought a landing net on a long pole for bringing the kings on board. The ring that held a web basket on the end of the pole was round when we began. Tom hung over the side of the bow with the long pole extended. He searched the water for any sign of a king. He shoved the opening of the ring under a king the minute a ripple in the water gave any hint of a fish. If the king hadn't tangled in the web, the salmon slipped away from the net and fell into the basket. He'd cheer and haul the king on board over the side. Even when the web tangled the king, he took no chances and brought the once-round ring elongated through the rollers. The mangled landing net that saved countless kings never left my boat. Tom sent a couple of the kings to Merrie for their freezer, and we gave our one priceless sockeye to Red for her birthday barbeque.

Fishing for only six hours twice a week, even with the travel time, left the gillnetters with more time off than usual. I stayed in the house a month before I packed the last of my belongings and moved to a room in the fishermen's bunkhouse at the Orca Cannery. During the winter of 1945-46 NEFCO built the two-story bunkhouse. One or two fishermen lived seasonally in each of the fifty-three separate rooms. The bunkhouse sat on the town side perimeter of the property with a waterfall rushing along the far side. The roar of the falling water blocked the sound of the generators that kept the plant in operation. When Linda and Clifford moved into the bunkhouse, not everyone endorsed the idea; however, the fishermen adjusted, and a few brought their wives north. The men framed off one of the toilets and a shower for the women. When I moved in, the women presented me with a key to the lady's room.

The move from a house into one room was a challenge. My room had a double bunk built off the floor. I filled the space under the bunk with a bookcase, desk, and chair. I gave things away and packed my bunkhouse room to the ceiling. I had moved often through the years, but the house at home plate had been my permanent base. I resisted the move, but living at the cannery was convenient. Everything I owned was in my room, tied to the dock, or in my locker. The window stayed open, and I listened to the thunder of the waterfall and predicted I would live in that bunkhouse room every season for the next twenty years.

HISTORICALLY CAMA SETTLED the price of spring and summer salmon with a signed contract before the gillnetters went fishing. That year the processors paid $1.40 a pound for the kings and promised to pay for the reds retroactive to the final contract price. Gillnetters targeted king salmon and tried to allow the sockeye to escape and spawn, and because we caught so few, no one worried about the price. When Fish and Game opened the season at Coghill, we felt the devastating error of not having a CAMA contract signed for sockeye, pink, and keta salmon. The gillnet and seine boats were ready to go catch fish, but none of the canneries wanted to buy our salmon.

"A good supply of sockeye is predicted in Bristol Bay, and those fish will flood the markets," the canneries reported.

For decades CAMA had been powerful in price negotiations, but that season it wasn't even able to declare a strike for lack of an offer to buy at any price. The fishermen were powerless. Before the previous season, NEFCO sold the cannery at Orca to Chugach Alaska Fisheries. An unofficial part of the deal was how NEFCO's fishermen and many of the employees stayed at Orca. When the ownership and management changed, nothing else missed a beat. A local native corporation owned Chugach instead of a Japanese corporation. We thought local ownership might begin a change in the industry with better prices for the fishermen. When talking salmon price offers, Chugach was silent too. We learned the Japanese brokers also controlled the Chugach markets.

No one had made any money and the fishermen were desperate, but without a price, the majority of skippers stayed in town and waited for any price offer. The first week, CAMA reported two boats fishing at Coghill, the next week eight, and then sixteen. Those gillnetters ran their salmon into Whittier and loaded the reds on the train, sold them in Anchorage, flew them to markets in Seattle, or sold them to tourists.

The CAMA members labeled those gillnetters scabs, and they were non grata in town. A list of boats fishing or anchored at Coghill hung in CAMA's window on the main street. The next week, the window displayed enlarged photos of the scab boats fishing. The emotions of the fishermen were strong. Tensions grew, along with the stack of bills, while the season and opportunity to earn money escaped.

The Bristol Bay fleet was on strike with a few scab boats fishing. An Anchorage newspaper ran an article about the statewide sockeye crisis. Inspired by the article, we designed a clenched fist of power holding a salmon, RJ cut a template, and we stenciled it on our T-shirts.

Alaska is the main producer of Pacific salmon for the world. The fishermen thought that other than Mother Nature and sustainable management, they were in control of the salmon production, because they owned the fishing permits. That year the fishermen learned the Japanese dictated the harvest, because those companies owned the local canneries and they controlled the salmon markets. The processors gave fishermen a strong reminder of that fact.

Cordova was in the midst of a depression. No one had any money. The season reminded the town businesses of how dependent the local economy was on the fishermen. More than two-thirds of the gillnetters weren't in town. They didn't buy parts, groceries, or gas or keep the bars and restaurants crowded during closures. They didn't employ net menders, mechanics, welders or rent housing or pay for moorage in the harbor.

Every fishing season is different, but that season was unrecognizable. The Coghill sockeye run was at the peak of the season, and we were stuck in town. None of the processors showed any interest in purchasing sockeye salmon. Weeks continued without any price discussions. In the four-week season on the Flats, gillnetters fished thirty-six hours and then we sat on the beach without a market for a month.

Local canneries purchased salmon from other areas of the state. Tenders brought the loads to the Cordova canneries for processing. The sight of those tenders rubbed salt in the wounds of the local fishermen and crew members. They stayed in town and waited for any price offer.

Summer brought the pink and keta salmon runs. After most of the Coghill sockeye swam up the river, negotiations with the canneries began. The canneries wanted the pink and keta, which dominated the catch so late in the season. The canneries offered CAMA a price, and the fishermen went fishing.

I switched to my pink net and ran to Coghill with Mick and Karen. We were a month late crossing the Sound. The mountainsides covered with snow all winter were brown when we usually arrived in June. The hillsides were already a lush green when we finally arrived. The most noticeable difference was the spring chill missing from the air. Summer arrived before we did.

We set our nets in Port Wells and rejoiced at the abundance of salmon. The seiners fished in other parts of the Sound, and the largest cannery tenders bought their salmon. The tenders that bought salmon from the gillnetters were small, filled fast, and headed for town before reaching the river.

Mick called me on the radio when he discovered the problem. "A tender with room in its fish hold is hard to find."

I picked my net and ran down Port Wells. When I found a tender, the skipper told me his boat was full. I begged him to buy my salmon.

"I need to calculate my final tally of the fish I already purchased. If you want to wait for the total, I might buy a few more," the skipper said.

The fishermen hadn't fished for more than a month. We thought we had the opportunity to catch fish and pay our bills; instead we faced a struggle selling our salmon. The problem was difficult to accept. That tender bought my salmon, but not one more. Once the fishermen caught the buildup of salmon, the tenders didn't fill up as fast and we enjoyed a few weeks of lucrative fishing. The quantity wasn't enough to substitute for the lost Flats and Coghill sockeye seasons, but the earnings helped everyone with their basic expenses.

My bills were going down, until my transmission went out. I was powerless, drifting in Port Wells. My hydraulics worked, and I was able to retrieve my net, but I had to set it with wind power. When I told Mick, he came by and towed my boat alongside his so I could set my net intentionally, which worked well when the winds were gentle. The next day a tender headed for Orca towed me in for repairs.

In town I called south and ordered a new transmission. My engine was famous for tranny trouble, maybe because bow-pickers use reverse more often, and not always at a slow speed when we set or tow our nets. The beach gang pulled the boat and set her on blocks in the warehouse. I removed the lower unit and climbed into the bilge. I opened the shop manual and read. I felt as though I was reading a foreign language. My frustration overwhelmed me. I put the book down. Close to tears, I straightened my back and told myself, "Pull up your big girl boots. You can figure this out." I knew I needed to remove the engine to exchange the transmission. Determined, I decided I could look at the engine and figure out what to disconnect to remove it. After I spent hours in the bilge, the beach gang used a crane to lift the engine out through a hatch in the cabin roof.

After I switched transmissions and reinstalled the engine, the beach gang lowered the *Luna Sea* into the water. I started the engine, heard a horrible clang, and shut her down. The noise sounded internal, metal, and horrible. I had no idea what I had done, but the problem sounded serious.

I went to see the port engineer, who offered to look at the engine. He found I had bent the dust cover. It was hitting the flywheel. "In a boat, you don't need to worry about a dust cover," he said as he inserted a wedge of wood that solved the problem.

I ran the boat back to Coghill. When the season on the Sound closed, the gillnetters moved to the Flats. We were optimistic about silver season paying the remaining bills.

I ran my boat to Egg Island. A few miles shy of the anchorage, I heard Ed King call on the radio. "*Luna Sea, Chinook*. You pick me up?"

"*Chinook, Luna Sea* back, yeah Ed, I hear you. How're you doing?"

"I'm over here watching you run past me."

Puzzled, I slowed the boat and looked around,

"I'm north of you," he said.

"Okay, I spot you."

"I'm alone in here, and there're two good sets. I'll direct you in if you want."

I agreed. Ed had his boat anchored in a hole I had never struggled through the shallow water to reach. I appreciated an opportunity to learn anything from the old-timers, especially about a new fishing hole.

"Continue your course east. I'll watch and signal when to turn north." Ed told me. He directed me around the shallow sandbars. His ability to judge the location of the channel from a distance impressed me. Ed trapped in the winter. At Coghill he told me impressive stories about his experiences in the early days before statehood. After I tied to his skiff, he told me about his adventures when he worked as a guide.

In the morning we stood on deck, sipped coffee, and looked at the tide book, the wind, and the current and planned our first set. Ed pointed to the markers farther up the channel to the north. He told me where he planned to set his net and where I should set mine. A brisk wind blew, but any day rain didn't fall was pleasant weather on the Flats. I untied the *Luna Sea* and idled down the channel. Ed pulled his anchor and idled not far in the opposite direction. The tide went out and exposed the sandbars around us. The channel became narrow, and with the shallow water, the tide slowed much earlier and continued with a gentle current. When the tide ran hard, we anchored, ate a meal, and relaxed until the current slowed.

Early Tuesday someone on the radio reported a net drifting without a boat. The skippers listened. Everyone expected a frantic and relieved gillnetter to respond, asking for the location. The radio remained painfully silent. The gillnetters couldn't tolerate the radio silence. They searched for a boat without a net.

A skipper spotted a cabin skiff, the *King James,* inside the main channel at Egg Island without a net. The gillnetter pulled alongside the skiff. He hollered and knocked on the side of the cabin. Everyone listening to the radio felt the chill of no response. Someone called the Coast Guard and reported James Olsen, the skipper of the *King James,* as missing. A Coast Guard helicopter in town flew out and began a search from the air. If anyone had seen Olsen go overboard, they could have rescued him, but minutes are critical in those silty, frigid waters. The distance between the net and the boat left the fishermen with weakened confidence that James Olsen was alive, but no one gave up hope.

The helicopter flew east, west, and south of us, searching the surrounding water and sand. Despite the noise from the helicopter, I heard a bird screech. I went to my front deck and saw the bird, about the size of a crow, caught in my net close to the bow. I was nervous about suffering pecks when I cleared the bird from my web. I remembered what my neighbor told me about wild animals, "Never show your teeth. Don't smile."

By hand I pulled in the lines beyond the bird, which left the web in between slack. The net had caught the bird, but it wasn't tangled. It didn't peck me when I picked it out of the net and set it on the gunwale, the upper edge of the boat side. The bird seemed dazed by the experience and content to sit and gather its wits. I went into my cabin and pulled out a bowl of fish I had saved for sandwiches. I laid a scoop of the fresh flakes next to the bird. It showed no interest. Breadcrumbs and a dish of fresh water never sparked any interest either.

The tide turned, and it was time to pick my low-water set. The bird sat perched near my controls. When I stopped to pick a coho salmon, the bird stood. It walked along the gunwale to where it enjoyed a better view of the salmon. I was delighted to see the bird walk, but worried because it didn't fly away. I pulled in the net, and the bird paced. When I picked another salmon, the bird stopped and watched. The routine continued while I picked fish for the entire one-hundred-fifty-fathoms. When the buoy ball on the end of the net came on board, the bird squawked and flew off. It circled low above me before it flew out of sight. Watching it fly away unharmed made me smile.

The helicopter continued to survey the area. The search for a member of the fishing fleet formed a gloomy cloud on the morning. A few hours into the flood tide, boats ran the channel toward Whitshed. A gillnetter spotted the missing skipper on a sandbar. The helicopter recovered and flew James Olsen's body to town.

Olsen and his brothers fished all their lives out of Cordova. James fished alone. No one knew what happened. The pile of engine tools and eyeglasses on the stern gave a hint. People guessed he'd switched his net from the stern, where the water splashes against the flat surface, to the bow to work on his engine but slipped and fell overboard.

The stern pickers often switched their nets to the bow, where the boat drifts more comfortably holding the net against the wind. I had switched numerous times with my skiff.

The loss of a fellow fishermen is easier to hear and accept when I can blame something. I want something to explain the loss, anything to differentiate between him and me. Losing James Olsen, I had a slip of his foot to blame. The simple action was too familiar and hard to accept. We lost him on the inside waters, which threatened me more than losses on the gulf did.

I accepted that one day death might happen to me. Knowing someone died every year let me know the threat was real. Believing I wouldn't be the one lost allowed me to leave the harbor. Deep inside I knew that one day I *could* be the one, and I considered the other ways I might die if I didn't fish. We all die, but knowing I might die any day made the end of life more real, more immediate. Knowing I might not be around the next day kept me more in the present and unwilling to let things remain unresolved. Accepting that I could die any day gave me a unique perspective on living.

CHAPTER FOURTEEN

WHILE I MENDED my net on the dock during the closure, Tabor came by and told me about his good catch. On Sunday I followed him to Softuk. The profitable fishing made me stay. After two weeks I flew to town during a closure and heard the ferry schedule had changed. The coho run and market remained strong, but I craved more understanding of mechanics. I decided to quit fishing early, catch the last ferry to Whittier, and arrive in Anchorage in time to attend fall semester. One problem—my boat sat anchored in the slough at Softuk. Tabor offered to use his boat to fish for the week, run my boat to town, and winterize it. He once worked at an outboard shop and would perform a better job winterizing than I knew how to do.

"You should fish the morning opener and fly in," he suggested.

"No, you better try fishing my bow-picker. If I wait I'll miss the ferry and be late for school."

Tabor flew out on a floatplane Sunday, grabbed my toolbox off the *Luna Sea*, and put it on the plane. I met the plane, grabbed my toolbox, and drove onto the ferry. When the ferry docked in Whittier, I followed the other vehicles onto the train to Portage. From there I drove forty miles on the highway to Anchorage.

My nephew Bob, one of Desiree's older brothers, accepted a job transfer to Anchorage. We shared an apartment halfway between his office and the college.

Bill Tiedeman was a buyer for a chain store and supplied village residents with everything needed for life in remote Alaska. He spent most of his time away in communities new to my ear such as: Scammon Bay, Hooper Bay, and Unalakleet. When he came to town, he stayed with his brother about a mile away, and came to visit me.

Sewall flew to Anchorage on his way to his new cannery at Egegik and stopped to visit. In Kodiak he processed crab, shrimp, and bottom fish, before he moved to Bristol Bay for salmon. His visit was short, but we knew we'd see each other at Christmas.

WHEN I FINISHED the semester at school, I flew to Seattle and stayed with my parents. After the holidays I flew back to Anchorage. I worked days in an office assisting with an audit and attending real estate classes at night. Mother Nature controls salmon seasons, and my brief history told me I needed another more dependable way to earn money. I enjoyed working with numbers and people and thought a business doing real estate, insurance, bookkeeping, and taxes would be welcome in Cordova. I would have to study in Anchorage for a few years, but school was an enjoyable winter occupation.

After passing the Alaska Real Estate Exam, I wanted to go home to Cordova. The schedule was too early in the spring to include the voyage by ferry from either Seward or Whittier. My one option was to catch the ferry in Valdez, a hundred miles by air, three hundred by road. Bill happened to visit for a few days, and I was delighted when he agreed to ride with me. Bill escorting me to Cordova was a tradition. We left Anchorage in the morning. The Volkswagen climbed the passes in the slow lane. We didn't roll down the last pass into Valdez until twilight. We parked in line at the ferry terminal hours before the scheduled departure. People crowded the space in between the waiting vehicles and visited with old friends. Sylvia, ahead of us in line, had known Bill her entire life. They both grew up in Cordova. She gillnetted and assumed the job of skipper on her dad's seine boat when he retired the previous season. She drove thirteen hundred miles on the Alcan *alone*, which made me feel silly complaining about my three-hundred-mile drive.

Bill and I slept through the night on the ferry and arrived in Cordova in the morning. After we enjoyed breakfast at a cafe, we lingered on the main street and visited with old friends. Everyone in town talked about the herring season. Fish and Game witnessed spawning in the Sound earlier than ever before. The seiners fished for three days, caught their quota, and returned to town. The short season was unexpected but a welcome change from the tradition of weeks on the Sound anchored and waiting. The wild kelp fishermen complained that the herring spawned on seaweeds that weren't marketable or on good kelp covered with dirt or silt. We heard stories on the street about becoming rich and of disaster. At the end of herring season, the processors paid the fishermen five million dollars, which fueled the spring economic boom.

Late that afternoon we drove the VW to Tom's place. With the birth of Tom and Merrie's daughter the previous fall, the family moved from the tent to a home in town. Their son, Jesse, was old enough for a job as a seine crew member. Tom hoped he could persuade his mom, Edwina, to babysit so Merrie could join them seining. He knew Edwina wouldn't even consider living in the tent.

We stayed and enjoyed dinner at Tom's trailer, one of many in town that Guy, the local sales agent, had shipped and sold for temporary homes the year of the earthquake. The residents built large additions onto the trailers, which doubled the footprint and made the "houses" permanent. Tom's, fifty-four by ten-foot had a lean-to the same length and twelve feet wide. The front door opened to a room with hangers and hooks for raingear and a chest freezer for home-packs. Another room had laundry facilities, and down the hall were four bedrooms and a bathroom. The large kitchen hosted a dining area with a table that sat six and more often than not held a crowd around it drinking industri-al-strength coffee. In the spacious living room around the wood stove were three couches for visitors, where Bill and I spent the night. Tom derived immense pleasure in having a home to offer, because housing remained in short supply.

Bill enjoyed his visit, but his job demanded his time. He caught the plane back to Anchorage the next day. I drove him to the airport and then drove to Orca, unlocked my bunkhouse room, and looked around. I saw everything as I had left it the previous fall. My surroundings felt familiar, yet unfamiliar, because of the passage of time.

My boat was in the warehouse, and because it didn't need the maintenance a wood boat requires, preparation to launch was days shorter. The beach gang lowered the *Luna Sea* into the water. I climbed down the ladder, cruised into town, and tied to a float in the harbor.

Mornings when I headed from the bunkhouse to the harbor, I stopped at Tom's trailer for coffee. I found him, with Floyd, JD, and Willie around the kitchen table, drinking the second or third pot of coffee. Tom filled the extra bedrooms with visitors and friends when his family wasn't in town. In the spring when the gillnetters fished the Flats, Floyd and his brother, JD, stayed in two of the four bedrooms. When the boats moved to the Sound, Merrie, Jesse, and Elizabeth moved in for seine season. Tom's mom, Edwina, stayed in the fourth bedroom. At the end of the seine season, Edwina continued her travels around Alaska in her motorhome, Tom's family returned to Washington, and the gillnetters returned to the Flats for silver season and to Tom's for shelter.

Most conversations around the kitchen table were about the new gillnetters' cooperative. The previous season's fiasco, sitting on the beach unable to fish until the red salmon were in the lake, caused the fishermen to question the methods of their livelihood. Different ideas of how to sell their salmon sprang up in every fisherman's mind. Most of the fishermen weren't willing to trust the sale of their catch, once the tender lifted the salmon from their fish hold. The fishermen knew the one constant every season was the price dispute with the processors. The story was old. The canneries and fishermen shared a history of fighting about price since the first processor made a purchase. Decades earlier, the government sent federal mediators to settle a strike. They reported the canneries were robbing the fishermen. From that day forward, fishermen suspected the processors continued to rob them. The previous season those long-simmering, bitter feelings intensified when the boats sat tied to the dock for a month without any price offer.

Fishermen grumbled about what they couldn't do, but a few were enthusiastic about change. They experienced enough bad results with the foreign control of the salmon markets. Those gillnetters wanted to catch, process, and market their salmon on the domestic market. They organized a cooperative because they never again wanted to sit on the beach, not fish, when the season was open. When people have passion, they find success. A group of gillnetters, Tom, Floyd, Sylvia, and James among them, organized The Copper River Fisherman's Cooperative, CRFC. A few with vision, enthusiasm, and drive grabbed the rest of us for the ride. James, with an inability to hear "no" and inexhaustible energy, drove the co-op to happen. He became the CRFC's president. Tom and Floyd were staunch promoters and board members determined to make the co-op succeed.

The co-op business plan required a minimum of forty members who paid $750 each to cover the essential costs of beginning the business. An ice machine was the first priority and most expensive. I wanted the co-op to succeed, but its market focused on salmon from the Copper River. I was passionate about fishing in the Sound. I occupied a cannery locker and a bunkhouse room and enjoyed winter boat storage at Orca. Tom and Floyd continued to coax me every morning at coffee, until I decided to help the co-op with a few salmon and $750. They understood the cannery was my main market, but they were desperate to raise the startup capital.

The co-op leased a building from the city located on the end of a dock in the harbor. In the spirit of defiance, Tom painted CRFC in fat red letters twenty feet tall on the sloped tin roof, announcing the co-op presence to the canneries. The board hired a brokerage firm to sell the salmon and Peggy to coordinate the logistics from boat to market. The energy of the people involved was invigorating and magical. May 15 was no longer the rule for the opener. On May 1, Fish and Game announced the Copper River would open Monday, May 18, for thirty-six hours instead of the historical forty-eight.

"Beginning May 18, we're already three days late," the gillnetters whined.

The mood at the CAMA meeting was one of urgency to talk about price and hear about negotiations. Fishermen knew price talks began after we heard from Armin, who had grown pinks for the seiners at San Juan and was setting his bait for the gillnetters. "PWSAC can build a hatchery that develops a fishery at Coghill from early June until late September," Armin said.

For me his promises of an extended season on the Sound meant less time on the Flats. For those who fished the Flats, Armin's promises meant less competition, if boats departed earlier for Coghill. The CAMA membership gave Armin the go ahead to investigate building a hatchery on Esther Island. The final decision was up to the PWSAC board, but Armin understood having the support of the fishermen behind him was critical. The CAMA members reaffirmed their support for the voluntary assessment, and discussions turned to price.

The co-op members knew the co-op could pay a price higher than the canneries offered, so they thought they were legitimate in going fishing. The other five hundred gillnetters voiced anger at the position of the co-op. CAMA members believed they would lose their strength to negotiate if the co-op members fished before the canneries signed a contract. The whole concept of salmon sold in the market instead of at the tender conflicted with gillnetters age-old ways. CAMA members talked about not agreeing to an asking price in an attempt to keep the co-op boats from fishing. News spread around town that the co-op boats were going fishing on Monday. With the market strong, CAMA settled the price before the opener.

The co-op wanted to produce the highest quality salmon. The members planned to dress the fish when we caught them. We built V-boards to lay the salmon on for easier cleaning. Dressing the salmon worked for those of us in calm water with a limited catch. The opening set at the east end of the Flats proved cleaning the catch wasn't feasible.

Bob Christensen had gillnetted for years. That spring, retired from gillnetting, he tendered for the co-op at Softuk with his seine boat the *St. Elias*. Through his binoculars he saw the end of the nets come out of the water. Red salmon filled the nets. Bob knew the gillnetters would pick until their boats were full. If the boats had to stop fishing and clean the salmon while other gillnetters reloaded their boats, his tender would remain empty. Bob changed plans to accommodate the large catches. He loaded the *St Elias* with iced whole salmon and headed for town.

Fish and Game announced it wouldn't schedule a second opener that week.

The second week the announcement of one opener told the highliners, the fishermen that catch the most fish, they had to pick salmon, not waste time cleaning them. The added work required more time, space, and a crew. The size of our boats made processing impractical. The discussion ended when we heard a quality report. Our cuts were inconsistent, which yielded a lower grade in the marketplace. Bob Christensen's load of professionally processed salmon received the highest grade and price. The co-op members agreed they were better at catching than at processing. From then on, the tenders brought iced salmon to town where a crew repacked them in totes of fresh ice. Peggy chartered DC-8s to fly the salmon to Anchorage for processing.

The third week, the Fish and Game manager increased the weekly period from thirty-six to forty-eight hours, and the next week the opener lasted sixty hours. For those of us who fished inside the sand islands having only one opener per week cut our income in half. We caught most of our salmon on the opener and the first low-water set. For the remainder of the period, we set our net for hours then days of torturous scratch fishing. More boats moved outside to fish in the gulf.

The new area biologist managed the fishery like a dog marks a tree. None of the historical data mattered to him. The previous management had been logical and predictable. Sixty-hour fishing periods weren't logical or historical. The changes in the fishing schedule and not understanding why made me feel discouraged. For example, the manager delayed the opener at Coghill. On Saturday I looked at the number of sockeye past the weir and was surprised when he refused to open the district on Monday. He didn't give any credit to the historical escapement patterns.

Salmon respond to various things; most we don't notice or understand. We know salmon sense and react to changes in barometric pressure. Many times half the reds shot up the river to Coghill Lake after a hard rain or high tide. Each salmon family is distinct. An obvious difference in salmon is how far up a river the fish travel before they spawn. The Copper spans hundreds of miles, with various distinctive streams or lakes where the sockeye spawn. Different families swim through the fishery as early as May and as late as August. At Coghill the river is an afternoon hike from the lagoon, and the sockeye are in the lake in less than a month.

Sunday after the boats headed to the Flats, the manager announced an "emergency" opener at Coghill, with a deluge of salmon at the weir. The sockeye were so thick Fish and Game opened the area in College Fjord that had been previously closed until July. The department scheduled the opener before the period on the Flats closed. Most gillnetters never heard about the Coghill opener. Fewer than a hundred boats ran across the Sound. Those of us who did hear about it caught more fish than usual. We rejoiced when salmon continued to stream up the fjord. Fish and Game extended the fishing period another twenty-four hours.

My life and attitude changed that week at Coghill. Gillnetters arrived late, and with the buildup of sockeye and less competition, I caught more salmon on the opener than I had caught previous years in the first week. Sockeye flooded in while gillnetters picked fish and enjoyed the sunny weather. With the reduced size of my fish holds, I tried to deliver often. I didn't want to miss fishing time while I searched for a tender. I sold most of my salmon to Chugach at Orca, but with the good catch, I sold to all the tenders when they cruised past my boat.

The co-op never planned to send a tender to Coghill, but the co-op boats saw the high-catch numbers and the lack of interested buyers. A member called the co-op office and asked Peggy if she could find a market and a tender for at least one load of sockeye. Peggy called Whittier and hired the *Itzwoot* for our tender. She rode the ferry to Whittier, where she expedited the salmon by train to Anchorage for processing. With the strong market, Peggy continued to send the tender. Many of the gillnetters stayed on the Flats or went seining. With the reduced competition and the strong run, my catch began to pay for my boat. When the red catch dropped off, the strong pink and keta runs kept fishing exciting.

Fishing the *Luna Sea* for a week the previous fall had changed Tabor's thoughts about bow-pickers. Over the winter he built his own, the *Mocha Java*, both longer and wider than the *Luna Sea*. I fished near Jeanie and Tabor at Coghill for most of the summer. During pink season, I spent a closure eating and sleeping with my boat tied to the empty *Mocha Java* anchored in Island Bay.

When Jeanie and Tabor flew out from town on Sunday evening, the pilot brought Red on the same plane. She escaped town for a couple of weeks and had a standing offer for a vacation on the Sound.

When they landed at our anchored boats Red said, "I've seen the *Luna Sea;* I want to see how she performs."

Tabor said, "We saw an amazing number of salmon in Unakwik from the plane." He was hardly able to talk because he was so excited.

Red unrolled my chart.

Tabor pointed to the district on the chart. "It's right next door."

Ready to explore a new area, Red and I pulled our anchor and with the *Mocha Java,* made the one-hour run. Unakwik Inlet is the fjord east of Port Wells, separated by high mountains with numerous glaciers. The inlet is narrower but similar to College Fjord, with glaciers at the head and drifting icebergs. The radical difference is the shallow reef that divides Unakwik Inlet. The reef crosses the inlet like a partition. The inlet is miles long and fathoms deep, but at the reef the shores narrow and the water gets shallow. Parts of the reef go dry at low water. The deepest passage across is between fifteen and thirty feet, depending on the tide. In a short distance the bottom drops off to hundreds of feet and then hundreds of fathoms. The water moves freely up and down the fjord until it hits the reef. The flow of the water becomes restricted and causes confused and turbulent currents, including whirlpools. At times on the ebb, because of the strength of the tide and the glacial melt-off, the water flows over the reef, and resembles rapids. Traveling across the reef was quick but bizarre.

"Believe me, you don't want your net to drift anywhere near the reef," Tabor warned us. "The bottom has pinnacle rocks with jagged edges that love to shred nets. If your net drifts across, the repairs will cost more than the penalty for drifting out of the gillnet district."

Once across the reef, we saw salmon jumping everywhere. I had never seen so many salmon. They were thick. A few of them jumped and flew through the air constantly. Throughout the night we slept to the music of splashing salmon. *Plop, plop,* they fell back into the water after they jumped. We pulled our anchor in the morning and looked around. We couldn't decide on the best spot to set. Salmon jumped out of the water everywhere.

We nicknamed Red Humpy Hawkeye, because of her vocalizations. "Jumper!" she yelled when she pointed to a swirling school. Each time she saw a salmon in the air, she called out, "Jumper! Jumper!"

The salmon jumped everywhere around us. We were unable to calm down enough to set the net. Once we set the net, we questioned, with the salmon so plentiful why aren't other boats fishing. Are we fishing in a closed area? The thought tortured us. I called and checked in with Tabor. Without voicing our concern, I dropped a hint. Tabor and Jeanie had asked themselves that same question and understood. We both pulled our net and went to find a tender.

The reef divides the inlet north and south into two fishing districts. The seiners fished in both districts. Fish & Game restricted the gillnetters to the northern waters. We knew the area below the reef was open to the seiners. We thought the gillnet district at the top of the fjord was open, but an opener with tons of salmon and not another boat in sight?

We found the *New St. Joseph*. We knew Mike, the skipper from our summer at Eshamy. We confided in him our experience. "Do you know if the area above the reef is open?" I asked.

"I don't know any reason why the area isn't open, but I'm not sure," Mike responded. He radioed the Fish and Game office in town and asked what areas were open rather than asking if Unakwik was open. He thought he drew less attention to the district that way regardless of the answer. We stood stiff and silent in the wheelhouse and listened to a woman read the announcement over the radio. At the end of the radio call the silent tension in the wheelhouse broke into giddy laughter. Our muscles relaxed and smiles returned to our faces. We rubbed our hands together imagining the schools of salmon waiting for us. We delivered the salmon from our first set, which Fish and Game had confirmed were legal, and ran back for more.

After we caught the buildup of salmon, we needed a strategy. Tabor tried a set he knew was lucrative for sockeye. Red and I knew nothing about the area. We pulled out my chart and looked for what might be a fishy point. We found an outcropping of rocks where we set a few fathoms of net to see how fast the current pushed us toward the reef. The net drifted at a slow pace. When we set the entire net, a couple of feet of cork line pulled under. Unfamiliar with the waters, we were concerned about rocks snagging the lead line. A few tense moments passed before the cork line returned to the surface and bounced with salmon. We held our breath each time the net went down. When the cork line resurfaced wiggling, we sang shouts of joy and danced on the deck. Each time we pulled in the net, we picked a bunch of pinks and a few keta.

Tabor and Jeanie stopped on their way to another point to give us their report. The famous sockeye set produced few pinks.

The current changed three hours early by the tide book. Without ever stopping, our net drifted in the opposite direction into the rock pile. Pink salmon swarmed from the bay above us and swam around the rocks. The net exploded with salmon. The splashing caused the water around my net to boil. In spots where the cork line went down, it wasn't coming up. The net was too heavy with salmon to float. Pinks swam over the sinking cork line. Tabor and Jeanie, with their net on the reel, looked sick and sped off to set their net. Red and I picked salmon and cheered. For the first time in history, and the last, we caught more pinks that day than Jeanie and Tabor.

With our boats loaded each evening we searched for a tender willing to buy our catch. That week, the peak of pink season, the seiners harvested more than a million salmon a day. The tender fleet was busy buying tons of fish from the seiners. We were more of a pest with the meager number of salmon we offered for sale, yet we sold our load every night. The question was how far south we traveled before we found a willing tender. The pink salmon came in thick, and we loaded our boats every day. The *Mocha Java*'s length and beam paid off because it packed more salmon. We fished a rock we named Pink Paradise. Jeanie and Tabor made an impressive fishing team and consistently delivered more salmon than I did. The strenuous work and routine of a boatload, day after day, felt satisfying. Our nights of sound sleep were guilt free.

At the *New St. Joseph* one evening, a Fish and Game research technician offered to unload our salmon. We agreed to someone else doing our work while we sipped hot chocolate with a splash of peppermint schnapps and looked on. The technician searched for marked pink salmon from the Cannery Creek Hatchery, below the reef. When he began he doubted any of our salmon were from there. He believed the hatchery fish never crossed the reef. When he finished he concluded our entire catch originated from the hatchery. The origin of our catch explained why the fishing boats were missing. The salmon we caught were from a new run of salmon created by the state hatchery. That year was the second year of returning pinks and was double the amount from the previous year. The hatchery pinks returned well after the wild sockeye were up the river.

When the season slowed, my nephew Bob began his vacation. Red and I picked him up in Whittier on the weekend. The season was near the end. We expected to fish for a few days and run to town. Bob planned to ride with us to Cordova and fly south from there. The three of us squeezed onto the *Luna Sea*. Bob, a marvelous cook, spent his day at the stove while Red and I picked salmon and loaded the boat. One morning when our nets came up nearly empty, we knew the hatchery run was over. We fished the morning tide, found a tender, and with the *Mocha Java* headed for town.

The *Luna Sea* followed the *Mocha Java* down the fjord. Red, Bob, and I moved into the cabin when the rain began, but we thought nothing of the showers. Father south our boats began to bounce. A storm blew in the Sound, but we hadn't felt a whisper of wind in the sheltered terminus of the fjord. We experienced the severity of the wind at the bottom of the inlet when the water tossed our boats. We traveled close to the northern coastline and ducked inside of islands for protection whenever possible. We ran behind Glacier Island, north into Valdez Arm, across the shortest track of open water, to the inside of Goose Island, where we peeked out the other side. When Tabor saw the turbulent water in front of Knowles Head, he turned the *Mocha Java* around. I followed him behind Goose Island. We anchored our boats and waited. We hoped the water in front of Knowles Head would calm when the tide went slack.

Tabor offered to ferry Bob on the larger *Mocha Java* for the last critical leg of the run to town. At high water slack, we secured everything in our cabins and turned off our stoves. I pulled my anchor in. Bob leaped onto the *Mocha Java*, and we braced ourselves for a wild ride. The wind blew hard, and the seas grew tall. Our boats bobbed like corks. Red and I ran the *Luna Sea* behind the *Mocha Java*. In front of Knowles Head, cruising at less than half speed, the *Luna Sea* flew through the air, plunged into the water, and shot walls of spray into the air before the bow pounded through the next swell. Bob reported he looked back and saw our lower unit from under the bow of the boat when it flew through the air. The trip was horrible. We were thankful when we tied the boats to the dock in Cordova's harbor.

The storm intensified. The lake in town rose one inch each hour. Before the night ended, the town flooded around Lake Eyak, including the city airport. Most skippers, when they flew to their boat, left their vehicle keys with the air service office or in their vehicle. The air service folks moved those cars and trucks to higher ground. The vehicles without keys filled with water.

In one day more than sixteen and a half inches of rain fell, and it continued to pour. Bob and I drove the road to Orca until a rockslide blocked our passage. We parked the car a safe distance from the slide and hiked across the fresh pile of rock. We arrived minutes after the stream next to the bunkhouse became a raging river and developed a new course, running through the door of the bunkhouse. Some quick thinkers threw up a sheet of plywood to block the doorway. They tore up the floorboards to let the water out, saving the bunkhouse. Bob and I gathered the things I needed from my room and hiked to the car. We wanted to reach town before we witnessed any more effects of the rain.

"This is the worst summer storm since '58," the old-timers claimed.

With the town flooded and the wind howling, Bob cut his visit to Cordova short. He caught the first available flight to his other destination, hydroplane races in sunny Seattle. With the road blocked and the boat tied in the harbor, I stayed in town at Red's apartment high on the ski hill. The rain and wind persisted. Fifty-nine inches of rain fell in the first two and a half weeks of August.

Throughout the days of rain and wind, boats tried to reach the harbor. The supply of food ran low, and skippers felt anxious. On days when the weather calmed, gillnetters made a dash for town. To make the journey in the gulf from the east, a boat had to travel west until the captain spotted the Egg Island light. Unknown to some, the navigational light was out.

One boat that tried to make the trip from the Bering River district to town searched for the Egg Island Light. Desperate but unable to find it, he ran his boat closer to the breakers. His steering failed. He ran to the inside helm, the rear steering responded. Relieved, he maneuvered away from the breakers. He hadn't located the light and the wind blew a steady forty with gusts of fifty to sixty knots. Steering a course from inside proved difficult with his compass mounted at the front helm. He ran the boat away from the beach to deep water, to ride out the storm.

The skipper had talked to a fisherman on the CB radio who then called the Coast Guard and requested assistance for his friend. When the Coast Guard helicopter arrived at the boat the seas were immense. At times the boat floated higher on the swells than the helicopter flew. The skipper watched the lights of the helicopter go in and out of sight in the enormous seas, and then the helicopter disappeared. The helicopter had gone down. In the darkness the skipper searched the water. The water laid quiet in the fuel spill. He searched but couldn't find any of the helicopter crew members. Throughout the night the boat drifted toward the entrance of the Sound. The helicopter floated through the entrance and washed up on Storey Island, in the middle of the Sound. Later searchers found the bodies of two crew members on the beach at Montague, an island at the entrance of the Sound. The search for the other two crew members continued.

The loss of the helicopter crew filled the fishermen and the townspeople with grief. The skippers suffered guilt and anger about the loss of four of their heroes. Everyone wanted someone to blame. Some people in town blamed the skipper. When he returned to town unharmed, he bore the brunt of the anger.

A Coast Guard official commented in an article in *The Cordova Times* about the accident. He reassured people that the accident wasn't anyone's fault. The helicopter malfunctioned, he wrote and that fishermen shouldn't hesitate to call for assistance.

Everyone shouldered a deep pain at the loss of four brave men who fishermen consider their heroes: Lieutenant Ernest "Pat" Rivas, thirty-three, of Alameda, California; Lieutenant Joseph G. Spoja, thirty-one, from Helena, Montana; Aviation Machinist Mate First Class Scott R. Finfrock, twenty-five of Fresno, California; and Aviation Machinists Mate Third Class John H. Snyder Jr., twenty-one, of Bethlehem, Pennsylvania.

CHAPTER FIFTEEN

THE CO-OP MEMBERS met on the dock in front of the CRFC building to discuss silver season. The local canneries offered such an excellent price that the co-op board decided CRFC couldn't afford to buy. Members fished for the traditional processors.

Monday morning I was on my boat at Egg Island when my alarm clock rang. The fog was so thick, my eyes strained to see my net on the reel. A cloud sat on the surface of the water and drizzled. I made a thermos of coffee while I looked out the window and dressed, unable to see another boat or my own bow. With the opener minutes away, the thick fog rendered me blind.

Standing on the front deck in my raingear with my engine warm, I grabbed the anchor line but debated pulling it. The tide was high and ebbing, the worst time to get stuck. The boat wouldn't float for hours. I'd miss low water, my most productive set. I let go of the line, drank more coffee, and waited for the dense fog to lift or shift enough for me to see my surroundings. Cozy on my bunk, I was reading a book when I heard someone call my name, loud and clear. I stood and looked out the window, expecting to see a boat drift by with the person on deck who called to me. Walking out on deck, I heard nothing. After listening for a few more minutes, I returned to the cabin and sat on my bunk, confused by the voice I'd clearly heard. Hours passed before the fog lifted. Visibility improved early enough for me to set my net. The catch was good, and the coho run appeared strong.

WHEN I MOVED into the bunkhouse I had to give up my telephone. During the closure Bruce, Bill Tiedeman's brother, called people in town looking for me. Eventually he found me at Tom's trailer. Bruce told me, "Monday morning Bill departed Anchorage with two coworkers headed for a store in Grayling. The Cessna they flew in is missing."

Hearing those words made me collapse into a chair. His words knocked the wind out of me. Monday morning? Was it Bill who called my name? I immediately dismissed the idea. If Bill made his way to the ground, he could survive. I refused to give up hope.

"Searchers reported a few sightings that week, but none of them turned out to be the plane. A pilot spotted people in the search area around noon. I'm hoping the group is Bill and the other passengers," Bruce said optimistically.

The next morning Bruce reported, "The searchers confirmed the people seen were remote campers." I continued to call Bruce when I was in town on the closures. We heard fewer and fewer reports about Bill and the Cessna.

THE CANNERIES QUIT buying salmon a week into the season. Our coho market ended before the run peaked. Fishing was open, and a healthy run of coho salmon was available. The fishermen were eager to catch more silvers. They met at the CRFC building on the dock.

"The coho run just began. We want to fish. Can the co-op provide a market?" the members asked. "This is precisely why we need the co-op."

Peggy made telephone calls and met with the co-op members the following morning. She reported what our catch would sell for when it was ready to leave Anchorage. With a guesstimated value, the members agreed they wanted to fish that week for that price. When people on the street heard the co-op was going fishing, the membership climbed from forty to seventy. Gillnetters joined without being disloyal to a cannery. Other gillnetters felt so intensely opposed to the co-op that they quit fishing.

With the local canneries not buying, most of the gillnetters wouldn't fish. People who planned to fish for their freezer, canner, or smoker would stay close to town. The co-op planned to send two tenders to the far east end. The co-op members decided where they'd fish and paid a fee for space on that tender. Tom ran the *Sugar* to Softuk. I followed him with Floyd and James. The weather made a dramatic change. The rain stopped for a couple of weeks and the winds blew less than fifteen knots, which was surprising weather for the fall and uncommon for the Flats at any time of year.

The silvers were bright, firm, and plentiful. We loaded our nets and the tender's fish hold. We caught more than our share, because we didn't divide the catch with the customary number of boats. Floyd ran his boat with a load of salmon into town with the loaded tenders. Once there, he helped Peggy move the salmon from the dock to the airport.

The silver run held strong. The price stayed steady. News traveled to Valdez, and the next week cash buyers headed to the fishing grounds after they heard about the good catch and the lack of buyers.

On the closure I anchored my boat in the slough, flew to town, and called Bruce. The reports about Bill's plane were frequent at first with a few sightings that offered Bruce hope. Planes scoured the area of Rainy Pass, but he heard fewer and fewer reports.

I continued to call Bruce every closure when I was in town. One time when I called from Tom's trailer, Bruce said, "The officials called off the search without a trace." He sounded defeated but remained optimistic. "The Christian Pilots Association will continue the search as long as it receives donations to pay for fuel."

"You can begin with this," Tom said with a heartfelt smile as he reached in his pocket and handed me a crisp hundred-dollar bill. "This is my secret party stash. A contribution to find Bill is appropriate. We know he'll throw a carousing party."

I appreciated his optimism. I tried to visualize Bill safe somewhere in the wilderness. I was sure he'd delight me with laughter while he teased me about how absurd I was to worry about the "Iron Indian."

AT THE END of the season the cannery manager at Orca determined boat storage space based on the number of deliveries the boat made that season. My small fish holds turned out to be beneficial because I made many deliveries. I moved my boat into the warehouse at Orca, locked my bunkhouse room, caught the ferry, transferred to the train, and drove the VW to Anchorage, where I became a real estate agent. Bill's friend Terry met me for dinner. Our meeting was painful without Bill to joke and laugh with us. Anchorage felt unfamiliar without Bill.

For Thanksgiving I flew south to celebrate with my family and stayed for Christmas. While in Seattle I enjoyed dinners with Sewall. He took a week of vacation, and we painted his living and dining rooms. Before flying back north I attended a commercial boat show where distributors displayed and sold the latest products. Two devices, the Loran C and the VHF radio were cutting-edge. The Loran C, a navigational tool, would tell me the location of my boat when I couldn't see. The VHF radio allowed me to communicate with other boats from a farther distance, call the Coast Guard for assistance, or call a Mayday. Most valuable to me, the radio would give me a current weather forecast. After a profitable season, I bought both.

Weather forecasts were hard to hear before VHF radios. Most of us depended on the tenders to pass on the latest forecast the skippers heard on the single sideband radio. Alaska mariners depended on Peggy, a woman in Kodiak, who became famous because she broadcast the best marine weather reports available. Her husband, Oscar Dyson, a well-respected man across the state, pioneered the Alaskan crab fishery. He'd fished since the end of World War II and harvested everything he could market. His boat covered more distance in a season than most of us would ever travel.

Oscar installed a radio at his home and called his wife, Peggy, from far off in the stormy Pacific or the frozen Bering Sea. He and other fishermen called Peggy on a regular basis from waters around the state and reported their locations and observations. With her knowledge and the mariners' information, she broadcast an excellent report of the current weather with a reliable forecast. If a low was approaching, mariners wanted to hear Peggy. With a VHF radio, although I couldn't hear Peggy, I received the next best, the NOAA marine forecast.

Through the winter we heard no information about Bill Tiedeman's plane. It never landed at Grayling. The Christian Pilots Association searched for the missing plane whenever the weather allowed, but winter had set in.

I continue to listen and hope for a discovery some year when mushers from around Alaska and the world run the Iditarod Trail through Rainy Pass.

CHAPTER SIXTEEN

SEWALL AND I visited in Seattle and Anchorage in the winters and wrote to each other during the summers. Although we learned we both grew up in Seattle less than a mile from each other, we had never met until we were at Orca. After five years we married, knowing our long-distance relationship would continue for another fishing season.

Before we separated to fly north, we drove to Bellingham to visit Tom and Merrie. Tom worked through the winter with a friend, Paul, and from a basic hull built a boat that Tom could gillnet and seine. The thirty-seven-foot *MJB*, named for Merrie, Jesse, and Betsy, was in the water and running. Tom and Paul were busy completing what they could before they ran the boat north. Tom invited us for a cruise around Bellingham Bay, breaking in the engine. When we docked in the harbor, Sewall and I drove to Seattle. He went back to work, and I caught up with Willie. He was excited to take me for a ride around Lake Union in his new factory-finished forty-two-foot boat, the *Monde Uni*. Anticipating record returns of pink salmon, most of the seiners bought a new boat with a larger fish hold.

The following week disaster shocked the salmon industry. A can of pink salmon packed in Alaska caused the hospitalization of a Belgian couple with botulism. Weeks before the opener, the FDA recalled more than fifty million cans of Alaska salmon distributed throughout the world.

I had bought a car for showing real estate, I parked it in the yard of a friend in Anchorage. The ferry stopped in Whittier, and I made a short drive to the train in the VW. The departure was my first time leaving Anchorage without Bill. I suffered the painful loss of my older, wiser blood brother.

I RETURNED TO the bunkhouse, launched the boat, and made daily stops at Tom's trailer. "You must give up your alliance with the cannery and commit your catch to the co-op," Tom pleaded.

"I'm dependent on the cannery for a summer market on the Sound." I replied.

He tilted his chair back on two legs, "The co-op was successful, and we're growing in strength." His chair plopped back onto four legs when he leaned forward, "The co-op needs loyal members. When we capture more of the market share, we can buy all of your salmon."

The co-op and Chugach shared my catch. I had grown dependent on the cannery facilities, the purchase orders, the boat hoist, and its port engineer. Losing storage and the benefits of the cannery wasn't conducive to considering independence.

"You could begin by moving out of the bunkhouse. You can stay in Betsy's room until seine season," Tom proposed.

The services the cannery offered were hard to ignore, and I enjoyed the camaraderie of the Orca fleet. On the other hand, the times when the traditional processors refused to buy our salmon made the co-op a necessary investment. Moving toward independence, I moved out of the bunkhouse and into Betsy's room until Coghill season.

The botulism scare made the market too uncertain for anyone to commit to a price for pink salmon. CAMA agreed to a price contract for kings and reds. Fish and Game opened the Copper River season on May 17 for thirty-six hours. The co-op members threatened to go fishing. On the first period, tension among the fishermen and the loyalty some co-op members felt toward CAMA kept all but six boats in the harbor. Tensions among the gillnetters escalated. CAMA settled the price before the Thursday night opener, but it didn't alleviate the tension.

When Sewall heard I was pregnant, he guessed I wouldn't fish for the season. That thought never crossed my mind. The baby would be born months after the season closed. We reached a compromise; he insisted Red join me for the season. I enjoyed her company, and the season was perfect for a crew member's help. The Department of Fish and Game predicted good runs of sockeye and kings on the Flats. More valuable would be her help at Coghill.

Fish and Game collected fish scales from the catch to determine the age of the salmon. The sockeye at Coghill were four and five years old when they returned to spawn. Most years five-year-old sockeye comprise eighty percent of the run. The previous year's good return was eighty percent four-year-old salmon. I hoped the five-year-old fish would return and set a new record.

The boat was ready to leave the harbor, but a dry wind gusted. The predicted forecast sounded grim. Richey moored the *Camelot* across the float from me. He stopped at my bow on one of the trips from his truck to his boat. "When are you heading out?" he asked.

"I don't know if I am. The forecast doesn't sound good."

"How are you ever going to be a gillnetter if you don't fish the storms?" He chuckled.

"My father asked that exact same question. He told me he caught the most salmon during the storms."

Richey nodded. "The salmon hit hard in a blow."

He climbed aboard the *Camelot* and started the engine. While it warmed, he made another trip to his truck for more supplies. He untied his boat, climbed on board, and shifted into gear. "You better go out at least to fish low water," he called to me when he pulled away from the dock.

"Good fishing," I hollered.

In the afternoon when the rest of the boats headed out, Red and I decided to go as far as Whitshed and peek around the corner at the weather. The predicted storm seemed late. At Whitshed we decided to continue to Egg Island, hopeful we could make a few sets before the weather became too wild. We loaded up with reds on the opener.

Friday at low water, the weather wasn't bad, and we caught quite a few king salmon. The wind began building with the tide. We listened to the latest forecast while we watched the weather deteriorate.

We heard about a boat, the *B J*, which capsized. Another skipper saw the incident and rescued the captain within minutes. On the radio gillnetters reported that the wind and swell caused chaotic water in the gulf. The wind became intolerable. We anchored, waited for the tide to cover the hump with enough water to travel, and dashed into town.

SATURDAY DISBELIEF FILLLED the harbor when people saw the *Camelot* hadn't returned to its harbor slip. Someone saw Richey with a load of salmon Friday near Strawberry Bar. Another gillnetter couldn't stand by with the *Camelot's* harbor stall empty. He went looking for Richey. The searchers flew and found the *Camelot* destroyed on the Hawkins Island beach. Richard T. Hinde was missing. No one saw the boat roll. The news was hard to accept. Richey fished for thirty-two years and raised two sons fishing. He knew the channel well and traveled through Strawberry Bar numerous times. The fishermen guessed the cause must have been a rogue wave, a massive one to have rolled the *Camelot*.

I thought about Richey's confidence when he left the harbor with a smile. He was one of the old-timers who came up with good solutions to problems, especially for stoves. He maintained an attitude that made everyone believe the best was about to happen. I missed him. Richey left behind his wife, Shirley, and his two sons, Ron and Larry. I hoped his sons hadn't heard about the tragedy over the radio.

CHAPTER SEVENTEEN

THE GILNET FLEET fished two twenty-four-hour periods, shorter than we fished in the past, but perfect for me because we fished twice a week. With the brief openers, Red and I fished hard, day and night. Hours into a twenty-four-hour period, we were exhausted. We knew fishing closed soon, and then we could sleep. We pushed on. Six hours before the closure, Fish and Game announced a twelve-hour extension. Another eighteen hours of work sounded impossible. We anchored and took a short nap.

Red and I fished at Egg Island, Pete Dahl, and Softuk. We used the Loran-C to record the location of the buoys at the bar entrances. The new technology told us our approximate location in a big ocean, but the Loran wasn't precise enough to mark the small channels inside the bars. We were at Softuk the week before Coghill opened when we heard about a low-pressure system headed our way. The fear of missing the Coghill opener, with the boat stuck at Softuk because of weather, made us scurry to Egg Island. The next period, the wind blew. Red and I stayed in town, changed nets, scrubbed the hull, and loaded the cabin with food, mosquito nets, suntan lotion, and an extra cooler for a long summer at Coghill.

Sunday afternoon with light winds, we headed for Port Wells. We were disappointed on the opener because of our tremendous expectations. With the sun shining, we were satisfied to pick a few sockeye while we drifted among the icebergs. On Tuesday the Coghill catch remained slow. Wednesday a few gillnetters talked on the radio about going back to town early. "We can run to town, switch nets, and catch the Thursday night opener on the Flats."

I teased Red and asked her if she wanted to go. We both laughed at the idea of trading the pleasure of drifting in the Sound for a beating on the Flats. Wednesday night and Thursday morning, boats departed. The remaining skippers relaxed. Our nets drifted out of shape without many salmon. Most of us enjoyed a vacation from the Flats. We drifted, dreamed, and dried out in the sunshine.

Thursday afternoon the sockeye flooded in on a wave. We woke to the arrival of reds. The activity of the boats increased. Salmon swam in from every direction. The boats near the river numbered few enough that we didn't feel crowded. The aggressive boats had returned to the Flats. The remaining skippers smiled, picked sockeye, and exchanged shouts and hoots of excitement.

Lloyd Montgomery, one of the Orca fishermen, knew Sewall from days in the NEFCO office. He knew I was expecting a baby. "Baby needs a new pair of shoes," Lloyd chanted every time he cruised past us.

The sun warmed us, and the gentle wind kept the boat off the net and the bugs away. We drifted with the slow-moving current. Music blared from my deck speakers. The net splashed with salmon. In the hot sun we pulled in the net without raingear and watched the fish holds fill with red salmon.

When the weather is pleasant and the catch is plentiful, fishing feels exhilarating and intoxicating. The experience etched itself in my memory. The high feels like winning a championship game or finishing final exams. Fishermen are optimistic gamblers. When fishing is at its worst and I'm scratch fishing and dirt broke, I draw on those memories of abundance and know another profitable catch is a few sets away.

We worked nonstop and pushed our bodies to the limit because we knew the period ended that night, and for three days we could eat, sleep, and resupply. Another announcement came. A huge return of sockeye swam past our nets and up the river. The technician at the weir counted record schools of sockeye swimming into the lake. The manager extended the opener until Friday night.

A flood of sockeye hit our net every set we made. We set the net and sat in the warm sun to enjoy a short break Thursday afternoon. After an hour, or maybe two, a boat passed and saw our net drifting near the boundary line. He suspected we had fallen asleep. He intentionally threw a wake. The *Luna Sea* rocked abruptly. The motion startled us awake.

The punishment for illegal fishing can include a fine, the loss of your catch, and the boat if the offense is serious. In a small community the shame of cheating can be even more painful. When we opened our eyes and saw where the net had drifted, the adrenaline charged us faster than any cup of black coffee. Without gloves or raingear I pulled the knob for the hydraulics and began to pull in the net. Red grabbed a couple pair of gloves and rushed to the bow. She handed me a pair as she ducked under the net to reach the far side of the bow. Once she was clear of the net, I spun the reel again as fast as the pump would allow, stopping briefly to pick salmon. We retrieved the net minutes before we drifted past the marker.

On Friday the manager extended the period through the weekend, which meant we could fish without a break for another seven days straight. We weren't that greedy. We needed a break, and we needed more food. Late Saturday, Red caught a floatplane into Cordova for the night and stocked up on groceries. I ran the *Luna Sea* into Whittier for a shower, hot food, laundry, and a walk on dry land.

We met at Coghill Lagoon on Sunday afternoon and began another action-packed week. We caught sockeye so fast that we were concerned about unloading them. Red and I listened to the tenders talk on the radio. When a tender came close, we picked our net and ran to meet the boat. We lost fishing time, but we saw other boats anchor with a load of salmon and wait half a day or longer until a tender reached the river.

One afternoon when we picked the net, we filled the fish holds. We were unaware of any tenders on their way to the river. We ran the boat down the fjord. Through the binoculars we spotted the *Drag-on*. The tender with a crew of two drifted north of Esther Passage. Sally, the captain, was part owner, with Emily, the engineer. Neither Sally nor Emily talked on the radio because they were both busy on deck. They bought salmon for North Pacific Processors. We hadn't sold to them before, but any tender looked good when my fish holds were full. The *Drag-on* had room and bought our load. By the end of the extended period, the fishermen caught more sockeye than the fishermen caught most years during the entire season at Coghill. The catch continued to set records.

Pinks swam into the Sound, and CAMA called the gillnetters to town. CAMA wanted the gillnetters to stay on the beach, not fish, and strike for a pink price. I felt outrage that CAMA wanted me to quit fishing when the sockeye catch and escapement were setting new records. The district closed for the weekend, and I flew into town to protest.

I went to a CAMA meeting and announced, "I won't sit on the beach for a pink price in the middle of a record harvest of red salmon. I'm not catching any pink salmon."

"You must not know how to catch salmon if you're not catching any pinks. The Sound is full of them," one fishermen hollered at me.

"I don't need to know how to catch pinks. I'm plugging my boat with sockeye. I can offer my support by not selling a single pink, but I refuse to quit harvesting reds."

I resigned from CAMA, left the meeting, and flew to my boat. I made everyone aware of the five-gallon bucket and salt that I flew out with me. I could layer filets with coarse salt in the bucket to preserve any pink salmon I might catch. My father loved salmon. He rinsed the salted pink fillets, added a shot of beet juice for a rich color, and sliced the salmon thin.

AT THE END of the previous season with the salmon moved to Anchorage, Peggy had gone back to writing independent stories. That winter she began to work for CAMA. Her co-op friends planned to fish, which made her job at CAMA difficult. The co-op members were the younger gillnetters who explored new ways of selling their salmon. The majority of the fishermen were staunch members of CAMA. In their opinion the co-op was destined to fail. They believed the traditional way they delivered their catch and received the contract price was the only way business worked. CAMA members thought fishing Coghill with the co-op buying sockeye should constitute breaking a strike; however, the situation didn't fit their old definitions. The relationships between the co-op members and the fishermen with traditional markets continued to deteriorate. The conflict tore families apart.

Tom and Willie were co-op members, but more important to them, they were seiners. Seiners made twice what they earned gillnetting. The previous years with the record returns of pinks, a seine season was worth three or four times a gillnet season. Willie and Tom stayed in town to strike for a price on pinks but supported the co-op gillnetters harvesting sockeye.

Monday morning, none of the traditional markets purchased salmon. The co-op provided a market and saved us again. Lack of a market didn't force us to sit on the beach and miss the harvest of a record sockeye return. The period began without many salmon. A few boats lined up at the marker for the opener, but the skippers disappeared when the first boat had a poor catch. The boats spread out across and down the fjord.

Red and I made a brief set the way the skippers set their nets when the boats lined up. None of the boats showed any interest in the point. We had the marker set to ourselves. We began to fish the point instead of the marker line. We drifted for about twenty minutes and then pulled in the net. A passing boat stopped and asked for a catch report. We had caught only half a dozen sockeye. He continued his run south.

The river runs hot and cold with salmon. People must possess patience if they want to fish at Coghill Point. Red and I loved to fish the area because of the scenery. We were familiar with the eagle nested in a treetop on the point. We understood the different currents that can turn a net in circles, and we were patient.

We set the net again and tried to perfect the set. Without other boats close by, we didn't worry about someone making the set on the marker line and corking us. We knew fishing was quiet everywhere by the lack of activity up and down the fjord. We set our net from the opposite side of the point and powered into the current, dropping the net overboard. The net drifted away from the lagoon toward the fjord. The current went slack. With the water quiet, our net inched in the opposite direction, toward the lagoon and the boundary marker. Without many salmon, we knew we could pull the net in minutes if it drifted too close to the marker line. The current pushed the cork line closer to the fishing closed marker.

We stood at the bow ready to pick the net when the current stopped, switched direction, and washed our net away from the marker. A school of sockeye swam out of the lagoon with the new current. At first the salmon struck close to the shore. They followed the cork line out, and the water exploded along the length of the net like a string of firecrackers. Our net swung around the point, drifted up the fjord and out of the sight of the other boats. We pulled the net and filled our fish holds halfway. We ran the boat back to the point. The sockeye poured out of the lagoon.

I called the tender to pick up our catch. We didn't want to alert the rest of the boats. "We are cold fishing alongside these icebergs. We need hot coffee, but we ran out of diesel for the stove," I said.

"We're at the pass headed in your direction," the skipper on the *Gandil* replied.

We watched the salmon hit our net. We had caught a boatload. An hour passed. We searched the southern horizon, but the tender was nowhere in sight. "We're desperate for some hot coffee, and we're freezing," I whined.

"Yeah, I'm headed north," the *Gandil* skipper assured me. "The skippers who ran from town are slowing me down. They need gas."

Red and I picked sockeye out of our net but wondered where we were going to store them. Both fish holds overflowed. The salmon began to cover the deck. We positioned the fish hold covers to block the pile of salmon from interfering with the operation of the reel.

A floatplane flew above us. We were sure the passengers represented CAMA. They saw a bird's-eye view of our deck-loaded boat. When the plane flew low and banked, Red extended her arms and displayed a sockeye. "They're all sockeye," she yelled.

The people inside the plane couldn't hear her, but we hoped they understood her message. If they snapped a picture, we hoped anyone viewing the enlargement would appreciate her message. We never saw any pictures of the deck-loaded semi-scabs in the CAMA window, but they did post a list of the boats. Most were co-op gillnetters, but the list included a handful of seiners who delivered their fish to private markets.

We searched the southern horizon for the *Gandil*. We laughed at our dilemma. With our fish holds full and salmon on the deck, the cabin door no longer opened. Half of our net remained in the water full of sockeye. I crawled through the window into the cabin, handed two cups and a thermos of coffee to Red, and climbed back out. After we sipped our coffee in the sun and laughed at our predicament, I reached through the window for the radio mike. Red and I knew the demand for gas overrode our need for stove oil. Our sob story was a low priority.

"When will you be here?" I pleaded. "I need you to unload my catch."

Within minutes other boats raced in around us like a swarm of bees and set their nets. James ran his boat toward us. When he ran past our short net, another school of sockeye hit. Red and I cringed. He thrilled at the sight. "You're loadin' up," he howled from his front deck.

"Set your net! Cork us! Catch the reds before any more hit our net," we begged him.

The *Gandil* steamed up the fjord. We set the half of our net on the reel back into the water. The tender pulled alongside and drifted near our net while we unloaded the salmon. We breathed easier when the level of the *Luna Sea* rose in the water. All that weight turned into money. By the time we delivered and cleaned the boat, our net had drifted into a sea of growlers. We looked farther up the fjord and saw the waterway full of ice.

We dodged icebergs and picked in a hurry the few fish from the half of the net we laid out to deliver. We picked the remaining net while we drifted into the slushy water. We pushed chunks of ice away and inched the net on board while we picked sockeye. With the net on board, we ran the boat down the shore, around the point to the lagoon. There we found the *Gandil* anchored. We delivered our catch, washed the boat, and dropped the anchor. The tide had changed, we had caught the buildup of sockeye, and we were exhausted. We knew the rest of the evening would be anticlimactic.

The co-op boats fished the week without competition from eighty percent of the gillnetters. The catch that week paid for my investment in the co-op. The following week, CAMA settled the pink and keta price, and the entire fleet fished. The canneries hated the co-op and increased the divide between fishermen with traditional markets and those in the co-op. Historically the canners agreed to a price contract and bought from every CAMA member. That year the processors decided to buy salmon from their *list* of preferred seine boats, not co-op boats. Some co-op members were unaware they were without a market for their seine catch. Tom, a founding co-op board member was one of them.

The *MJB* caught a boatload of salmon and pulled up to the closest tender with the crew psyched and ready to deliver their catch. They learned Tom lacked a market. He was in shock. He'd never experienced a problem selling his salmon. He called on the radio for another tender in the area. The radio remained silent. He couldn't believe his situation. He couldn't sell his catch, even after he stayed on the beach in support the strike with the other seiners until the processors signed the contract. Tom needed to sell his salmon while they were fresh, but he couldn't find a buyer. The volume of salmon the seiners caught was more than the co-op could handle, which made it useless for a market.

Tom became quite vocal when he wasn't happy. He knew wasting salmon was illegal. Unable to sell his catch he called the protection officers on the radio in desperation. He threatened to throw the load of salmon overboard. If the protection officer arrested Tom, the state would confiscate his salmon and sell them. The tenders wouldn't refuse salmon delivered by the protection officers. Tom could find a better solution after he unloaded his boat, but with a boatload, he had a limited amount of time to search for options. He was happy to give the salmon to the state instead of watching them rot. He screamed wild threats on the radio.

The protection officers found a tender skipper who agreed to buy his catch if he transported them across the Sound. Tom and Merrie traveled through the night. When they arrived the skipper at the tender told them the salmon were too old. They tossed pink salmon overboard like dollar bills while the *MJB* traveled across the Sound headed for town. The memory became one of the worst of Tom's fishing career.

Before he reached town, the entire fleet and the governor in Juneau heard news of Tom's radio rants and threats. Before the season, seiners claimed the predicted run of salmon exceeded the canners' capacity. The canners wanted to keep their supply exclusive and claimed they had plenty of capacity. When the canners refused to buy Tom's salmon, the governor signed an official order that allowed foreign processors to come into the Sound and buy salmon. Tom refueled and turned around. He knew he could sell his second load of salmon. A floating Korean processor waited to buy any seiner's catch.

Red and I sold salmon to the co-op, Chugach, North Pacific, and any buyer with a tender in the area. The processors weren't using a preferred fisherman list when buying from the gillnetters.

The following week, the sockeye catch dropped off. The sockeye were in the lake and the pink salmon were swimming up the fjord. We headed for town with a half bucket of salted pinks for my dad.

The beach gang pulled my boat at Chugach and moved it into a warehouse. Instead of fishing silvers, I winterized the *Luna Sea* and flew northwest to Bristol Bay. After Sewall closed the cannery in Egegik, we flew to Anchorage, picked up my car, and drove via Fairbanks and North Pole to Haines, where we caught the ferry south. We stopped in Bellingham and stayed with Kris and Jym for the night. In the morning we completed the trip to Seattle. I promised years earlier that I would never live in a big city. Funny what love changes.

That fall our first child, Sam, was born. Nights with an infant are tough. I thought sleep deprivation was extreme when I fished. Parents don't enjoy a closure to catch up on their slumber.

RELATIONSHIPS HAVE ROOTS and branches. Sewall decided our family needed roots. He traded six months in Seattle and six months in Alaska for twelve months at a job in Seattle. The change was beneficial.

The stress of preparing a cannery in remote Alaska had caused Sewall to eat Tums by the pound and wear a mouth guard at night.

Sam grew and changed daily. The Commercial Fisheries Entry Commission didn't consider breastfeeding a reason to miss the season and lease my permit to someone else. The thought of being away from Sam made me ache. My sister offered to care for Sam while I was in Alaska and Sewall was at work. I planned a schedule of short trips throughout the season. My first trip was in late April, after the herring boats departed for the Sound and before the gillnetters arrived. In that week I wanted to prepare the boat, complete any unexpected repairs, and then fly to Seattle and stay until the opener.

When the time came for my flight north, I felt worse than when I headed into gale force winds. I tried not to feel anything. I had seen families fish together on the Sound, and the experience seemed valuable for the children. I wanted to give that experience to Sam. My passion for Prince William Sound and my goal of fishing with Sam in the future held my focus.

When I arrived in Cordova I found Floyd and JD living at Tom's while they prepared for the halibut season. They had opened and warmed the trailer. JD came out and greeted me, "Well, didn't you time your trip right? This is the first break in the weather we've had in a month." JD knew how harsh the wind had blown and how much snow had fallen, because he and Floyd spent most of the month longline fishing for cod.

Tom was on the *MJB* harvesting kelp on the Sound. When the rules outlawed hooks for harvesting kelp, he skipped a few years, until he realized how much he missed witnessing the birth of spring in Prince William Sound. A determined man, Tom bought a hookah and dry suit before he learned how to dive. Cutting the kelp involved shallow water diving. He confirmed he could dive deep enough to harvest. He invited professional divers who kept him too busy on deck to dive, a relief to his friends.

After a successful year, the co-op bought Bayside, Fred Pettingill's cold storage plant and the Whitney Fidalgo property next door, with land to store boats and a building with two floors of lockers. Behind the

Whitney building stood a dock equipped with a hoist for the gillnetters to use. Bayside included a large dock for the tenders.

Over the next few days I prepared the boat. When she was ready and the tide was high, the beach gang jacked up my boat and slid a dolly under her. The thick wood timbers on the warehouse floor creaked when the heavy dolly rolled out of the warehouse and down the dock. Harold turned on the switch, lifted the straps cradling my boat, and lowered it into the water for what I didn't realize would be the last time. I climbed down the ladder, ran my boat to the harbor, and parked in my slip. After I loaded my net and some nonperishable food, the *Luna Sea* was ready, and I caught the plane to Seattle.

Tom called and reported, "When price negotiations began the processors cried, 'The fresh market is bad, and the canned market is worse.' They claimed the supply of pink salmon is plentiful around the state. Sales of canned salmon are down, and inventories are building. The price doesn't look good."

The price CAMA accepted for sockeye from the Copper stayed below a dollar, at ninety-five cents a pound. The kings were a dime more. The one positive thing about the contract was that the tension didn't build between the co-op and CAMA members because all of the gillnetters were going fishing on the season opener. Tom called me with the news, and I flew to Cordova in time to catch the tide to the Flats. The weather prediction called for moderate winds for the opener on Monday and a blow that night. I ran to Egg Island and intended to catch some salmon and slip into town before the wind blew a gale.

While I was anchored Sunday night the wind picked up. Monday the wind and water jerked my boat and me around wildly. The new forecast predicted the wind speed to come down that afternoon. I fished on the opener and through the first low water. Instead of the wind lessening, it blew harder. I threw my anchor and listened to the fishermen joke on the radio about the weather predictions. The skippers decided one of the weather stations must have malfunctioned to broadcast such inaccurate forecasts. The latest report called for variable fifteen knots by morning.

The high winds never diminished. In the morning I ran to town with two kings and sent them to my parents. After a shower I looked in the mirror and saw bruises covered my body. The abrupt movements of the boat had bounced and slammed my body around during the stormy weather. I hadn't noticed the impact at the time. I was too focused on my net, equipment, and location to notice. The bruises weren't serious or painful, just a reminder of the previous day and how much I hated to fish in stormy weather. I decided then that although I claimed to be a fisherman, when the wind blew a gale, I preferred to be a fisherlady, and the gulf in a gale was no place for a lady.

With one period that week, over the closure I began to move my belongings out of my locker at Orca to a double locker I shared with Tom in the co-op's Whitney building. The co-op properties met the processing and storage needs of the members. The office manager found an insurance company to write a fleet policy to insure our individual boats. The co-op members switched from cannery purchase orders to personal credit cards. To declare independence from the traditional processors, the co-op needed to buy and market all five species of salmon.

Our investment in a processing plant made production numbers critical. The expenses to process the first salmon through the production line cost a ton of money. The second salmon splits the fee to half a ton. For the co-op to pay a competitive price, the members needed to supply enough salmon to reduce the unit cost of processing. We were convinced the co-op could pay what the local processors paid. Our brief history strengthened the old suspicion that the processors robbed us.

On the weekend the co-op celebrated its success with a picnic called Eat Your Losses. With the boats moved out of the yard, we set up tables and barbecues. The employees thawed and cooked Fred Pettingill's inventory that he'd left in the plant freezers. The fishermen, plant workers, and people from the community enjoyed barbequed salmon, cod, and halibut. The sun shone and spirits were high.

Another low-pressure system moved in on Sunday. The wind blew hard enough for me to keep my boat tied to the dock. I despise the action of a storm. Before I had a child I was cautious about fishing in storms. Since Sam's birth I was borderline paranoid. With the abbreviated time to fish each week, I wished I could commute from Seattle. I would have heard the forecast and stayed home.

We fished thirty-six hours a week. The long closures were torturous because I ached for my family so far away. To ease the ache I stayed busy. I emptied my locker at Orca and moved my nets to the co-op. At the end of the third opener, I saved enough salmon for a home-pack and flew south. Sewall, Sam, and my sister Sue survived my time away. I enjoyed being with my family and the warmer weather. When I heard the catch reports, I knew I should be fishing, but the choice between sixty-hour periods on the Flats or time with my family was easy.

TWO DAYS BEFORE Coghill opened, I returned to Cordova with a couple wet-lock boxes loaded with fresh fruits and vegetables. I found one of my favorite co-op tendermen, Rick Johnson, who loved melons. I remembered to bring some vine-ripened ones for him. Jon Bosch, the new beach boss at the co-op, enjoyed the strawberries I brought for him. Those people make fishing possible when fishermen are desperate. A fishermen can never treat them too well.

I ran the boat to Coghill, but my catch was disappointing. On Wednesday I went to Unakwik. I hadn't fished at Unakwik for sockeye, but I enjoyed fishing there for pinks. I was glad I moved, because I caught three times the number of sockeye, but not enough to make me feel okay about being away from Sam.

The number of sockeye in Coghill Lake appeared right on target before the season. Yet the catch the first week was the worst for that week in ten years. Fish and Game cut our fishing time in half. When the catch and the escapement remained less than desired, we ran our boats to town. Closures because of lack of fish are hard but mandatory, because we know escapement is necessary for our future. The gillnetters spent a week in town before Fish and Game announced a short opener at Coghill. The catch was one of the lowest recorded for the district. Fish and Game closed the area for another week, and I caught the first plane south.

Tom called when the Coghill district opened to catch surplus pinks and keta. I flew to Cordova and ran my boat to Coghill. That night I drifted, enjoyed the quiet, and thought about waking that morning in Seattle and the dramatic difference between my two worlds.

Fish and Game opened a bay within the Eshamy District. The State of Alaska's new hatchery at the head of Main Bay provided a run of pink salmon. I ran south with about two dozen drift gillnetters for the opener. Thirteen set netters dotted the shoreline within the bay. Some set gillnetters acquired a Forest Service permit, which allowed them to construct a seasonal camp on the beach. With leased beach sites, the set netters' life looked quite romantic, a campsite in the wilderness with the job of picking an anchored net never far from home. I thought set gillnetting might be a better fishery for children, but if I traded a drift net for a set net, I would never see Coghill, my favorite scenery on earth. After the fishermen caught the buildup of pinks, most of us returned to Coghill where we harvested keta at twice the weight and price of pinks. In early August I ran the boat to town and caught the southbound plane.

BEFORE THE SEASON I planned a fourth trip for silvers, but I couldn't stand the thought of leaving Sam again. I was away from him for less than a month at a time, but the whole season I felt tortured. To fish silver season I needed a new net. I used that excuse to miss the season.

I stored my boat outside at the co-op yard, instead of inside the cannery warehouse. I hired Schultzy to pull my boat out of the water on his trailer. Howard, with his portable hoist, lifted my boat and set it on blocks. Tom's boat builder, Paul, built an A-frame I could reassemble each fall. Tom and I stretched a heavy tarp over the frame. With cans of spray paint we labeled the tarp "Luna Sea" in tall letters along the side. The silhouette of the tarped boat looked like a shark, with the dorsal fin at the high point of the frame. With cans of paint at our fingertips, we couldn't resist adding shark teeth at the bow.

I flew south on the next plane. The investment in a coho net would have paid off because half of the spring gillnet boats fished, and the season lasted until the end of September. I wasn't disappointed, because I knew the torture I avoided.

The co-op bought salmon spring, summer, and fall. The business future appeared promising for both production and marketing of salmon. Mike Bristol developed markets for our salmon domestically and in Europe. The CRFC tenders used a dedicated radio channel and cultivated a diverse group of gillnetters into a unit. The co-op replaced the security of the traditional processors with a new independent version. To celebrate the success, members organized a fishermen's ball. After a buffet dinner of seafood, RJ entertained the audience with humorous stories about the season. He passed out Sammy Salmon Awards "for conspicuous performance while engaged in questionable activities related to the fisheries" to people who experienced unusual events that season. Some incidents were milestones, a few heroics, but most an episode of embarrassment.

Without canning facilities and with a limited fresh and frozen market for pinks and keta, the co-op couldn't compete with the canneries. The volume the seiners harvested made dependence on the co-op to process their catch impossible. Tom searched for a market for his seine catch through the winter, while I paid off my numerous airplane fares.

Peggy quit her job at CAMA and moved to Seattle. She freelanced until she landed the job as associate editor for a seafood business magazine. I was excited to have her living close by, but my life changed with the birth of a child. Sam consumed me, and my other relationships suffered neglect. I considered not fishing for a season or two. The fixed expenses I incurred regardless of whether I fished or not made fishing necessary. I thought about selling the boat to avoid the insurance, storage, and maintenance and not fishing for a few years.

"If you sell out, you'll never be able to buy back in," the old-timers warned me.

CHAPTER EIGHTEEN

FISH AND GAME predicted strong salmon returns, and any thought I had of not fishing evaporated. Tom had been north for more than a month when I arrived in Cordova with web for a new net. At the co-op yard the fierce winter winds shredded most of the boat tarps; the wind ripped off others completely. The heavyweight tarp on the *Luna Sea* sat snug. Removing the tarp turned into a struggle because of its weight. I tied lines to the tarp and used Tom's truck to pull the tarp off.

Paul built the storage frame with notched lumber that fit on the hull and cabin. He connected the pieces with bolts, nuts, and washers, which made the frame easy to store in my locker each spring and reassemble in the fall. Before I dared loosen a single nut, I pulled out a wide felt marker and labeled every joint. When I reassembled the pieces after months in storage, I knew the frame would be a puzzle. I hauled the lumber to the locker and found a pile of boat equipment to carry back. After a dozen more trips I had my boat loaded.

When the lower unit and propeller were on, I called Schultzy and Howard. Howard's portable hoist lifted the *Luna Sea* onto one of Schultzy's boat trailers that he towed to the harbor and backed into the water. I backed the *Luna Sea* off the trailer and away from the shore. Floating on the water made my spirit sing. The air felt icy cold, too early in the season to think of endless hours in the breeze as desirable. The short ride in the harbor quenched a thirst I'd suffered all winter. I repaired the reel and hired Marcene, a local net specialist, to hang my new net.

Tide books dictate our schedules, but that year reading a tide book correctly demanded extra thought. The previous year, Congress allowed four of the five time zones in Alaska to switch to one. In October when Daylight Savings ended, Cordova changed to Alaska Standard Time without changing its clocks. Publishers print tide books more than a year in advance. From October 1983 through December 1984, the tide books for Central Alaska were off by an hour. We knew to add or subtract an hour. Whether to add or subtract to the tide book or the clock caught everyone by surprise at least once during the year.

The price for our spring kings and reds bounced back above a dollar. The tide forced the boats to run out for the season opener on Sunday afternoon. I ran to Pete Dahl and tied to a couple of boats. Kenny skippered one. I knew him from Morpac. Sue, new to the fleet, skippered the other. A woman added to the fleet was welcomed by me and over the years more single women joined the fleet.

After we shared a hot dinner, I prepared to drop my anchor for the night, my engine refused to start. I called the co-op office on my VHF radio. The beach boss, Jon, answered.

"Will you please send a starter out on the first available parts flight?" I begged.

I was thrilled Jon worked at the co-op. He was willing, energetic, and positive. Strawberries were a small investment for a favor on a Sunday night. The floatplane arrived, and I exchanged the starter before I went to sleep. I felt relieved because of the timing. If the starter had lived one more cycle, I would have discovered it broken minutes before the opener when my net caught more kings than I'd caught the previous year. The previous season the gillnetters harvested a record number of kings, but for me, the season was my worst. I knew being away from Sam wasn't going to be any easier, but I hoped I could keep my focus on fishing, and then maybe the season would be less painful.

Earlier in the year the navigational buoy marking Egg Island broke loose of its anchor in a storm. After mariners reported the light missing, the Coast Guard replaced it. On the season opener a few unlucky gillnetters destroyed their nets when they found the missing buoy on Egg Island down shore from the beached *Indian*. Until the pieces sanded over, the gillnetters avoided the light and the *Indian* when the nets drifted the outside beach of Egg Island.

After two weeks the Department of Fish and Game suspected a weak return and closed the Flats. The next week, the manager scheduled a thirty-six-hour opener on Sunday. A Sunday? No one remembered a fishing period that ever opened on a Sunday. When Tom heard the announcement, he convinced himself that with the long closure and the unusual call by the manager, the opener must be urgent. "We're going to load our boats," he said with a thrill.

Tom's friend Mack flew to town and crewed for a halibut trip. He planned to leave for Seattle on Sunday until he heard Tom rave about the opener. He convinced Mack an enormous number of fish must be available for Fish and Game to open fishing on a Sunday. Paul went fishing with Tom, and Mack, expecting to load the boat, joined me for the opener.

That season Tom gillnetted either the *Resin Detra* inside with a king net or the *MJB* outside in the gulf with a sockeye net and crew. On previous openers, he decided to fish for kings or reds and left the other boat in the harbor. Certain there was a buildup of kings or reds, he couldn't stand the thought of making the wrong choice. Unable to commit he ran the *MJB* towing the *Resin Detra* to Copper Sands. Paul stayed on the *MJB* anchored above the markers on the opener while Tom fished his skiff. Without many kings, he decided the surplus must be sockeye. He ran above the markers, anchored the *Resin Detra,* and drove away in the *MJB* with Paul in search of the big buildup of sockeye. Mack and I stayed behind Copper Sands. Monday we heard Tom was fishing inside Pete Dahl. The size of the *MJB* made fishing inside the bars difficult. We hoped the catch was too plentiful for him to waste time switching boats.

"Why a Sunday opener?" The fishermen questioned at the end of the period.

Everyone was disappointed and confused. The gillnetters expected such a large buildup of salmon that Fish and Game couldn't wait until Monday for us to fish. The gillnetters harvested fewer salmon than they had caught on either of the previous two openers. The loudest complainers about the Sunday opener were the Russians. Americans of Russian descent, the hardworking group practiced a traditional lifestyle and kept to themselves. They were part of a branch of Russians who traveled and searched the world for religious freedom. The group had moved to Red China, Hong Kong, and Brazil before they settled in Oregon and Alaska. The Russian gillnetters fished spacious stern pickers that many lived on with their families. They couldn't fish on Sunday for religious reasons. Fishing on Sundays had never been an issue. The Russians, along with the rest of the gillnetters, wondered what caused the urgency to schedule a Sunday opener. We sat in town for a ten-day closure and speculated why and remembered how much we missed the predictable Ralph Pirtle.

About the time everyone lost hope in the Copper River salmon, the fish began swimming past the counter in strong numbers. The manager opened fishing for twenty-four hours. I went to Egg Island and fished, but I ached to be with Sam. I had lost my focus on fishing. All I thought about, day and night, was an airplane that could transport me to Seattle. In the morning, I ran across the Hump, which made a flight that day possible. I had never fished inside Strawberry, so I watched for snags while the cork line drifted, ready to pick it up at a moment's notice.

A salmon wiggled the cork line. A sea lion cruised past my boat. He wasn't hungry, or he'd have eaten the salmon without me ever seeing him. He wanted some entertainment. He surfaced and rolled while he swam toward the salmon. I flipped on my hydraulic switch, raced the motor, and pulled the net out of the water at warp speed. I idled for a few minutes and waited for the fish thief to leave. He appeared to be gone when I put my net back into the water. The minute a salmon struck, he surfaced. We both raced for the salmon. When the net caught two salmon, we each picked one.

I didn't mind feeding him, but the damage he caused when he ripped the salmon from the web meant I would have to spend time on the dock for repairs. One time the sea lion pulled out a king and ripped a bite out of it while he hurled it into the air. He dove into the shallow water, recovered the fish, and flung it into the air again as he ripped loose another bite. His feast was entertaining and lasted until only crumbs for the birds remained. The troublesome sea lion was just the excuse I needed. I pulled my net and ran to the tender.

The *Harry B,* with Wally as skipper, was tendering at Whitshed. He quit gillnetting after he decided he liked bigger boats. He owned a fleet of vessels that spent much of the year fishing for halibut, cod, and crab, and summers tendering salmon for the processors. Wally's boats were the favorite tenders among the co-op members because the vessels were well equipped and large enough to accept deliveries in the ocean. Wally installed huge fenders on the sides of his tenders. The bumpers held the boats a safe distance apart and protected the sides. I pulled alongside and a crew member tossed me the tie-up line, more of a rubber strap, which lessened the yank when boats surged while tied side to side.

I delivered my salmon and ran to town while I had the tide. Late that afternoon I caught the plane south to see my family with a couple of boxes of fresh salmon, a few missing a bite or two from the sea lion. I enjoyed the days with my family soothing the ache that had festered for nearly a month.

WITH FRESH GROCERIES on board, I ran the *Luna Sea* across Prince William Sound, set my net in Port Wells, and turned off the engine. My surroundings felt magical. The motion of the boat gently rocking, the grand scenery, and the serenity quenched a thirst in my spirit. Life in the city meant quietness was impossible to find; I missed the tranquility I experienced fishing.

After a couple of weeks fishing at Coghill, I ran to Unakwik. Sewall and Sam were flying to Cordova to visit for a week. Fewer jellyfish plagued the water in Unakwik. Because I didn't know the weather in advance, the protected fjord made wind less threatening. I flew to town, and Saturday Sewall and Sam arrived.

"I found nowhere for a man to change a diaper. I had to improvise," Sewall said.

A floatplane flew us to the *Luna Sea* on Sunday, where we settled in with all of Sam's stuff. Boats stow weight low for stability. The cabin with the shelves at floor level and at Sam's chest height positioned his entire world at his fingertips. Sharing a limited space with his mom and dad, where he saw everything and accessed most anything, made Sam feel secure and relaxed. His Burt and Ernie Gas Station turned the front deck into his playroom when the net was out. At a year and a half, he loved life on the *Luna Sea*.

The fresh air and the gentle motion of the boat often rocked Sam to sleep. I had made a hammock for him and positioned it so that if he fell, he landed in the double-size bunk below. Every morning when he woke he was delighted to roll out of his hammock and dive-bomb us. Life felt perfect with Sam and Sewall on board.

Midweek, with the weather calm and the prediction favorable, I ran the boat south. I was more interested in showing Sewall the beauty of where I lived in the summer than in catching salmon. At the bottom of the fjord, the *Luna Sea* turned west and plied between islands, past gravel beaches and steep rock cliffs. Sewall commented on the trees near the shore. Gnarly and stripped of needles on the windward side, they grew despite exposure to the persistent wind. I ran the boat north to my favorite scenery on earth, south of Coghill Lagoon with a view up College Fjord. With my landing net we scooped chunks of glacier out of the water and enjoyed cocktails while the sun dropped behind the mountains. Noisy glacier ice cubes popped and rolled in our glasses and released air bubbles. Life was good. A couple of hours before we met our plane on Friday, I called the skipper of the *Dawn L* on the radio.

"We just arrived from town. We're busy buying salmon at the south end of the district," Tim reported.

Our plane would depart before he reached us. We picked large chunks of ice, broke them into smaller pieces, and packed them around our salmon. We anchored the boat in the passage where Tim and his crew member, Kyle, could transfer our catch at their convenience. Kyle kept the chunks of glacier and gave the slow-melting ice to gillnetters at the south end of the island for their coolers.

We flew to town and enjoyed the weekend Fourth of July celebrations. The Fish and Game manager predicted a plentiful harvest of pinks and observed them in higher than imagined numbers, earlier than expected. He opened the entire Sound for salmon seining July 2, but the majority of the seiners stayed on the beach, striking for a price on pinks and keta.

When Tom sat on the beach until the canneries signed CAMA's contract, the processors denied him a market. Throughout the winter he and other co-op seiners developed an independent market. They had a tender, a floating processor, and a freighter anchored, ready for the seine season to open.

Sunday afternoon Sewall and Sam caught the plane south, and I flew to my boat at the north end of the passage. I had caught more sockeye at Unakwik so I ran back for the Monday opener. While I fished I reminisced about the previous week, which made fishing painful without Sewall and Sam on board. I fantasized about how much we would enjoy fishing together when Sam was older.

Minutes before the opener, I saw a productive set, but without the boat that usually set there. I grabbed the opportunity and slapped out my net at seven o'clock sharp. After ten minutes the boat that homesteaded that point drove his boat over to his set. He couldn't believe his eyes. He must have run his boat from town and miscalculated the time or experienced boat trouble that delayed him. He wasn't happy to see me on *his* set. He cruised alongside my boat and demanded, "Pick up your net."

"No."

"I'm going to tow your net out of my way if you don't pick up."

"It's illegal for you to touch my net."

"Then I'll tow your boat," he threatened.

I told him to go bother the boat on the other point, which a good-sized karate expert skippered. I wasn't going to budge. The homesteading skipper, known as one of the bad boys according to the stories I had heard made me feel a bit intimidated. While he went on with his threats, I considered his possible actions. He had to tie onto my boat to tow it. I'd untie the line. I then thought of how he could lasso a cleat and put his boat in gear, making the loop impossible to unfasten. I'd cut the line. When those thoughts rushed through my mind, I walked into my cabin and picked up my radio mic. I stood at my cabin door and pretended to call a Fish and Game protection officer. "Fish and Game Protection, this is the *Luna Sea*."

Long pause.

"Fish and Game Protection, this is the *Luna Sea*."

Pause.

"Yes, officer, I wanted to ask about someone threatening to move my net."

Pause.

"Yes, he is threatening me now."

Pause.

"We're at the north end of Unakwik on the east side."

Pause.

"No, only threats."

Pause.

"Yeah, I'd go for that. Thanks. *Luna Sea* out."

I made sure the other skipper could hear me talk. He of course didn't hear the officer. I think he considered I might have a better radio with a farther range. He must not have wanted to take a chance, because he left me alone.

The sockeye run remained strong later in the season than usual. The Cannery Creek hatchery supplemented our late sockeye run with keta and pinks. I fished another two weeks before I ran to Coghill in search of more salmon. Not finding enough to pacify the ache I had for Sam, I ran the boat to town and flew south for a week.

I RETURNED AND joined the gillnetters fishing in the Eshamy District. On the opener a hundred drift gillnet boats fished, five times more than when Red and I had first fished there. The area seemed unfamiliar with the large crowd. The hatchery transformed the catch into an unfamiliar fishery. We were there to catch wild sockeye, but the dominant catch consisted of pink and keta from the Main Bay Hatchery.

Toward the end of the Eshamy season while setting my net the shifter cable broke. I was glad it broke while the transmission was in neutral because to reach the shifter at the rear of the engine, under the bunk was a challenge. It was the end of the week, I was tired, and felt defeated. I picked up my net, reached under the bunk, shifted my boat into forward gear and ran it into town. When I neared the boat harbor I reached to the stern and shifted the transmission out of gear. My boat coasted to the dock.

In my harbor slip I replaced the cable. Tom flew to town for parts and found me on my boat. He helped me load my coho net onto my reel while he bragged about another tremendous seine season. In spite of the strong catch, the streams overflowed. Fish and Game reported exceptional pink salmon escapement around the Sound.

The dry and sunny summer that year was also exceptional. The creeks began to dry up. The water temperatures began to rise. The heat caused the oxygen levels to fall. Salmon began dying before they spawned. The stream conditions threatened to destroy the strong run of salmon. Before the sunny weather caused a disaster, the rain returned and reversed the situation. When the rain began, the seiners quit fishing.

Tom switched to gillnetting and suggested we run to Pete Dahl. I agreed until I heard the new forecast. The prediction called for a strong northerly wind. I expressed my reservations to him.

"It might blow down the Copper, but we don't intend to travel that far. The mountains to the north will protect us," he reassured me.

Tom was correct. I had never experienced a bad northerly wind on the Flats. I never fished at Kokenhenik. There, the gillnetters look up the mouth of the river rushing south between the mountains to the gulf.

I anchored in Pete Dahl Slough. Tom ran fifteen minutes farther to King Salmon Slough. We were on the fishing grounds ready to fish the morning opener with time to relax. I lit the oil stove and crawled into my bunk with a book about child development. When the stove warmed the cabin and the oven, I prepared dinner.

The conversations on the radio were about the wind and the wild seas. A brisk wind blew where I anchored, but farther east outside Kokenhenik the wind howled down the Copper. Hearing reports on the radio, I was glad my boat was up the slough on the anchor. The fall wind has more chill, and when it blew from the north, the chill felt extreme.

After I ate dinner, the skipper of the *Silver Load*, Dan Lowell, came on the radio with urgency in his voice. He'd pulled Stanley, skipper of the *Five O,* from the water.

Dan expressed concern about Stanley surviving until the weather allowed a plane to fly him to the hospital. Stanley's boat and crew member, Bruce Coventry were nowhere in sight. "I saw an orange blob, right before I nearly ran over Stanley. He is weak and shivering. I dressed him in dry clothes and wrapped him in a sleeping bag." Boats in the area helped with the search.

A mariner called the Coast Guard and reported an overturned black hull drifting east of where Dan had pulled Stanley from the water. The Coast Guard radioed for mariners to watch for the semi-submerged hull. The *Five O* was similar to Bean's *Equinox* with the steering station in the stern of the cabin. Stanley's son saw the beating his father experienced and had given him a flotation suit. That suit was the reason he'd floated and survived.

Stanley told how a monstrous wave smashed the side of the *Five-O*. He looked back and saw another wave even more massive. He hollered to Bruce, and both men hit the deck. The wave thundered down on the *Five-O* and killed both engines. The violent wave launched both men fifty yards from the boat and forty feet from each other. They tried to swim to the boat, but after Stanley swallowed gallons of salt water, he gave up. He watched the *Five O* float away. He caught a glimpse of Bruce when he disappeared under the surface. While Stanley floated alone in the ocean, he worried he'd never survive. He knew Bruce was dead, and then the *Silver Load* nearly ran over him.

The Coast Guard helicopter and the boats searched the empty waters until dark. A tender, the *Dalmatia,* found the *Five-O* and towed it farther east to an anchorage protected by the Martin Islands. At first light the search for Bruce resumed.

Thirty-year-old Bruce Coventry had flown to Cordova from Bellingham and seined earlier in the summer. That trip was his first to the delta. I wondered if Bruce was as naïve as I had been on my first trip to the Flats. The search continued but his body was never recovered, which must have made the loss hard for his family in Washington to believe.

CHAPTER NINETEEN

SILVER SEASON OPENED with one hundred and fifty fewer boats fishing. The schoolteacher fishermen were in school and the Puget Sound boats had gone south to fish. The channel looked as though the other four hundred gillnetters opened at Pete Dahl. Nets flew into the water. Boats crowded each other. The skippers set their nets across one of the five different channels, which ran from inside the bar to the grass banks. A few gillnetters homesteaded those channels, but for the opener, other boats invaded. Everyone was extra competitive because of the crowd.

I waited in line at the marker, but at the last of the ebb and my turn, another skipper raced over and set his net. People around me were as outraged as I was. They encouraged me to cork him. Some conflicts make me fight to the end but setting so close to the marker and his net made me think of the threat or possibility of catching a net, his or mine, in my propellor. Instead I left when the water was deep enough. The space in my channel behind Copper Sands had less salmon but fewer boats to compete with, which was more desirable to me. The gillnetters fished for silvers for eight weeks. I fished more than the previous year, but called an early end to my season and flew home for the winter.

ARMIN WORKED ON his plans for the hatchery at the south end of Esther Island. When the fishermen, processors, and community volunteers transformed the San Juan cannery into a hatchery, Armin had arranged financing backed by the CAMA voluntary assessment of two cents per fish. For the new hatchery the state required the fishermen commit two percent of their gross salmon income to guarantee the loan. During the winter, PWSAC held meetings in communities around Alaska, in Seattle, and in Bellingham to promote an aquaculture tax to guarantee a loan for the new hatchery. "It will be the largest hatchery in the world. We can raise all five species of Pacific Salmon. The fishermen can fish in the district the entire season," Armin claimed.

I loved the idea of fishing all season on the Sound and helped spread the word about the meetings with numerous phone calls to people I knew and total strangers.

When Armin sold the idea of aquaculture, nearly the entire seine fleet also gillnetted. The gillnetters who didn't own a seine permit usually crewed for the seine season. In the decade since Armin peddled his aquaculture idea the fishermen had changed. Fewer than half of the seiners also gillnetted. A fourth of the gillnetters held a personal stake in seining. The fishermen and their common economic interest in Area E changed from a group of salmon fishermen into two distinct groups based on harvest methods: gillnetters and seiners. Armin was determined to sell the idea of a mandatory assessment to the fishermen. He didn't care whether a person gillnetted or seined, he had something in his plan for everyone.

PWSAC hired boats to harvest salmon that returned to the San Juan hatchery. The hatchery used some of those fish for brood stock, eggs to fill the incubators for the next generation. PWSAC sold the additional salmon to cover the hatchery budget. The seiners harvested the surplus, which contributed about five million dollars of pinks and some keta to the seiners each year. The seiners also harvested pink and keta salmon from the state hatchery in Unakwik Inlet. The *Mocha Java* and *Luna Sea* caught a few of those salmon too. The previous couple of years both drift and set gillnetters harvested salmon from the hatchery at Main Bay.

Armin predicted, "In ten years Esther hatchery will contribute ten million dollars of keta and coho and an additional five million in pink salmon."

The fishermen experienced Armin's promises in their pockets. The proven benefit of hatcheries made his proposed assessment seem like an investment instead of a tax. I was delighted when the fishermen voted to support the mandatory assessment, secure the loan, and build a world-class hatchery on Esther Island.

SEWALL AND I found out we were expecting our second child before I went north. Sewall was less anxious, having seen my cautious fishing routine and didn't insist I take a crew member. I'd spent the winter with Sam attending swim lessons and co-op preschool.

Preparing to go back to Alaska, I heard from shocked mothers. "How can you intentionally leave your child?"

I felt shamed by their reactions. My dreams of a future with Sam and the new baby spending summers in Alaska and fishing with me made staying home impossible. I knew what I wanted for my family, and I had solid support from them. Swimming lessons had ended, and my mother would continue with preschool. Sam gave her purpose and meaning, since my father had recently passed away.

THE CALENDAR TOLD us the month was May when I arrived, but snow covered the ground. Fresh flakes covered the boats in the co-op yard, and deep snow accumulated around them. Before I called Schultzy and Howard, to lift and haul the *Luna Sea* to the harbor I needed to dig the snow around the boat to reach it with the trailer and truck.

The old-timers laughed when I whined about the snow I had to shovel. They recalled a spring when the snow had been many feet deep. One old-timer told me, "People had to remember where they had parked, or they dug out the wrong boat."

Chapter Nineteen

The new harbor was a hot topic. Cordova doubled the number of boat slips. More of the skippers could lease a boat slip and enjoy a safe moorage. That winter Schultzy had built a boat trailer for the *Luna Sea*. He named it the Luna Lander. I hired Howard to lift my boat for the last time, while Schultzy backed the Luna Lander under her hull.

Fish and Game announced the season opener for Monday, May 13, the earliest date most of us had ever fished. Snow fell during the opener. The sight of a white beach, which normally meant breakers, startled me and had me doing numerous double takes. Fishing with snow falling didn't seem possible, but slick, icy decks made me aware of the reality.

I had heard from old-timers that years earlier, when they fished on May 1, they caught an early run of kings. The first period convinced me the tale was true. We caught the tail end of that legendary run.

Another period, I fished in Pete Dahl Channel. Larry, an old-timer who homesteaded Pete Dahl, passed me in his skiff and pointed at Mount St. Elias. The sky was clear in every direction to the horizon, and Mount St. Elias stood proud. Surrounded by blue sky, a halo cloud hung around the peak. I didn't see the cape often, and that day was the first time I saw the mountain with that halo-cloud formation.

At low water the wind was still. I had a tough time deciding from which end of my net I should pick. Within ten minutes the wind blew forty knots from the southeast. I struggled to pull my net while I maneuvered my boat to stay off a sandbar. I pulled the end of my net, put the boat into gear, powered away from the beach, and ran up the slough. There I saw Larry and half a dozen boats that fled to the anchorage ahead of me. When enough water allowed us to travel, we were headed to town. While I waited, I thought about the cloud around Mount St. Elias. Was Larry teaching me something when he'd pointed to the peak? Maybe he meant to alert me, thinking I knew what that cloud meant. I laughed at my interpretation, because at the time I thought the beauty of the scene impressed him.

After fishing another two and a half weeks, the torture I felt being away from Sam exceeded my limit, I hand delivered a home-pack to my family.

MY SCHEDULED WEEK in Seattle lasted two weeks. I ran the *Luna Sea* to Coghill. Twelve different buyers competed to buy salmon from about one-hundred-fifty boats. The price went up to a dollar fifty for reds. I moved the boat to Unakwik at the end of June because of the sheltered waters and lack of jellyfish there. Sewall and Sam were flying to Cordova for a week. Sam was more active at two and a half years old, so fewer jellies was important.

They arrived on Saturday. We prepared for bed that night and made a bed for Sam next to mine at Tom's trailer. I applied almond oil on my pregnant stomach.

Sam gently tapped and then caressed my belly. "Hi baby, it's Sam, your brother."

I loved Sam's interest and excitement about having a brother or sister. Life was satisfying with my family beside me. We fell asleep with me dreaming about fishing the week with them.

IN THE MORNING having coffee Tom said, "Jesse and I are going to Unakwik to gillnet for the week before we switch nets and go seining. We can haul you, your family, and Sam's load of supplies.".

The weather was perfect for a daylong cruise across the Sound. We brought additional food and prepared a couple of meals during our trip. People on workboats miss meals or choke them down in a rush. Most of the time food on a workboat is cold or burnt. When the crew has time to eat on a workboat, meals become a celebration. Traveling across the Sound with Tom, Jesse, Sewall, and Sam gave me reason to celebrate. When we arrived at Unakwik, we boarded my boat and left more than half of our supplies for Sam aboard the spacious *MJB*.

In the morning my net loaded up with pop weed kelp that drifted out of the bays. Sam delighted in pushing the clumps of kelp through the scuppers and watching them float away. He loved when we caught salmon and often looked at them in the fish hold. One afternoon we delivered our catch while Sam napped. When he woke he checked the fish hold, found it empty, and became frantic.

"We sold the salmon to the tender," Sewall explained.

Sam wasn't satisfied with his explanation. I told him we have to sell the fish for money. I handed him a pack of gum that I had hidden before he arrived. "The tender gave us gum for you. The captain traded the gum for the salmon."

He looked at the gum and thought for a moment. He agreed the trade was acceptable and a smile returned to his face. The next time we delivered to the tender *Harry B.* I introduced Wally to my crew and slipped him a pack of gum with my permit card. When he brought my fish ticket, he presented the pack of gum to Sam and thanked him for the salmon. The concept delighted Sam. He wanted to catch more fish.

The evening of the fourth of July Tom and Jesse went to the beach and built a fire. The island was perfect with a sloped gravel beach too small for bears and exposed to the breeze, which kept the bugs away. We anchored the boat near the island. Jesse, eleven years old, drove out to the *Luna Sea* in his inflatable skiff and taxied us to the shore. We lit fireworks and sparklers while we ate hotdogs and s'mores. Sam reacted to the burning sparklers with silent wide-eyed amazement interrupted by bursts of excited squeals.

An evening on the beach was uncommon. We shared food, friendship, fireworks, and the ability to stretch our legs and walk. After the celebration we stayed anchored for the night. Early in the morning we unloaded the supplies Tom had stored for us. The *MJB* departed for Cordova.

We delivered our fish to a tender on Friday night, anchored the boat, and while we waited for our plane, we cleaned the boat. Sam ran out of pop weed to push through the scuppers. He became bored and without my knowledge carried things out of the cabin, dropped them through the scupper, and watched them float or sink.

I finally saw what he was doing. "Oops! There goes the sunscreen. No, it floats. Only weeds and sticks go out the scuppers," I explained. "For the float-or -sink game, you can drop things in this five-gallon bucket."

Sewall scrambled to recover the things that floated. I valued the magic of Sam's fascination, but I needed those things. The bucket stood chest high for Sam with plenty of depth for things to sink. He played the game until the plane arrived. He thrilled at the flight.

We enjoyed the weekend in town together. On Sunday Sewall and Sam flew home and I flew back to a cold, vacant boat. I had emptied it of any nonessentials to accommodate Sam's extra stuff, and without it, the cabin was hollow. Noise echoed. I was miserable.

On Thursday I delivered my catch to the *Dawn L.* I shed my wet boots and raingear, sat at the helm with a cup of coffee, pushed the throttle forward, and began the run to Coghill. An island jutted out from the western shore at the bottom of the inlet. The chart showed a submerged rock on the outside of the island marked "PA," which means "position approximate." The marked location gives no reassurance to mariners. I stepped out to the forward steering station and navigated the rocky passage on the inside shore. I slowed the boat and focused on the water under my bow and searched for kelp, mussels, or barnacles, which signaled rocks. Once I was through the passage, the shore widened, and Prince William Sound stretched out before me.

Once I moved away from the glaciers, the air lost its chill. I stayed on the front deck, leaned on the throttle, and ran west another few miles. Music blared from my deck speakers. The *Luna Sea* traveled an hour without another boat in sight, but when I arrived at Coghill, a crowd of gillnet boats marked the boundary line.

Above the music from my deck speakers, I heard the shrill of my smoke alarm. I whipped around for a glance at the cabin. Thick smoke billowed out the door and windows. Fiberglass boats can burn in a heartbeat. I veered toward the closest boat in case I needed to abandon ship. My alarm wailed. The skipper on the other boat burst out of his cabin, and I caught his attention. I wasn't going to die. If I jumped into the icy water, he'd pull me out. I extended my trembling hand inside the cabin. The tips of my fingers reached and turned the key. The engine shutdown.

Schultzy on the *Hypnotic*, rushed alongside, threw his bow line around my bow cleat, and leaped on board. "What did you do?"

When the smoke cleared we found no flames, but the unmistakable stench of burnt rubber permeated the cabin. I pulled off the engine cover and Schultzy climbed in next to the engine.

He pulled out a spark plug. "Oh, yeah, you've got a problem. The cylinders are full of salt water."

The water intake had sucked in some weeds or a jellyfish that plugged the cooling system. I couldn't read my gauges at the helm from the front station, and with the stereo speakers blaring, I didn't hear the engine alarm. The engine became so hot that it burned the rubber exhaust flaps. When I shut off the engine without the flaps, the engine sucked salt water through the exhaust into the cylinders. The *Luna Sea* was dead in the water.

"You need a tow to town. The *Alliance* is going in tonight. How about if I tow you over there?"

Schultzy towed the *Luna Sea* to the *Alliance,* a sixty-three-foot boat in Wally's tender fleet. Greg, the skipper, agreed to tie my boat behind the *Bella Donna,* another broken-down gillnet boat the *Alliance* already had in tow. The *Luna Sea* would arrive at the outboard shop in the morning. I might return to fishing with the engine repaired by afternoon.

CHAPTER TWENTY

LATE IN THE evening we were underway headed east. The *Alliance* planned to meet and resupply the *Dawn L* with gasoline and groceries about an hour into the trip. The *Dawn L* would stay, buy more salmon, and supply the fishing boats while the *Alliance* delivered the salmon in town. I stood at the stern of the *Alliance* and watched the *Bella Donna* and the *Luna Sea* in tow. The wind had been calm for the previous few days and the surface of the water was flat. The sun settled beyond the mountains behind us. The silhouettes of the boats disappeared when the islands cut off more of my view.

The tenders met and their deck lights lit the dark sky. I helped the crew tie the boats together. When the lines were secure, Greg shifted the *Alliance* into gear and resumed his course to town. Chris, the *Alliance* crew member, passed the gasoline nozzle to Tim, skipper of the *Dawn L*. He stuck the nozzle into the red five-hundred-gallon auxiliary gas tank chained to the back deck. The crews passed boxes of food from the freezer and more boxes from the back deck. I knew the crew was in a hurry, and I intended to help them transfer supplies, but when I stood back to let Chris pass, my belly, more than six months pregnant, hung out so far that standing back didn't help. I turned sideways. The crew had a well-practiced routine. I was in their way. I walked around the stern of the *Alliance* into the galley.

Patti, the skipper of the *Bella Donna,* and Janet, her crew member, were cooking tacos. I was about to offer food from my boat but remembered the *Alliance* was in gear, and my boat trailed behind on the end of a taut towline, impossible for me to reach. I sat at the galley table, picked up a magazine, and settled in for the all-night ride to town.

A brilliant flash filled the open galley door, followed by a deafening concussion. I leapt to my feet. The three of us in the galley stood momentarily paralyzed and speechless, looking at each other with wide eyes. We heard glass break in the wheelhouse above us and crashing noises on the front deck. We ran out the rear door. Flames engulfed the port stern quarter and lit the darkness. We rounded the cabin on the starboard side to escape the intense heat and rushed toward the bow. A ball of flames ran to the side and jumped overboard. Was that the captain?

The raging fire also consumed the stern of the *Dawn L,* where gasoline continued to pump. Half a dozen fifty-five-gallon drums surrounded the fuel tank. Empty of gas but full of vapors, the drums exploded, catapulted, and landed on the front deck of the *Alliance.* With no emergency equipment in sight, Patti and I spotted a six-foot rubber bumper that hung along the side of the boat. We began to untie the lines that secured it to the *Alliance.* The fender would float high, and I hoped the florescent pink color would be easy for rescuers to spot.

"I'll find the radio and call a Mayday," Janet yelled as she ran toward the wheelhouse.

Another explosion shook the boat. Patti and I climbed over the side rails, still untying the bumper. Janet ran from the wheelhouse and joined us outside the rail. Our best chance of survival in those frigid waters was if we stayed with the burning vessels. The fire would draw rescue boats. The moment we had the lines unfastened, I wound one of them attached to the fender around the rail of the *Alliance.* Another thunderous blast rocked the boat. Without a word Patti, Janet, and I held onto the bumper and dropped into the water. I kept a grip on the line that tethered the fender to the rail of the boat. The *Alliance,* with the autopilot engaged, idled across Prince William Sound at about three knots and dragged the three of us alongside, clutched to the fender.

"The propeller is trying to pull my legs under," Patti shouted.

The massive *Alliance* propeller sucked in the water and everything else from around the hull, including us. I pulled my legs up, because a fetal position is best to prevent hypothermia, and I feared the propeller's suction. The smoke thickened. In the still air the motion of the *Alliance* wasn't enough to keep us clear of the smoke. I feared it might be toxic to my baby. I buried my face in the shirt that covered Janet's shoulder and filtered the air I breathed.

Another explosion, and burning embers rained down on us. I knew that staying with the boat was the first rule of ocean survival, but I didn't want to burn. Flaming debris showered down on me. I tightened my grip on the line that held us alongside the *Alliance* and tipped my head backwards into the water. Better cold than burned.

An even larger explosion rolled a carpet of flames across the dark expanse in front of us. The water was on fire. If we continued to hang alongside, the *Alliance* would drag us through the flames. Against all conventional wisdom, I released my grip.

EARLIER THAT EVENING prepared for the morning seine opener, Mike anchored the *New St. Joseph* in a bay south of Unakwik and retired for the night.

His visiting brother-in-law enjoyed the quiet evening on deck. He went into the cabin, brushed his teeth, and headed for his bunk, when something led him back out on deck. He stepped out of the cabin and saw a fireball that hadn't been burning minutes earlier. "Fire!" he yelled to Mike.

The crew sprang from their bunks, and Mike started the engines. With the anchor pulled, he set a course toward the flames while he continued to dress. Mike had installed a new engine in the *New St. Joseph* and maintained low and varied speeds for the break in. The urgency he felt at the sight of the distant fire made him disregard caution for his equipment. The *New St. Joseph* steamed toward the fireball under full power. Mike called the Coast Guard to find out whether anyone had made a distress call. Other boats tuned in to receive information about the red-orange ball on the clear night horizon. He described the location to the Coast Guard when the fireball broke in two. One remained stationary, while the other proceeded on a southeasterly path. Neither burned less brightly.

In the distance, but in front of the two fires, Mike saw lights move up and down in the water. The *New St. Joseph* came alongside the lights, which turned out to be strips of reflective tape on a survival suit. The crew pulled a man on board and found him seriously burned. The survivor was in shock and unable to talk. He suffered with burns on his hands, neck, head, and back. Mike didn't recognize the man but saw *Luna Sea* written across the back of the survival suit. Mike and his crew searched the dark horizon for the *Luna Sea*. When the crew spotted her, Mike ran alongside and fastened a line. On board he found Tim and Kyle from the *Dawn L*.

"We recovered one person in a survival suit," Mike told them. "He's below with multiple burns on his body."

"He's Greg, skipper of the *Alliance*. The *Alliance* and the *Dawn L* caught fire while the boats transferred gasoline," Kyle said. "The *Bella Donna* and *Luna Sea* were in tow behind the *Alliance*."

"The power of the blast threw me into the air," Tim told Mike. "I stood at the stern of the *Dawn L* at the time of the initial explosion but landed in the water, way clear of the boat."

"I heard the explosion when I opened the chest freezer on the flying bridge," Kyle said. "The lid protected me from the blast. When I shut the freezer, I saw the entire stern of the *Dawn L* engulfed in flames. I jumped into the water with Tim."

"We saw Greg climb onto the *Luna Sea* and cut her loose," Tim said. "We knew if we made our way onto the *Luna Sea*, we'd be safe."

The lines that held the *Dawn L* to the *Alliance* melted. The boats separated. The *Alliance*, on auto pilot, motored into the Sound. The blazing *Dawn L* drifted into the *Luna Sea*.

"The intense heat of the burning vessel must have tortured Greg's burnt skin," Kyle said. "We watched him wrap his arm around a survival suit and jump overboard."

Greg hadn't seen Tim and Kyle struggle in the dark water. The hulls of the *Dawn L*. and the *Luna Sea* were dissimilar in both length and depth, which caused them to drift differently. Kyle and Tim watched the boats drift apart, and they swam toward the *Luna Sea*. When Tim reached the boat he untied a buoy and helped Kyle. They climbed on board and changed into dry clothes. They were cold but in good condition.

They told their story, and Mike relayed information on the radio to the Coast Guard while he ran his boat to the *Bella Donna* in search of survivors. The *New St. Joseph* pulled alongside and secured a line. Mike found Patti and Janet on the front deck searching the water for Greg. He found me in the cabin helping Chris change into dry clothes.

When I saw Mike's familiar face, an overwhelming sense of relief filled my body. The threat of dying ended. We were safe. I had known Mike for years and respected him and his skills as a mariner.

Mike felt relieved to find the skipper of the *Luna Sea,* the first boat he'd identified from the survival suit. He was full of questions. Mike thought he was searching for three people. When he found four, he drilled us about who was on which boat and the boats involved. Mike wanted to ensure people searched until they rescued everyone.

Chris, Janet, and Patti followed Mike on board the *New St. Joe*. I sat at the helm of the *Bella Donna,* paralyzed from the experience.

Mike returned and insisted I come drink some hot chocolate or tea and warm up in his galley. I feared the initial explosion had killed Kyle and Tim. When I walked in the cabin and saw them huddled in sleeping bags around the galley table, I was thrilled.

"You're alive! I thought you were dead," the three of us screamed in unison.

Kyle said, "We climbed onto the *Luna Sea* and felt terrible when we changed into your clothes, because minutes before the fire, you were at the stern. We hadn't seen you leave and concluded you died in the explosion. When the others entered the galley, it seemed to confirm our fear."

A smile brightened Tim's face when he stood and dropped the sleeping bag warming him to the floor so we could see what he was wearing. "What do you think?"

We erupted in loud laughter. We were happy to be alive. Laughter came easy, but the sight of Tim, the skipper of the *Dawn L,* dressed in maternity clothes pushed us into hysterics.

Patti explained how we might have died, but when the flames burned in the water and we cut loose of the *Alliance,* Chris stumbled out of nowhere. "He hoisted himself hand-over-hand on the towline to the *Bella Donna* and cut it loose," Patti said.

Patti had bellowed orders to Chris, like a drill sergeant, "Lower the outdrives, start the engines." Alarms blared, but she told him, to ignore the alarms. "Cut the *Luna Sea* loose."

Chris said, "It's not there."

My boat was missing, but the fact was insignificant. Chris steered the *Bella Donna* toward us. We recognized he'd never operated a small fast boat and feared he might run over us. Patti signaled him to stop. "Shutdown the engines. We're close enough. We'll swim to you."

We hung onto the fender and swam alongside the *Bella Donna.* Patti extended her arms, and Chris lifted her straight up out of the water. Janet and I swam to the back of the boat and used the lower unit to climb onto the boat. Once on the *Bella Donna,* I changed into Patti's dry clothes. My body was larger than Patti's and being pregnant made her petite clothes a bad joke.

Chris was below with Greg, receiving medical attention. When I helped Chris into dry clothes, he told me a metal fifty-five-gallon drum had struck him in the original explosion. In flames he'd lowered himself between the two boats to extinguish his clothes. He cut one of the lines that held the tenders together and emptied a fire extinguisher on the fire, but it had no impact. He went to the other rail and found us alongside. Chris told me he might have a broken hip. With the pain in his hip and the burns on his skin, he impressed me with how well he'd followed Patti's commands.

Troy, an EMT-trained gillnetter, saw the blast, cut loose of his net, and sped to the scene with his emergency bag. The *Dawnbreaker,* the *Cory Ann,* the *Seabrook,* and other boats in transit altered their course when the ball of fire erupted. Boats with EMTs arrived on the scene and offered assistance. Having medically trained people assist was a relief, because Greg's burns were severe.

The autopilot guided the *Alliance* with golden flames into the middle of the Sound. The other boats gathered at the *New St. Joe.* The *Dawn L* continued to drift, her fiberglass hull burning. Resources weren't available to fight either fire, so the concern focused on the safety of the seven survivors. We heard a Coast Guard helicopter would fly out and transport the injured people to the hospital. Greg and Chris needed medical attention. The crew thought the injured should include me, because of my pregnancy.

The Coast Guard evacuates people by hoisting them in a basket into a helicopter while it hovers above. That journey sounded worse than riding in a boat lifted by a hoist. The passenger must wear a life jacket in the basket. People might land in the water before they see the inside of the helicopter. I could live without that thrill. Word came that the helicopter could transport three survivors. I persuaded Mike that I felt fine and that Janet, because of smoke inhalation, should be the third person.

Mike went on deck and told the crews of the boats tied alongside to prepare their decks for the helicopter. "Batten down for eighty-knot winds."

The crew gathered life jackets for the three injured people to wear in the basket. The Coast Guard requested that the *New St. Joseph* transfer the injured to the *Seabrook* because of the size of its back deck. Both Greg and Chris suffered burns, but we worried more about Greg when the Coast Guard hoisted him away.

Mike offered to anchor my boat and tow it to town on his next trip in and suggested I fly to town with Patti, Kyle, and Tim. I accepted the offer. I only wanted to feel warm. Mike's brother-in-law lent us pairs of thick wool socks. We huddled around the galley table of the *New St Joseph* wrapped in sleeping bags and sipped hot chocolate. We tried to lose the chill we felt deep in our bodies.

We talked as only people who have shared a trauma together can. The shock and relief forced us into an unusual state of mind. We talked frankly about life and death. The puzzled and surprised faces of the *New St. Joe* crew told us we weren't acting normal. We understood they might be shocked, but we found stopping impossible. Our words relieved our stress, while we tried to make sense of what happened.

A floatplane left Cordova at first light. The four of us babbled about our experience until the plane landed at the *New St. Joseph* and flew us to town.

The *Dawn L* burned to the waterline and sank. When the plane flew past the *Alliance,* we watched it continue to burn. The fire burned hot enough to melt the aluminum doors. When the floatplane landed on the lake in town, Wally waited for us on the dock. He drilled us with plenty of questions. His skipper and crew member were in the hospital with serious burns. We shared warm hugs, gave what information we had, while Wally drove us to the hospital for a quick check.

The doctor found the inside of my nose was singed, and I was hypothermic. He told me I could leave. The previous night, everyone had expressed concern because of my pregnancy, but the doctor checked me and didn't acknowledge the baby. I questioned him.

"Your baby is fine. You suffered less from hypothermia with your extra layer of fat, because of your pregnancy."

"May I hear the baby's heartbeat?" I asked.

The steady pulse reassured me.

From the hospital I walked to Tom's trailer. Edwina was living there with Elizabeth known as Lizzy, not Betsy. They were sympathetic and comforted me. "Here, I'll add another heavy wool blanket to your pile." Edwina said as she covered me on the couch.

I appreciated more layers and thanked her. Bundled in multiple layers of clothing and under several blankets, I still felt the chill deep in my body.

Tom and Willie were seining, but they both called on the marine operator and congratulated me on cheating death.

When I heard the sound of fireworks, my baby flipped around, prepared for another explosion. I sympathized with mothers who live in war zones.

The doctors in Valdez flew Greg to a burn center in Anchorage. The doctors said the fire forcing Greg to jump into the water had been the best emergency treatment for his burns. Nurses at the burn center reported that the EMT who applied Greg's bandages helped lessen his injury.

Wally flew out to board the *Alliance* when the fire burned out. The flames had turned into mere smoke. At first the boat looked ready for Wally to board, but he watched it sink.

ABOUT THE TIME my body temperature returned to normal, I heard the *New St. Joseph* arrived in town. With the harbor skiff I towed the *Luna Sea* to her slip. My boat earned the title of hero. With an engine full of salt water she still saved three lives. She showed effects from the experience. The plastic navigation lights had melted into a splat on the roof of the cabin. The fire bubbled and scorched the shift and throttle knobs, and the front windows had multiple cracks but remained tight. The intense heat melted my net into a blob on the reel. The white corks resembled roasted marshmallows. Dry chemical dust from a fire extinguisher coated every surface.

I removed everything from the cabin, scrubbed what I could, and discarded the rest. I hired Maureen, a woman who worked odd jobs in town, to wash the cabin. No matter how well she cleaned, more of the dust settled, and she cleaned again.

I thought about calling and telling Sewall about the explosion. The conversation would be easier in person when I could reassure him that the baby and I were fine. The newspaper in Valdez ran a front-page article, and I decided I had better tell Sewall before he heard the story from someone else. "Earlier in the week my boat broke down and I had to get a tow to town. We encountered a problem on the way in," I told him.

"What happened?"

"The *Alliance* and *Dawn L* blew up. The baby and I are fine. I'm just glad you and Sam weren't on the boat."

"What did you say?"

"The *Alliance and Dawn L* burned. They were transferring gasoline. I am, ah, we are fine. The flames scorched my boat a bit, but I'm fixing it."

"When are you coming home?" Sewall asked.

"I don't want to end the season with memories of the explosion. I need to go out fishing."

"If you must," Sewall said reluctantly.

THE OUTBOARD SHOP installed new exhaust flaps and made other repairs to my engine. I replaced the melted plastic lens covers and wires for the navigational lights. Maureen cleaned the cabin three more times. I cut off the melted net and loaded my coho net. The *Luna Sea* needed the windows replaced, but I needed to order them from down south.

I found the *New St. Joseph* before it left the harbor and returned the socks the crew gave me, each filled with a bottle of wine.

With the *Luna Sea* cleaned and repaired, I ran to the Flats and made the opener. Again the dry chemical dust settled. I tasted it in the air and in the back of my throat. I wanted to leave the gas tanks full, but the thought of pumping gas frightened me. If the gasoline exploded, I knew I didn't want to refuel on the Flats. I returned to town that evening and retired for the season with memories of peaceful drifts behind Copper Sands with ideal weather.

The main fuel dock in Cordova sat a mile north of town, at the bottom of tall pilings, where the current rushes by. The outboard shop sold gasoline in the boat harbor for a premium price. I have a reputation for being frugal, but I willingly paid top dollar for the comfort of pumping gasoline in town, in between the shore and a harbor float, in shallow water without any current and close to the hospital.

I parked my boat at the fuel shed, but not before I'd bumped an overhang and knocked my stovepipe off into the water. I was a nervous wreck. Every minute I spent pumping gasoline and waiting to blow up made me miserable. I knew with my rational mind the gasoline wasn't going to explode, which allowed me to pump, but another part of me visualized the possibility, remembering my experience in the fiery water. I felt relieved when the tanks were full and I passed the nozzle back to the attendant.

I flew to Seattle and drove to Petrzelka Brother's shop with my window patterns. When the new windows arrived in Cordova, Paul installed them and leased the boat for the rest of the season, while I relaxed close to a hospital. He promised to have the *Luna Sea* fueled and ready for me to fish in the spring.

My focus switched from fishing to preschool and swimming lessons. Sam continued to rub my belly and talk to the baby. He was excited about a new brother or sister. That fall Steven was born healthy and alert. He slept well, not bothered by loud noise.

EPILOGUE

IF YOU THOUGHT that after that experience, I quit, you don't comprehend the hold fishing had on me. I fished for another twenty-five years and enjoyed fishing with the boys and enormous returns of salmon from the hatcheries. Life in Prince William Sound and Cordova became a nightmare when the Exon Valdez oil spill happened, the Copper River Fisherman's Cooperative, Chugach, and other processors went bankrupt.

The oil spill taught me I had a voice if I spoke up. The Alaska Seafood Marketing Institute, ASMI, appointed me to the Quality Committee, later the Technical Committee. The fishermen elected me to the board at Cordova District Fishermen United and the Prince William Sound Aquaculture Corporation, where I served as vice chair on the Executive Committee. PWSAC appointed me to a seat on the Copper River/Prince William Sound Regional Planning Team, a group that with Fish and Game worked on salmon enhancement planning in the area. I had an opportunity to spend a week in France with four other fishermen representing ASMI on a market familiarization tour. In 1995 The National Fisheries Institute, a nonprofit dedicated to education about seafood safety, sustainability, and nutrition, invited me to visit Boston and accept a Person of the Year award.

In winters I enjoyed my role as a school mom. My favorite projects were teaching F.U.N. (Finding Urban Nature by the Audubon Society) and the time I accompanied a class to the University of Washington, where the children received salmon eggs and milt. The children witnessed the teacher mix the two together in an aquarium at the school and then watched the eggs grow and hatch. In the spring I drove small groups of children to a stream where they released the baby salmon and watched them swim away.

Sewall shared my desire for our boys to experience life in Alaska. In the spring and fall he and the boys shared life as three bachelors, and in the summers, with their enthusiasm, I realized my dream of the boys fishing with me. On the closures, with a skiff and handheld VHF radio, Sam and Steven explored and found locations they were positive they'd been the first humans to discover. The three of us fit in the bunk until the boys were older and larger. I then built a bunk above the double bunk in the stern. In their mid-teen years, the boys took turns fishing with me. On a visit to the hatchery Steven watched the bears. Sam experienced Mount Spur's eruption when we raced to the anchorage and turned off the engine to avoid damage from the raining ash.

Sam and Steven enjoyed living in a big city and vacationing in the wilderness. When we didn't fish, we had other activities to entertain us. We went out the road to the sand dunes, where the boys rode their ATVs, or they sport fished with Guy. They went across the bay in a skiff to explore or to a party on Spike Island when Sam drove all invitees to the island.

When the boys were young I felt guilty leaving them. Now I feel the gift of summers in Alaska were the most valuable experiences I could have given my children. Schools don't teach the lessons they learned in the wild.

Sewall was pleased when I retired. Before I did, Steven fished with my permit one season. Neither of the boys wanted fishing as a career, which pleased me. I didn't want to worry about them.

Although I don't fish anymore, Tom, Willie, Peggy, and Red remain close friends, and my love for Cordova and Cordovans endures. Three of my five grandchildren live in Alaska, cementing my constant desire to return.

IN MEMORIAM

TO THE MEN lost during the years this book covers but their tragic loss was not included.

Jeff Pettingill

Doug Wentworth

Terry Allen

Keith *Brian* Gordaoff

Kenny Honkola

Bob Gill

ACKNOWLEDGEMENTS

I THANK PEOPLE in Cordova who encouraged me to write this book.

Thanks to Karen who read my first attempt and told me it read like a school report.

Thanks to early editors Tom, Peggy, Mick, Pete and Adam who painfully struggled to read my early chapters and gave me their honest opinions and constructive criticism.

Thanks to creative writing teachers Steve Lorton and Ariele Huff (who also edited) and fellow students who gave me ideas of how to improve my story.

Thanks to Bobbie Christmas at Zebra Communications who inspired me to keep writing and her editing that hopefully improved your enjoyment reading this book.

GLOSSARY

Bow of a boat is the front.

Briggs refers to a Briggs and Straton engine

CAMA The Cordova Aquatic Marketing Association.

CDFU The Cordova District Fishermen United. The political arm of CAMA

Closure refers to the times during the season when fishing is closed.

Corked is when a fisherman intentionally sets a net in front of another net, cork for cork and intercepts the fish.

Draft refers to how deep below the waterline the boat extends into the water.

Drift Gillnetter is a fisherman who sets a net of diamond shaped web that catches salmon by their gills while the net and boat drift.

Ebb refers to the tide going out, the direction of the water running out causing the depth to decrease.

Fathom is a measurement that equals six feet.

Flood refers to the tide rising, the water flooding in and increasing the depth.

Growlers are the smaller large chunks of an iceberg.

Hang a net is the act of tying knots to attach gillnet web to cork and lead lines.

Home-Pack refers to the fish a fishermen keeps for personal use.

Kicker is another word for an outboard motor.

Opener refers to when the season begins, or the time scheduled fishing periods are open.

Period refers to the time Fish and Game schedules the harvest of salmon.

Port refers to the left side of the boat. A hint, I was given to remember, port and left both have four letters.

Scupper is a hole in the side of the hull at deck level, that allows water to flow overboard.

Seiner means fishermen who use a purse seine to encircle salmon, close the bottom of the net and haul the salmon on board

Set Gillnetter is a fisherman who anchors a gillnet to the shore.

Sit on the beach is a local term meaning the fishermen didn't fish because of price or market.

Slough pronounced slou, is a secondary channel of a river delta that is flushed by the tide.

Slip is a parking spot at a dock for boats.

Spit refers to a sliver of land projecting into or under the water like a tiny peninsula.

Starboard refers to the right side of the boat.

Stern is the back of the boat.

Strike is when the fishermen refuse to fish, stay on the beach, because of the low price the processors offer to pay.

Strip a net the act of cutting all of the knots that hold web to the lines.

Thru-hull fittings are intentional holes in the hull with a hose connected to pump water overboard.